SLUGGERS!

HISTORY'S HEAVIEST HITTERS

Paul Adomites
Bobby Cassidy
Saul Wisnia

Publications International, Ltd.

Paul Adomites is the author of *October's Game* and coauthor of *Babe Ruth: His Life and Times* and *The Best of Baseball*. He was also a contributing writer to *Treasury of Baseball, Total Baseball,* and *Encyclopedia of Baseball Team Histories*. He served as publications director for the Society for American Baseball Research (SABR) and founded and edited *The SABR Review of Books* as well as its successor, *The Cooperstown Review.*

Robert Cassidy, a former collegiate baseball player, was an associate editor for *Inside Baseball* magazine and has written about major-league baseball for *Newsday* and *New York Sportscene*. He has contributed to the *Los Angeles Times* and the *New York Post*. He is the author of *Muhammad Ali: The Greatest of All Time* and co-author of *Boxing Legends of All Time.*

Saul Wisnia, a former sports and feature reporter for the *Washington Post,* currently writes for the *Boston Herald, Boston Magazine,* and *Sports Illustrated*. He is the author of *Wit & Wisdom of Baseball* and *Baseball's Prime-Time Stars* and coauthor of *Babe Ruth: His Life and Times* and *The Best of Baseball*. He was a contributing writer to *Baseball: More Than 150 Years, Treasury of Baseball,* and *Michael Jordan Scrapbook.*

Editorial Assistance: Michael Coulter, Marty Strasen, and Pete Palmer

CONTENTS

HISTORY OF THE HOME RUN

THE HOME RUN—like the knockout punch in boxing—is one of the most dramatic statements in sports. When a batter delivers a pitch into the seats, it is an emphatic display of skill, bat speed, and power. That explosive combination has forever fascinated fans of America's pastime.

In baseball the sluggers are the most revered players and the home runs are the hits that live forever. Peruse the decades of baseball history and the most memorable moments typically involve the home run: Babe Ruth's "called shot," Gabby Hartnett's "Homer in the Gloamin'," Bobby Thomson's "Shot Heard 'Round the World." The home run has also brought baseball back from the depths of despair.

The home run traces its lineage back 140 years. According to the *Home Run Encyclopedia,* the first home run ever recorded in a boxscore came off the bat of John Henry Holder on July 20, 1858, during an amateur game. The National League was formed in 1876, and the Chicago White Stockings' Ross Barnes was credited with the first home run on May 2, 1876. In the same game, just two innings later, Cincinnati's Charley Jones jacked a big fly.

During the inception of baseball, the home run was more of an oddity than a regular occurrence. There were just 40 homers hit during the National League's first year of play, slightly more than Mark McGwire accumulated by the 1998 All-Star break. Harry Stovey became the first man to reach double digits in homers (14) for a season, in 1883. A year later Ned Williamson smashed a record 27 long balls, but he benefited by playing in Chicago's Lake Front Park, where the left-field fence measured 180 feet from home plate.

Baseball in the "dead-ball era" was about pitching, bunting, basestealing, and hitting to all fields. The object of the batter was truly to "hit 'em where they ain't," as opposed to today's batters who strive

to "leave the yard." In 1911 baseball was introduced to a new cork-centered ball that was livelier than any ball used before. Offensive statistics began to rise. That season Frank "Wildfire" Schulte led the NL with 21 home runs, while Frank "Home Run" Baker topped the American League with 11.

Then along came Ruth. The Boston Red Sox were convinced they had a dominant southpaw pitcher when they added Ruth to their roster in 1915. They were correct. Ruth won 18 games in his first major-league season. But he also batted .315 and slugged four home runs.

The Red Sox were so impressed with Ruth's pitching prowess that they failed to maximize his offensive talents. In 1919 Ruth played the outfield and first base on the days he wasn't pitching, posting a 9–5 record on the mound while slugging a major-league record 29 round-trippers. Then he was sold to the New York Yankees in 1920, and the legend of the "Bambino" was born.

In 1920 Ruth batted .376 and blasted 54 homers. The following season he clubbed 59, and he finally reached his high-water mark of 60 home runs in 1927. The popularity of Ruth and America's obsession with the home run quickly delivered baseball from the devastating Black Sox scandal of 1919.

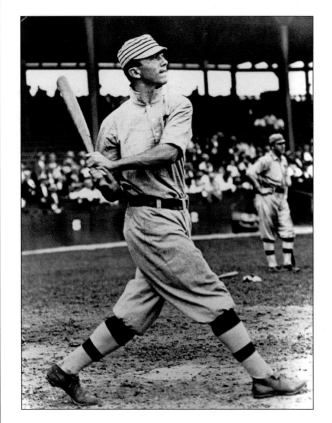

Frank Baker of the Philadelphia A's hit game-winning homers on successive days in the 1911 World Series. Thereafter, he was known as "Home Run" Baker.

Mickey Mantle (left) *was the most renowned home run hitter since Babe Ruth, clubbing 52 homers in 1956 and 54 in 1961. Hank Aaron* (right) *never hit 50, but he surpassed Ruth's 714 career homers in 1974.*

Ruth established the standards for home run hitters—60 in a season and 714 for his career. The first to launch an assault on Ruth's record was Hack Wilson, who hit a National League-record 56 homers in 1930. But Wilson may have benefited from another ball change. Baseball agreed to use balls with lower stitches for the 1930 season, which made it harder for pitchers to throw curves. In fact, the batting average of the entire National League was .303. The experiment lasted one season.

Others challenged Ruth as well. Jimmie Foxx (1932) and Hank Greenberg (1938) came closest with 58. Mickey Mantle eclipsed the 50-home run plateau twice (52 in '56 and 54 in '61). In 1947, in the National League, Johnny Mize and Ralph Kiner hit 51. Kiner hit 54 in 1949 and Willie Mays launched 51 in 1955.

Then came Roger Maris's 61 home runs in 1961. What should have been a wonderful season for Maris was one filled with torment. He and Mantle chased the Babe for much of the season. Unfortunately, many New York fans wanted Mantle, a Yankee icon, to break the record and others wanted it to last forever. Finally, on the last day of the season, Maris hit the record-breaking homer. His legacy, though, was tainted when Commissioner Ford Frick qualified the record. He ordered that the official record book state that Ruth achieved his 60 homers in a 154-game schedule while Maris played a 162-game slate.

While players mounted single-season assaults on the record, Hank Aaron was slowly hammering away at Ruth's all-time mark. Although Aaron never hit more than 47 homers in a season, he finished his 23-year career with 755.

The long ball became vogue again in the mid-1990s. In '96 three teams eclipsed the 1961 Yankees record of 240 home runs in a season: Baltimore (257), Seattle (245), and Oakland (243). Also in that season, a record 17 players hit 40 or more home runs, eclipsing the previous mark of eight players in 1961.

The culmination came in the magical 1998 season. McGwire and Sammy Sosa relentlessly pursued Maris's record. McGwire was the first to reach 62, then Sosa tied Mac days later. They finished the season with 70 and 66, respectively. In all, 13 players hit 40 or more home runs, and Ken Griffey Jr. (56) and Greg Vaughn (50) also reached the half-century mark.

Baseball, held in contempt by its fans following the 1994 labor dispute, was rescued this time by McGwire and Sosa—and, of course, the home run.

HANK AARON

Playing without noise or flash, Hank Aaron went almost unnoticed until he began knocking on the door of sports' most hallowed record—Babe Ruth's 714 lifetime home runs.

THE MAN WHO BASHED the most homers in baseball history didn't look like the archetypal slugger. At 6'0" and 180 pounds, he didn't seem to have the height or the heft to knock the ball far. And his unorthodox batting style would be impossible to imitate. But with his amazingly quick wrists, in-depth study of pitchers, and a body that was built for the long haul, "Hammerin' Hank" hit 755 home runs—41 more than the legendary Ruth—while using a bat that weighed 10 ounces less.

Aaron also hit for more total bases, 6,856, and more RBI, 2,297, than anyone else in the history of the game. Along with two batting titles, he won four RBI crowns and batted .300 or above 14 times. On the career lists, he's second in runs scored and third in hits. His 16 grand slams are second only to Willie McCovey's 18 for National League sluggers. In his 23-year career, he homered off 310 different pitchers. The hurler he victimized the most was snarling Hall of Famer Don Drysdale, with 17.

Above right: From the Negro Leagues to big-league immortality, Aaron made hitting baseballs a country mile look easy. Still, he never let his fame get to his head. "Babe Ruth will always be No. 1," he said after breaking Ruth's hallowed career home run mark. Below: Hitting off his front foot never posed a problem for Aaron, shown here launching his 700th career home run in 1973. Quick wrists helped the powerful slugger overcome any flaws in his swing.

Amazingly, he did all that with a batting style that no self-respecting hitting coach would ever try to teach. Aaron hit off his front foot. He could get away with it because of his remarkably strong and quick wrists. He said that he learned to hit that way as a kid when he practiced swatting bottle caps with a broomstick. "A bottle cap will change direction in an instant," he said. "You had to be ready."

Aaron began his professional career in 1952 with the Indianapolis Clowns of the Negro Leagues as a cross-handed batting shortstop. Since the integration of the major leagues, Negro League games resembled vaudeville acts more than baseball games. Some may have thought Hank's backward grip was part of the act. But a teammate suggested that he hold the bat the way everyone else did, and it worked: two homers in his very next game.

Aaron's talent was obvious to some right from the very beginning. As told in Jerry Brondfield's bio, *Hank Aaron . . . 714 and Beyond,* trainer Harvey Stone, who saw Aaron in his first minor-league season, said, "He was always something special, a natural-born hitter, with the greatest baseball instinct and the greatest pair of wrists I ever saw."

"My arrival in the major leagues was pretty dull," Aaron said in *The Sporting News* in 1970. "No drama, no excitement, absolutely none. I just arrived, and that was all."

There are those who would differ, however, including Ted Williams. At age 20, in his first major-league at-bat in spring training, Aaron walloped a homer off Red Sox Ike Delock over a row of trailers that bordered the outfield fence. Williams came running out of the clubhouse demanding to know who the person was who could make a bat sound that way when it hit a ball.

What Aaron probably meant by "dull" was that he had not been submitted to the pressure or media attention Jackie Robinson or other Negro stars had received. Aaron was shy, even aloof, and his style of play did not attract attention to himself the way a few other National League outfielders of the time did, such as Wille Mays, Roberto Clemente, and Frank Robinson.

In fact, Aaron was so unflashy, mellow, and relaxed that some suspected him of laziness. An article in a national maga-

Aaron will always be remembered for the long ball, but his
lifetime batting average of .305
sometimes gets lost in the home
run totals. Aaron captured two
league batting titles.

zine called him "The Talented Shuffler," a term that sticks in the throats of today's more racially aware people. But to the more discerning eye, that calmness meant something special—that Aaron wasn't there to make a show, but to perform, and for a long time. Aaron's first big-league manager, Charlie Grimm, said in David Porter's *African-American Sports Greats,* "He's not the spectacular type. Everything he does he makes look easy." Hall of Fame pitcher Robin Roberts said, "He could fall asleep between pitches and still wake up in time to hit the next one."

Curt Simmons, a nasty lefty, uttered a quote that several other people have laid claim to since, saying, "Trying to sneak a fastball past Hank Aaron is like trying to sneak the sunrise past a rooster." Hurler Claude Osteen, quoted in the Brondfield bio, was even more graphic: "Slapping a rattlesnake across the face with the back of your hand is safer than trying to fool Henry Aaron."

> **"Trying to sneak a fastball past Hank Aaron is like trying to sneak the sunrise past a rooster."**
> **—Curt Simmons**

Pitching around the most prolific 1–2 power punch in baseball history was a tall task for Braves opponents. Aaron and Eddie Mathews (right) *socked a cumulative 863 home runs in 13 summers together.*

BROKEN PLATES

Hank Aaron was the last major-leaguer to have played in the Negro Leagues. He felt the sting of racism long before the hate mail he received when he was chasing Ruth's lifetime home run record.

While he was just a teenager, his Indianapolis Clowns were rained out of a Sunday doubleheader in Washington, D.C. They had breakfast in a nearby restaurant. After they ate, the young Aaron listened as the restaurant workers broke all the dishes he and his teammates had used. "What a horrible sound," Aaron relates in his autobiography. "Even as a kid, the irony hit me: Here we were in the capital in the land of freedom and equality, and they had to destroy the plates that touched the forks that had been in the mouths of black men. If dogs had eaten off those plates, they would have washed them."

Aaron took it upon himself to make a difference. It's why his autobiography is titled *I Had a Hammer.* He spoke out frequently and fervently about the need for better opportunities for African Americans in baseball. He also founded the Hank Aaron Scholarship Fund and worked hard for organizations such as the Salvation Army, the Boy Scouts, one for fighting sickle-cell anemia, and Big Brothers/Big Sisters of America. The sound of those broken plates has never left him.

In his first three seasons, Aaron led the National League in doubles twice and hits once, won a batting title, and hit 66 home runs; his team finished third once and second twice. But 1957 was his breakout year. That season he topped all NL batters with 44 homers, 132 RBI, and 118 runs scored while batting .322. In late September, with the Braves struggling to hold onto first place, Aaron belted an 11th-inning homer to clinch the flag, the first ever for the boys from Milwaukee. He later said it was the most satisfying homer of his long career.

In the '57 World Series, Aaron proved he could perform when the pressure was on. He led all hitters in batting average, hits, runs, RBI, and homers. The upstart Braves (whom Mickey Mantle had unwisely referred to as "bush league") knocked over the powerful New York Yankees, dealing the Bronx men only their second Series loss in their last nine appearances. The Braves took the NL crown again in 1958, with Aaron totaling 95 RBI and 30 homers. The Yankees revenged the upset in the Series, although Aaron hit .333.

In 1959 Aaron had one of the great slugging years in history. His league-leading 223 hits included 46 doubles, seven triples, and 39 homers, which added up to a sensational 400 total bases—a level reached only once in the previous 17 years. His Braves tied for the NL title with the Dodgers and were toppled in a best-of-three playoff before they could reach the World Series.

But in the public's mind, Aaron was still in the back seat compared to the magical Mays, regal Clemente, and fiery Robinson. Over the next nine years, Aaron led the league in homers and RBI three times and in doubles, runs, and slugging average twice. When the Braves moved to Atlanta in 1966, the cozy dimensions of Fulton County Stadium pleased him, and he hit 44 and 39 homers during his first two seasons there. His team, however, had fallen from the peak, finishing fifth, sixth, or seventh every year from 1962 through 1968.

With his team seemingly headed nowhere, and his status as a quality ballplayer well established, Aaron was considering retirement early in 1969. But during spring training that year, while he rested a knee banged up by a Pete Mikkelsen pitch, baseball historian Lee Allen talked to him, pointing out how close he was to several impressive statistical marks, including 3,000 hits, some of Stan Musial's National League records, and Ty Cobb's lifetime at-bats record. (Of course, no one thought Ruth's 714 was reachable at that point. Hank had 510 homers, and Mays was way ahead.) Aaron listened quietly, then decided two things: He would continue to play to shoot at the records, and he would no longer keep quiet. Instead, he would use his status in the game to speak out against racial inequality, the tacit curse that had tortured him in his minor-league years and had kept him in the background in the bigs.

That year Aaron knocked 44 balls out of the park and the Braves went to the postseason, losing the first-ever National League Championship Series to the "Miracle" New York Mets. He hit 38 the next season, then 47—the highest he had ever attained in one year. He was still 75 homers behind Ruth, but now people were talking about Aaron, giving him his long-deserved due. He rapped 34 more circuit clouts in 1972, and in 1973, at the age of 39, he belted 40 homers in just 392 at-bats—the most anyone had ever hit in fewer than 400 trips to the plate.

Aaron began the 1974 season just one homer behind the great Ruth, and on April 8, 1974, he made the Babe move over, slamming his 715th off L.A.'s Al Downing. Few people noticed that in his first at-bat in that game, he walked and scored to break Willie Mays's NL record for lifetime runs, putting himself behind only Cobb and Ruth.

The pressure on Aaron had been tremendous. He said, as Roger Maris had when he surpassed Ruth's single-season homer record, that he was just glad it was over. "Babe Ruth will always be No. 1," Aaron said. "Before I broke his home run record, it was the greatest of all. Then I broke it and suddenly

the greatest record is Joe DiMaggio's hitting streak." Hank slugged a total of 20 homers in '74.

After the season Aaron returned to Milwaukee, now in the American League as the Brewers, to finish his career as a designated hitter. He tacked on 22 more home runs in his final two seasons to finish at 755.

Aaron, despite his unintimidating physical appearance, was a great slugger, not just in terms of homers, but by every other definition. In his 23-year career he set the major-league record for most years leading the league in total bases, with eight. Eight times Hank reached the 40-homer mark, and he averaged 33 homers a year over his 23 seasons. Eleven times he topped 100 RBI. Fifteen times he scored more than 100 runs—still the all-time record. Aaron especially prized the last stat, because Jackie Robinson had told him that the object of the game is to get on and get around the bases; home runs are only one way to accomplish that goal.

With Eddie Mathews, Hank formed the best 1–2 slugging tandem in history. During their 13 seasons together in Milwaukee and Atlanta, they swatted 863 homers and drove in 2,633 runs.

But, as quoted in John Holway's book *The Sluggers,* Aaron was true to his style when he stated that "ninety percent of my home runs came when I wasn't thinking homer." He was just playing the game.

Left: His modest early years in baseball seemed a distant memory after Aaron celebrated his 715th career home run in 1974. Babe Ruth's legendary 714 fell on a pitch by Al Downing of the Dodgers.

BY THE NUMBERS																
Year	Team	G	AB	R	H	2B	3B	HR	HR%	RBI	BB	K	BA	SA	SB	
1954	Mil-N	122	468	58	131	27	6	13	2.8	69	28	39	.280	.447	2	
1955	Mil-N	153	602	105	189	**37**	9	27	4.5	106	49	61	.314	.540	3	
1956	Mil-N	153	609	106	**200**	**34**	14	26	4.3	92	37	54	**.328**	.558	2	
1957	Mil-N	151	615	118	198	27	6	44	7.2	132	57	58	.322	.600	1	
1958	Mil-N	153	601	109	196	34	4	30	5.0	95	59	49	.326	.546	4	
1959	Mil-N	154	629	116	**223**	46	7	39	6.2	123	51	54	**.355**	**.636**	8	
1960	Mil-N	153	590	102	172	20	11	40	6.8	**126**	60	63	.292	.566	16	
1961	Mil-N	155	603	115	197	**39**	10	34	5.6	120	56	64	.327	.594	21	
1962	Mil-N	156	592	127	191	28	6	45	7.6	128	66	73	.323	.618	15	
1963	Mil-N	161	631	**121**	201	29	4	**44**	7.0	**130**	78	94	.319	**.586**	31	
1964	Mil-N	145	570	103	187	30	2	24	4.2	95	62	46	.328	.514	22	
1965	Mil-N	150	570	109	181	**40**	1	32	5.6	89	60	81	.318	.560	24	
1966	Atl-N	158	603	117	168	23	1	**44**	7.3	**127**	76	96	.279	.539	21	
1967	Atl-N	155	600	**113**	184	37	3	**39**	6.5	109	63	97	.307	**.573**	17	
1968	Atl-N	160	606	84	174	33	4	29	4.8	86	64	62	.287	.498	28	
1969	Atl-N	147	547	100	164	30	3	44	8.0	97	87	47	.300	.607	9	
1970	Atl-N	150	516	103	154	26	1	38	7.4	118	74	63	.298	.574	9	
1971	Atl-N	139	495	95	162	22	3	47	**9.5**	118	71	58	.327	**.669**	1	
1972	Atl-N	129	449	75	119	10	0	34	**7.6**	77	92	55	.265	.514	4	
1973	Atl-N	120	392	84	118	12	1	40	**10.2**	96	68	51	.301	.643	1	
1974	Atl-N	112	340	47	91	16	0	20	5.9	69	39	29	.268	.491	1	
1975	Mil-A	137	465	45	109	16	2	12	2.6	60	70	51	.234	.355	0	
1976	Mil-A	85	271	22	62	8	0	10	3.7	35	35	38	.229	.369	0	
Total	23	3298	12364	2174	3771	624	98	755	6.1	2297	1402	1383	.305	.555	240	

ERNIE BANKS

One of the last men to play in both the Negro Leagues and major leagues, Ernie Banks had a long career, one that centered on five nearly unbelievable slugging seasons.

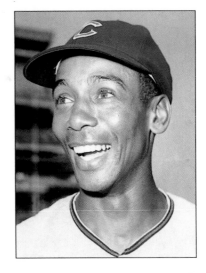

ERNIE BANKS HAD AN UNABASHED love for the game. "It's a wonderful day for baseball," he was fond of saying. "Let's play two!" Nevertheless, his sunny disposition didn't fool National League pitchers. At bat he was a terror. Even more important, he was a batting terror at shortstop, the home of glove men, not sluggers, for much of his career.

Ernie Banks, of course, had the distinct advantage of playing all of his home games for his entire career in Wrigley Field in Chicago, a great home run park not only due to the gusty winds off Lake Michigan, but also because every game there was played during the day. Every hitter will tell you that it's easier to see the ball, and therefore hit it, when you have the benefit of natural sunlight.

Banks's disadvantage was that he played for the Cubs, who were often below .500 and frequently in the cellar. And, once again, every hitter will tell you that it's easier to hit when you have good hitters around you in the lineup. Pitchers who don't have to pitch to you usually won't. And until the arrival of Billy Williams in 1960, Ernie was surrounded by hitters such as Walt Moryn, Dee Fondy, and Lee Walls —hardly names to frighten Don Drysdale or Sandy Koufax. But despite all that, Ernie never complained. He just loved playing baseball.

Like Hank Aaron, Banks didn't have the typical slugger's build. He looked like a shortstop: slim and lithe. But like Aaron, Banks had power that came from his strong, strong wrists. One teammate said he had "wrists right up to his armpits."

And because Ernie wasn't over-packed with muscles, he was durable. In his 19 big-league seasons, he played 150 games or more a dozen times—especially noteworthy when you consider that for seven of those years teams played only 154 games. In one stretch Banks appeared in 717 consecutive games, then the third-longest streak in National League history. After being an All-Star shortstop for seven consecutive years—setting the major-league record for homers by someone at that position—and playing more than 1,100 games there, he moved easily to first base. He stayed at the first sack for more than 1,200 games, making him one of only four players to appear in more than 1,000 games at two different positions.

Banks had played for the famous Kansas City Monarchs of the Negro Leagues for a couple of seasons when the Cubs picked him up for $10,000. He went straight to the bigs. In his first Wrigley batting-practice swing, he knocked one out of sight. He was just getting started. At age 22 he hit his first big-league blast off Gerry Staley of St. Louis. Before his career was over, he would homer off 215 more hurlers.

Over his career Banks belted 512 homers. Only 11 men have ever hit more. Five times he topped the 40-homer mark. His 1,636 lifetime RBI have been surpassed by only 18 others. He hit 12 grand slams, five of them in one season—a National League record. He drove in 100 runs eight times. Banks was twice chosen Most Valuable Player in the National League, in 1958 and 1959. And although his teams were not in last place those years, neither were they anywhere close to .500. The awards were simply recognition that Banks was playing at a level no one else was matching. And his competitors were no chumps: Aaron finished third to Banks in both of those years; the two second-place finishers were Willie Mays and Eddie Mathews.

Although Banks had a long and successful career, it was his performance in the years surrounding those two MVP titles that were almost unbelievable. Take a look: In 1955, just his sec-

Above right: Few possessed as contagious a smile as Banks, who loved his work and was driven to win despite spending most of his career on also-ran Cubs teams. "Let's play two" was his creed. Below: Whether lighting a cigar for his dad, Ernie Sr., on Father's Day or lighting up Wrigley Field with one of his 512 career home runs, Banks was a fan favorite in Chicago.

ond full season in the majors, he slugged 44 homers, drove in 117 runs, and batted .295. The next year he "slumped" to 28 dingers and 85 RBI, but still hit .297. In 1957 he powered 43 long balls and drove in 102 to go with his .285 average. In 1958 he tore the roof off: 47 homers, 129 RBI (both league-leading numbers), and a .313 average. Of course, they gave him the MVP title. He followed that with a 45-homer, 143-RBI, .304 season. He outhomered Mays and Aaron in 1960 with 41 taters, and knocked in 117.

Although he swatted 37 homers in 1962 and 32 more in 1968, and knocked in 100 or more runs three more times, the years 1955 through 1960 were the centerpiece of his marvelous career. He has never broken his allegiance to his team, still showing up at Wrigley with a Cubs cap and a smile.

Banks never played in a World Series, but his career did not lack for memorable moments, such as his 2,500th career hit (pictured) off Hall of Famer Bob Gibson of the Cardinals.

								BY THE NUMBERS							
Year	Team	G	AB	R	H	2B	3B	HR	HR%	RBI	BB	K	BA	SA	SB
1953	Chi-N	10	35	3	11	1	1	2	5.7	6	4	5	.314	.571	0
1954	Chi-N	154	593	70	163	19	7	19	3.2	79	40	50	.275	.427	6
1955	Chi-N	154	596	98	176	29	9	44	7.4	117	45	72	.295	.596	9
1956	Chi-N	139	538	82	160	25	8	28	5.2	85	52	62	.297	.530	6
1957	Chi-N	156	594	113	169	34	6	43	7.2	102	70	85	.285	.579	8
1958	Chi-N	154	617	119	193	23	11	**47**	**7.6**	**129**	52	87	.313	**.614**	4
1959	Chi-N	155	589	97	179	25	6	45	7.6	**143**	64	72	.304	.596	2
1960	Chi-N	156	597	94	162	32	7	**41**	6.9	117	71	69	.271	.554	1
1961	Chi-N	138	511	75	142	22	4	29	5.7	80	54	75	.278	.507	1
1962	Chi-N	154	610	87	164	20	6	37	6.1	104	30	71	.269	.503	5
1963	Chi-N	130	432	41	98	20	1	18	4.2	64	39	73	.227	.403	0
1964	Chi-N	157	591	67	156	29	6	23	3.9	95	36	84	.264	.450	1
1965	Chi-N	163	612	79	162	25	3	28	4.6	106	55	64	.265	.453	3
1966	Chi-N	141	511	52	139	23	7	15	2.9	75	29	59	.272	.432	0
1967	Chi-N	151	573	68	158	26	4	23	4.0	95	27	93	.276	.455	2
1968	Chi-N	150	552	71	136	27	0	32	5.8	83	27	67	.246	.469	2
1969	Chi-N	155	565	60	143	19	2	23	4.1	106	42	101	.253	.416	0
1970	Chi-N	72	222	25	56	6	2	12	5.4	44	20	33	.252	.459	0
1971	Chi-N	39	83	4	16	2	0	3	3.6	6	6	14	.193	.325	0
Total	19	2528	9421	1305	2583	407	90	512	5.4	1636	763	1236	.274	.500	50

BARRY BONDS

In 1998 Barry Bonds created a new category of offensive excellence— more than 400 home runs and 400 stolen bases. He is the club's one and only member.

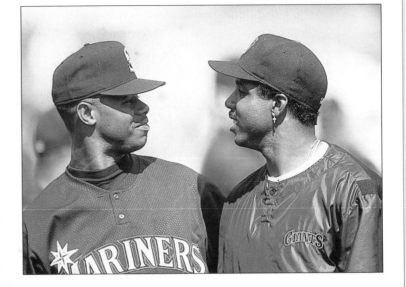

ONE CAN JUSTIFIABLY CLAIM that Barry Bonds is the Joe DiMaggio of his generation—the best all-around ballplayer on the field, day in and day out. Bonds is a consistent Gold Glove winner for his defensive prowess in left field. He's also a slugger who takes walks when pitchers won't pitch to him and turns them into doubles by stealing second base.

The greatest difference between the two, of course, is in the postseason. While the first four Yankee teams DiMaggio played on were World Series champs (and would be five more times with Joe on the team), no Bonds team has ever reached the fall classic.

Bonds came by his baseball talent naturally. His father, Bobby, played in the majors for 14 seasons, with eight different teams. On his mother's side, Reggie Jackson is a cousin. While most kids beg to pay their way into big-league parks, Barry grew up there. His godfather is Willie Mays.

Drafted out of high school by the Giants (who else?), Bonds gave an indication of his self-opinion when he turned down a $70,000 signing bonus (he wanted $75,000) and went to Arizona State University, home of many future major-league greats. He smacked 23 homers his junior year, but he dropped out after clashes with his teammates and coach. The Pirates drafted him eighth overall in 1985. Brought up from the minors on May 30 the next year, he still led all National League rookies in homers, RBI, stolen bases, and walks. He showed flashes of brilliance, hitting 25 and 24 homers his second and third years and stealing more than 30 bases three of his first four seasons. He homered in four straight games in 1987, and in '88 he had three two-homer games plus the ninth best home run ratio in the league.

Bonds came into his own with a remarkable 1990 season, winning his first National League MVP title at the age of 25. He's been a superstar ever since. That year he became the first player in major-league history to hit .300 while also slugging 30 homers, driving in more than 100 runs, and stealing 50 bases. His .565 slugging percentage led the league. He was also walked intentionally 25 times, a facet of his game that showed up more and more later. He was only the second player in history to hit 30 homers and swipe 50 bases in the same season. His Pirates won the NL East before falling in the League Championship Series.

In 1991 Bonds finished second in the MVP voting, but the Pirates again were bested in the playoffs, this time by Atlanta. He was just one RBI behind the league leader, and he led the NL in on-base percentage. His at-bat/RBI ratio of 4.4 was the best in the majors. Bonds garnered his second MVP Award in 1992 after another sensational year: .311, 34 homers, 103 RBI,

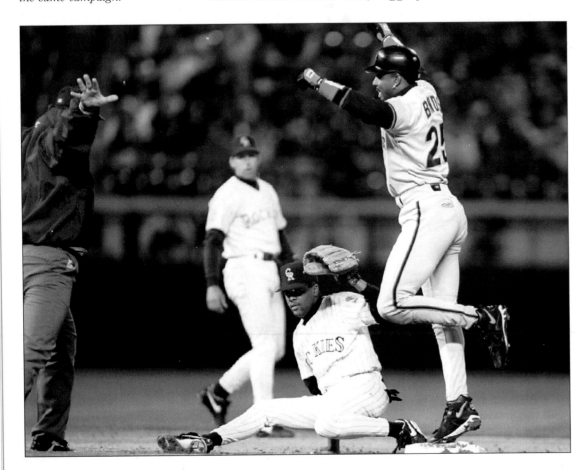

Now that he's the only player in history with 400-plus homers and steals, Bonds can aim for a new milestone—500 of each. Few would bet against him.

39 steals. But the small-market Pirates again flopped in the postseason, and Bonds went off in search of the richest free-agent contract in history. Not surprisingly, he got it.

Joining the Giants for the 1993 season, he outdid even his previous gaudy numbers, batting .336, homering 46 times, knocking in 123 runs, and swiping 29 sacks. He was the first player to lead the league in both on-base percentage and slugging average since Mike Schmidt a dozen years before. Naturally, he won another MVP crown. However, his Giants lost out to the Braves for the NL West title on the last day of the season.

Bonds's Giants finished last in 1995 and repeated the feat in 1996. That year Bonds became only the second man to hit 40 homers (he hit 42) and steal 40 bases in the same season. He scored 122 runs and was walked 151 times, setting a National League record.

The acquisition of needed pitching brought the Giants back into postseason play in 1997, helped along by Bonds's .291 average, 40 homers, 101 RBI, and 37 steals. He was walked "only" 145 times that year, 34 times intentionally. But the Giants were swept in three games in the Division Series by the wild-card Florida Marlins, who were on their way to winning the World Series.

In 1998 Bonds swatted 37 homers (33 fewer than Mark McGwire) but seemed to be adding a new dimension to his offense—doubles. For the first time in his career, he topped the 40 mark. A strong finish got the Giants into a tie for the wild-card berth. But in their one-game playoff in Wrigley against the Cubs, Bonds's team came up short again. Batting with the bases loaded in the seventh and again in the ninth innings, Bonds drove in only one run, and his team was knocked out of the postseason, 5–3.

Bonds may never reach the World Series, although the ultimate offensive milestone—500 homers and 500 steals—is well within his reach.

BY THE NUMBERS															
Year	Team	G	AB	R	H	2B	3B	HR	HR%	RBI	BB	K	BA	SA	SB
1986	Pit-N	113	413	72	92	26	3	16	3.9	48	65	102	.223	.416	36
1987	Pit-N	150	551	99	144	34	9	25	4.5	59	54	88	.261	.492	32
1988	Pit-N	144	538	97	152	30	5	24	4.5	58	72	82	.283	.491	17
1989	Pit-N	159	580	96	144	34	6	19	3.3	58	93	93	.248	.426	32
1990	Pit-N	151	519	104	156	32	3	33	6.4	114	93	83	.301	.565	52
1991	Pit-N	153	510	95	149	28	5	25	4.9	116	107	73	.292	.514	43
1992	Pit-N	140	473	109	147	36	5	34	7.2	103	127	69	.311	.624	39
1993	SF-N	159	539	129	181	38	4	46	8.5	123	126	79	.336	.677	29
1994	SF-N	112	391	89	122	18	1	37	9.5	81	74	43	.312	.647	29
1995	SF-N	144	506	109	149	30	7	33	6.5	104	120	83	.294	.577	31
1996	SF-N	158	517	122	159	27	3	42	8.1	129	151	76	.308	.615	40
1997	SF-N	159	532	123	155	26	5	40	7.5	101	145	87	.291	.585	37
1998	SF-N	156	552	120	167	44	7	37	6.7	122	130	92	.303	.609	28
Total	13	1898	6621	1364	1917	403	63	411	6.2	1216	1357	1050	.290	.556	445

JOE DiMAGGIO

In 1969 Joe DiMaggio was voted "Greatest Living Ballplayer." Forever known as the author of a 56-game hitting streak, he was also a feared home run hitter.

BASEBALL SUPERSTARS HAVE been adored, imitated, lionized, and mythologized. But none of them have carried the mystique of Joe DiMaggio. For a long time he was the greatest player on the greatest team; he even married America's most famous sex symbol, Marilyn Monroe. But it was something about the way DiMaggio's personality meshed so completely with his on-the-field performance—both quiet, dignified, and commanding—that sets him apart from all the rest. His numbers were excellent, although some have had better. It was the way he did it that made all the difference.

Of course, the one thing that comes to mind when someone mentions DiMaggio the ballplayer is his incredible 56-game hitting streak in 1941. (He also hit in 61 straight in the minors.) No one has ever come within 12 games of it. Although some historians have dismissed it as a "freak stat" (luck and timing have much more to do with a batting streak than quality), in truth it fit DiMaggio like almost no other stat could. Consistent performance raised to the next level—that was Joe DiMaggio.

DiMaggio's 361 lifetime home runs are nowhere near the top. Lesser lights like Graig Nettles and Norm Cash had more. Then again, Joe lost several years to World War II, and it must be remembered that he played his career in the caverns of Yankee Stadium, where it took a 400-foot clout to get near the left-field fence. He hit only 148 of those homers at home. But if you combine that home run achievement with another typically DiMaggio stat—strikeouts—you see something remarkable. En route to 361 homers, DiMaggio struck out only 369 times—in his career! That's a little more than two seasons worth of Ks for some of the game's more noted sluggers. In that remarkable season of 1941, he fanned only 13 times. He never struck out 40 times in a season.

DiMaggio was a one-man wrecking crew in 1948, winning American League MVP honors after leading the league with 39 home runs and 155 RBI.

DiMaggio's 361 lifetime homers fall short of the marks set by Ted Williams (left) *and Jimmie Foxx* (right), *but his place in baseball history does not.*

Even DiMaggio's batting style was one of understated excellence. He stood straight up, with as wide a stance as you'll ever see, and hardly strode into the ball at all. Try it yourself; it feels awkward. But with DiMaggio, it was pure poetry.

DiMaggio came to the Yankees because they could afford him. After suffering torn cartilage and pulled tendons, caused when he jumped out of a cab in San Francisco early in 1934, DiMaggio was considered damaged goods by scouts. The Yanks offered DiMaggio's San Francisco Seals $25,000 and five players for the young Italian slugger. But the contingency for the Yankees was that Joe would stay on the West Coast for the 1935 season, to make sure his leg was healthy. Joe scored 173 runs, knocked in 154, and batted .398. He passed.

DiMaggio came to the Yanks and set American League rookie records for runs scored and triples. The Yanks, who had slipped from dominance of the game—they had won just one World Series in the past seven seasons—moved right back to the top, knocking off the New York Giants in the 1936 fall classic. The next year DiMaggio drove in 167 runs and led the league with 46 homers. Lou Gehrig knocked in 159 himself, and the Yanks won their second world title in two years with Joe patrolling center.

The next year included more of the same. DiMaggio and Gehrig "slumped" to 140 and 114 RBI, but the Yankees still took the AL flag handily and swept the Chicago Cubs in the Series. Gehrig retired with a tragic disease in May 1939, but DiMaggio led the Yankees in home runs and RBI again—and led the league in batting with a .381 average. The Yankees swept their second World Series in a row. In the four years since

Before leaving to help the American cause in World War II, DiMaggio never hit below .305 in a season, nor did he drive in fewer than 114 runs in a campaign. Joltin' Joe won AL batting titles in 1939 and 1940.

Joe DiMaggio had joined them, the Yanks had won four World Series, losing just three games in all four. DiMaggio was a winner.

World War II cut more than three years from the middle of DiMaggio's career, but he was far from through. In 1948 he almost singlehandedly carried the Yankees to another pennant by walloping 39 homers and driving in 155—both league-leading efforts. Bothered by a persistent heel injury that responded to no treatment anyone could find in 1949, Joe still came through with one of his most impressive performances ever. In late June, with the Yanks again battling Ted Williams and the Boston Red Sox for the pennant,

DiMaggio's pain suddenly disappeared. He returned to the lineup in Fenway Park and belted four homers and knocked in nine runs in a three-game Yankee sweep.

DiMaggio's Yankees appeared in 10 World Series with Joe and won nine. In 1950 he became the first player to hit three homers in one game at the mammoth Griffith Stadium, but, of course, Joe was used to big outfields. Lifetime, he ranks sixth in slugging percentage.

BY THE NUMBERS														
Year	Team	G	AB	R	H	2B	3B	HR	HR%	RBI	BB	K	BA	SA	SB
1936	NY-A	138	637	132	206	44	**15**	29	4.6	125	24	39	.323	.576	4
1937	NY-A	151	621	**151**	215	35	15	**46**	7.4	167	64	37	.346	**.673**	3
1938	NY-A	145	599	129	194	32	13	32	5.3	140	59	21	.324	.581	6
1939	NY-A	120	462	108	176	32	6	30	6.5	126	52	20	**.381**	.671	3
1940	NY-A	132	508	93	179	28	9	31	6.1	133	61	30	**.352**	.626	1
1941	NY-A	139	541	122	193	43	11	30	5.5	**125**	76	13	.357	.643	4
1942	NY-A	154	610	123	186	29	13	21	3.4	114	68	36	.305	.498	4
1946	NY-A	132	503	81	146	20	8	25	5.0	95	59	24	.290	.511	1
1947	NY-A	141	534	97	168	31	10	20	3.7	97	64	32	.315	.522	3
1948	NY-A	153	594	110	190	26	11	**39**	6.6	**155**	67	30	.320	.598	1
1949	NY-A	76	272	58	94	14	6	14	5.1	67	55	18	.346	.596	0
1950	NY-A	139	525	114	158	33	10	32	6.1	122	80	33	.301	**.585**	0
1951	NY-A	116	415	72	109	22	4	12	2.9	71	61	36	.263	.422	0
Total	13	1736	6821	1390	2214	389	131	361	5.3	1537	790	369	.325	.579	30

JIMMIE FOXX

A world-class baseball trivia expert once said, "If you're ever stuck on a question about great hitters, guess Jimmie Foxx. He's the guy no one remembers."

THEY CALLED HIM "THE BEAST," and not for his attitude. In fact, he was one of the nicest guys around. Jimmie Foxx was simply fearsome-looking as he stood at the plate. He was only six feet tall, but his arms and thighs looked like tree trunks. He took psychological advantage of his build by cutting off his uniform sleeves, to highlight the muscles bulging there. Hall of Fame pitcher and noted wag Lefty Gomez said that "even his hair has muscles."

In his time Foxx was referred to as "the right-handed Babe Ruth." And in many ways he was as close to the Babe as any batter ever. Mention Gehrig if you like, but Lou never hit more than 49 homers in a season. Jimmie belted 58 once as well as 50 and 48. Foxx hit tons of home runs. When he retired, he was second behind the Babe with 534 homers, and he wasn't passed until Mickey Mantle did it in 1968.

Foxx was a feared hitter for average, too. He batted over .330 nine times. He has the highest batting average of all right-handers with more than 500 homers. He slugged over .700 three times and ranks fourth in career slugging percentage. His .749 slugging mark in 1932 is the eighth highest ever. Foxx was a productive slugger, too: He averaged 1.76 RBI per homer, the best among the top-10 homer hitters of all time. He drove in 100 or more runs 13 consecutive times, tying Gehrig for the all-time record. Seventeen times his homers came with the bases loaded.

But perhaps here is the most telling stat: In the 1930s, known ever since as the "Lively Ball Era," when baseballs allegedly went flying out of parks like butterflies, no one hit more home runs than Jimmie Foxx. No less an authority than Ted Williams said, "Next to Joe DiMaggio, Foxx was the greatest player I ever saw. When Foxx hit a ball, it sounded like gunfire."

So why isn't he remembered more? A 1990 biography of Foxx by baseball historian Bob Gorman is titled *Jimmie Foxx: Baseball's Forgotten Slugger.* Foxx played much of his career in Philadelphia, not New York. And even though his A's won three consecutive pennants and two World Series from 1929 to 1931, laying claim to being one of the greatest teams of all time, they don't resonate in memory the way Ruth and Gehrig and the Yankees do. Jimmie's baseball career had an unhappy ending, too. Problems with alcohol and wasteful spending left him destitute late in life. Tom Hanks's role as manager of the women's baseball team in the film *A League of Their Own* parodies Foxx, who held a similar job.

Foxx didn't just hit a lot of home runs; he hit them far. McGwire far. He twice hit homers completely out of Comiskey Park, one a blast that sailed over a factory behind the outfield fence. Wrote Gorman: "One day in May (1936) in Cleveland Stadium he hit a titanic shot which left the ballpark at the 417 mark in left field, traveled beyond a big Lux Soap billboard, went through the top of a huge oak tree and landed on a distant lawn!" While touring Japan after the 1934 season with a group of major-leaguers, Foxx hit one completely out of Tokyo Stadium. He was told that no native batsman had ever even hit one off the wall.

In June 1938 Foxx homered off the top of the huge scoreboard behind the left-field bleachers in Sportsman's Park in St. Louis. In spring training in Jacksonville, Florida, in 1934, he

Above right: Foxx made a mockery of Fenway's inviting left-field wall after being sold from Philadelphia to Boston. He hit 50 homers for the Red Sox in 1938, including 35 at home. Below: On those occasions when Foxx failed to homer, he was no sure out. He topped the AL three times in on-base percentage during a career that spanned 20 seasons.

swatted a ball that traveled 505 feet, even though some said it never got more than 25 feet above the ground.

But one of Foxx's longest homers is the source of one of baseball's greatest stories. The date was June 25, 1932, and Foxx was on his way to slugging 58 homers and driving in 169 runs that year. Foxx was red-hot as he stepped in to face the witty Lefty Gomez. The catcher called every sign he could, and Lefty shook them all off. The catcher went through the signals again, but Lefty said no to everything. The catcher walked to the mound. "What do you want to throw?" he asked. "Nothing," Lefty said. "Let's just hang around here for a while. Maybe he'll get a long-distance phone call." The baffled catcher responded, "Hell, let's just try to sneak a fastball past him."

Lefty reluctantly agreed, and Foxx hit it a mile. Lefty said afterward that it took him 20 minutes just to walk out to the spot where Jimmie's blast had landed. When he got there, he saw that the ball had broken the top half of a seat in the third tier of Yankee Stadium. Twenty more feet and it would have left the park completely.

On July 19, 1932, Foxx's 39th homer, a gigantic blast over the wall at the Athletics' Shibe Park, put him on pace to surpass Ruth's 60 homers in 1927. But the legend of that season grows deeper. Some historians have researched old records and discovered that in 1932 Foxx hit nine balls against screens in St. Louis and Cleveland that weren't there when the Babe hit 60. Foxx also hit two homers that season in games that were rained

Foxx's 496th home run came in 1940 and put him second on the all-time list, well behind Babe Ruth's 714. Despite finishing his career with 534, Foxx is sometimes overlooked when sluggers' names arise.

> "Next to Joe DiMaggio, Foxx was the greatest player I ever saw. When Foxx hit a ball, it sounded like gunfire."
> —Ted Williams

YOUNG FOXX

Jimmie Foxx built his immense muscles working on his parents' farm in Maryland. When he was only 12, he could toss around 200-pound bags of phosphate and lift a 200-pound keg of nails "without letting the keg touch my body," he recalled.

Foxx was also a tremendous athlete. In a 1923 track meet, he won the 200-yard dash and the high jump. At age 14 he was playing "semipro" baseball, earning a dollar a game. The next summer his huge homers were the talk of the Caroline County League, and in May 1924, at the ripe, old age of 16 years and seven months, he received a penny postcard that would change his life. It began, "You are invited to try out for the Easton professional base ball club." The card was signed by none other than Frank Baker, whose critical home runs in the 1911 World Series had earned him the mythical nickname "Home Run."

Foxx began his career assault on opposing pitchers when, batting eighth, he homered in his first game. In the playoffs at the end of the season against Martinsburg, he hit two homers in the first game at home and two in the second on the road. The *Eastern-Star Democrat* reported, "Fox (sic) knocked the ball over the center-field fence close to the flagpole. It was the longest home run ever made on these grounds."

out, and the homers disappeared from the record books. Add them up and Jimmie Foxx could have been the all-time single-season slugger, and Mark McGwire's 70 would have topped him by just one.

Foxx came to the majors in 1925 as a 17-year-old catcher, fresh from a season in the Eastern Shore League in which he batted .296 in 76 games—but also led all catchers with 16 errors. He batted just nine times in the majors that year and 32 the next, a season he spent partially in the minors. Old wizard Connie Mack, his A's manager, kept Foxx close to him on the bench to learn how the game was played. Mickey Cochrane, however, was settling in for a long career as the team's catcher. Mack put Foxx at first base for 82 games in 1927, but the youngster also played third, shortstop, second, and the outfield; he even pitched in two games. Foxx batted .323 for the season, although he hit just three home runs. Mack's A's finished second, 19 games behind the legendary Yankees.

In 1928 Mack bounced Foxx around some more, although Foxx wasn't complaining: 60 games at third, 30 at first, and 19 behind the plate. Foxx hit .327 with 13 homers and 79 RBI, and the A's sneaked to within 2½ games of the Yankees.

The next year the A's put it all together. The 21-year-old Foxx was given the first base job, and he responded in a big way: 33 homers, 118 RBI, a .354 batting average, and a league-leading .463 on-base percentage. Outfielder Al Simmons hit .365 and drove in 157 runs to lead the league. Cochrane hit .331, Bing Miller hit .335, and the Yankees failed to reach the World Series for only the second time in eight years. Foxx hit .350 with two home runs as the A's whipped the Chicago Cubs in five games in the Series.

It's no wonder Philadelphia dominated baseball in 1929, with Hall of Famers Al Simmons (right) *and Mickey Cochrane* (center) *joining a 21-year-old Foxx on a World Series champion.*

The Mackmen were unstoppable the next two years. In 1930 Foxx, Simmons, and Cochrane all topped the .330 mark. Foxx hit 37 homers, Simmons slugged 36, and Jimmie's 156 RBI were second only to Gehrig in the AL. The A's repeated as world champs. In 1931 Foxx hit 30 homers and drove in 120 as the A's took their third straight American League crown, although they were stopped in the World Series by the Cardinals. In the three Series he played in, Foxx batted .344 and slugged .609.

In 1932 Foxx had his 58-homer year, slugging 17 more than Ruth and 24 more than Gehrig. His 169 RBI, 151 runs, and .749 slugging average topped the league, too. He had 100 extra-base hits, and he was named Most Valuable Player. Yet, the Yankees still took the pennant. In 1933 the A's fell to third, but it was no fault of Jimmie's. He took the Triple Crown that year

Dizzy Dean (right) *was honored for his courage, but Foxx became the first AL player to win back-to-back MVP Awards after leading the league with 48 homers, a .356 average, and 163 RBI in 1933.*

with 48 homers, 163 runs batted in, and a .356 average. He actually would have won the year before if it had been played under today's rules; the 1932 batting champ, Dale Alexander, had only 392 at-bats. Foxx won the MVP for a second time in '33, making him the first American Leaguer to win back-to-back.

Foxx homered 44 times in 1934, then hit 36 long balls for a last-place A's team in 1935. Mack sold him to the Red Sox. He hit 41 homers his first year there, 36 his second.

Foxx didn't really take advantage of Fenway's short left field, though, until 1938, when he slugged 50 homers, 35 of them at Fenway. That same year, Hank Greenberg hit 58 homers. For his home run power, and his 175 RBI, Foxx won his third Most Valuable Player crown.

Foxx's 35 homers in 1939 led the league, and he belted another 36 the following year. In 1941 he was named to the All-Star team for the ninth consecutive year.

Foxx retired after the 1942 season, which he split between the Red Sox and Cubs. He was coaxed into returning to the Cubs for 1944, but he failed to homer in his 20 at-bats. In 1945 he ended his career with 89 games for the Phillies, but one

The muscular Foxx might have wondered where Ted Williams (left) *derived all of his power. Foxx finished his career with 13 more homers than "Teddy Ballgame" would hit.*

of his seven round-trippers that year created a memorable moment for at least one fan.

According to Bob Gorman's biography of Foxx, Jack Boyle, a longtime Ebbets Field vendor, saw the Phils play his Dodgers. "Jimmie Foxx hit a line drive over the glove of a leaping Tommy Brown at shortstop," Boyle said, "and the ball kept on rising until it landed in the upper deck in left-center field—a 'patented' Jimmie Foxx home run!"

BY THE NUMBERS

Year	Team	G	AB	R	H	2B	3B	HR	HR%	RBI	BB	K	BA	SA	SB
1925	Phi-A	10	9	2	6	1	0	0	0.0	0	0	1	.667	.778	0
1926	Phi-A	26	32	8	10	2	1	0	0.0	5	1	6	.313	.438	1
1927	Phi-A	61	130	23	42	6	5	3	2.3	20	14	11	.323	.515	2
1928	Phi-A	118	400	85	131	29	10	13	3.3	79	60	43	.327	.548	3
1929	Phi-A	149	517	123	183	23	9	33	6.4	118	103	70	.354	.625	9
1930	Phi-A	153	562	127	188	33	13	37	6.6	156	93	66	.335	.637	7
1931	Phi-A	139	515	93	150	32	10	30	5.8	120	73	84	.291	.567	4
1932	Phi-A	154	585	**151**	213	33	9	**58**	**9.9**	**169**	116	96	.364	**.749**	3
1933	Phi-A	149	573	125	204	37	9	**48**	8.4	**163**	96	93	**.356**	**.703**	2
1934	Phi-A	150	539	120	180	28	6	44	8.2	130	**111**	75	.334	.653	11
1935	Phi-A	147	535	118	185	33	7	**36**	6.7	115	114	99	.346	**.636**	6
1936	Bos-A	155	585	130	198	32	8	41	7.0	143	105	119	.338	.631	13
1937	Bos-A	150	569	111	162	24	6	36	6.3	127	99	96	.285	.538	10
1938	Bos-A	149	565	139	197	33	9	50	8.8	**175**	**119**	76	**.349**	**.704**	5
1939	Bos-A	124	467	130	168	31	10	**35**	7.5	105	89	72	.360	**.694**	4
1940	Bos-A	144	515	106	153	30	4	36	7.0	119	101	87	.297	.581	4
1941	Bos-A	135	487	87	146	27	8	19	3.9	105	93	103	.300	.505	2
1942	Bos-A	30	100	18	27	4	0	5	5.0	14	18	15	.270	.460	0
	Chi-N	70	205	25	42	8	0	3	1.5	19	22	55	.205	.288	1
1944	Chi-N	15	20	0	1	1	0	0	0.0	2	2	5	.050	.100	0
1945	Phi-N	89	224	30	60	11	1	7	3.1	38	23	39	.268	.420	0
Total	20	2317	8134	1751	2646	458	125	534	6.6	1922	1452	1311	.325	.609	87

LOU GEHRIG

The "Iron Horse," who died an early, tragic death, may have been the most consistently superior slugger of all time.

ONE OF THE MANY positive sidelights to Cal Ripken's consecutive-games streak was that many young baseball fans learned the story of the man whose record he broke: Lou Gehrig of the New York Yankees. It's a remarkable tale about an extraordinary man.

Gehrig's streak of 2,130 consecutive games played began May 31, 1925, when he pinch-hit for Pee Wee Wanninger. The next day he played first base in place of Wally Pipp, whose headache after a batting-practice beaning caused him to ask for the day off. Gehrig didn't take charge right away. Several times that year he was removed for a pinch hitter, and he didn't start the game on July 5 that year, although he did appear later.

We know now that Gehrig's streak could have used a few asterisks. Several times he batted in the first inning and left the game, just to keep the streak alive. But we have also learned that the ordeal was more physically punishing than we knew before. Late in Gehrig's career his hands were X-rayed, and doctors discovered 17 "breaks" in the bones of his fingers that had

healed without medical attention. He fractured a toe in 1934 but kept on playing. One day he was beaned, knocked unconscious, and sent to the hospital with a concussion. The next day he appeared in the lineup and, as the story goes, hit three triples.

In Gehrig's first full season as a Yankee, 1925, he hit .295, swatted 10 triples and 20 homers, scored 73 runs, and drove in 68 in 126 games. He would never again drive in or score fewer than 100 runs in a season until the fateful year of 1939.

Gehrig's consistency of excellence was almost beyond belief. He reached the 400 total-base level five times. In all of baseball history, that's been done only 22 times. Over an 11-year span in the middle of his career, he *averaged* 153 RBI a season. The 153-RBI mark has been reached only 33 times by anybody, ever. His RBI stats are even more remarkable when you consider that Lou batted behind two of the most notorious base-cleaners of all time—Babe Ruth and Joe DiMaggio.

Lou belted 493 home runs in his career, but no one got more out of them. He hit an all-time record 23 grand slams, 73 three-run shots, and 166 homers with one teammate on, giving him the highest RBI-to-homer percentage of any player with more than 300 homers. His lifetime slugging average trails only those of Ruth and Ted Williams.

One of the ways to evaluate a player is what historian Bill James calls "looking for the black ink." In *Total Baseball,* the official baseball encyclopedia, league-leading efforts are printed in black ink. Look at Gehrig's page and you'll be amazed. Thirty-six times the ink is black. What stands out are his five RBI titles and five on-base percentage crowns. But he also led the league in homers three times, doubles twice, and triples once. Three times he slugged more than .700. And late in his career his batting savvy increased, as he led the league in walks three years in a row, with never fewer than 127.

In 1927 Gehrig drove in 175 runs to set the American League record, breaking Babe's old standard of 171, set six years earlier. Then in 1931, Gehrig knocked in 184 to set the American League record, which still stands.

Gehrig was also the first American Leaguer to hit four home runs in a game, on June 3, 1932. And therein lies a tale or two. The story goes that after allowing Lou's first three homers

Above right: Watching the 1939 World Series must have been difficult for a failing Gehrig, who had been diagnosed with a fatal nerve disease that now bears his name. Below: Gehrig's consistency went well beyond his consecutive-games streak. He drove in at least 112 runs in 13 straight seasons, with a high of 184.

This home run in the 1937 World Series could not save the Yankees from a four-game loss to the Giants. The legendary first baseman socked the final 29 homers of his career the following summer.

in that game, Philadelphia A's pitcher George Earnshaw was yanked from the game by his manager, Connie Mack. Earnshaw had had enough and was eager to dowse himself in the showers, but Mack made him stay on the bench. "I want you to watch how [Roy] Mahaffey [who relieved Earnshaw] pitches to Gehrig," Mack said. Earnshaw watched studiously as Gehrig smacked his fourth homer of the game out of the park in deep center. "I see, Connie," Earnshaw said. "May I be excused now?" Gehrig came to bat a fifth time in that game, and only a leaping catch by Al Simmons kept him from hitting his fifth dinger of the day.

Ruth and Gehrig were a tandem the likes of which baseball fans had never seen. In 1927, the year Ruth hit 60 homers and Gehrig 47, the two of them *each* had more than any other *team* in baseball, save one. Over the next five years, they together averaged nearly 82 homers and 275 RBI a year.

In 1931 Gehrig popped three grand slams in a four-game stretch. Ruth and Gehrig finished the season tied with 46 homers, but Gehrig had lost one on a bizarre play. With teammate Lyn Lary on second base, Gehrig hit a drive into the stands so hard that it bounced back out and the center fielder

The 1935 MVP trophy was one of many honors Gehrig attained in a 17-year Yankee career. Lou amassed five seasons with at least 40 round-trippers and slugged a still-standing record 23 grand slams.

caught it. Lary, confused on the play, looked to the third base coach, who tried to signal him to slow down. Lary misunderstood, stopped dead, and ran back to second, just in time to see the relaxed Gehrig lope past him. Interestingly, those two runs cost the Yankees the game.

Gehrig was a monster in World Series play, too. The Yankees lost the first Series Lou and Babe appeared in together, 1926 vs. St. Louis. Ruth, after being walked in the ninth inning of the seventh game with his team down by one run, decided he'd try to steal second with hard-hitting Bob Meusel at the plate. He was caught, and the Yanks went down to defeat. But you couldn't blame Lou; he batted .348 for the Series. In 1927 the Yanks toppled Pittsburgh in just four games, although it wasn't the thrashing some writers claimed. Gehrig batted .308 with two doubles, two triples, and four RBI.

The 1928 fall classic *was* the Series in which the Yanks delivered a four-game thrashing, this time against the Cardinals. St. Louis tried to neutralize Gehrig by walking him six times, but it didn't help. He had six hits, four of them homers, drove in nine (one-third) of his team's runs, and slugged an unbelievable 1.727. The Babe did okay, too: a .625 average with 10 hits and three homers.

The A's of Jimmie Foxx and Al Simmons kept the Yankees out of the World Series for the next three years. It wasn't that Ruth and Gehrig were slumping; the A's pitching was just tougher. When the Yankees returned to the Series in 1932, they again swept in four games, with Gehrig leading all players in batting at .529, slugging at 1.118, homers with three, and RBI with eight.

LOU AND BABE

When sportswriter Fred Lieb asked Lou Gehrig how he felt about always being in Babe Ruth's shadow, Gehrig replied in typical fashion: "It's a pretty big shadow. It gives me lots of room to spread myself." But much has been made of the personal conflict between the two great slugging teammates. It's true that the two men could not have been more different as people. Gehrig was college educated, reserved, and soft-spoken. Ruth lived a life that could only be described as Ruthian, with outsized appetites for alcohol, cigars, women, and attention.

The two barnstormed several times after the regular season, with Ruth's team called "The Bustin' Babes" and Gehrig's "The Larrupin' Lous." Their relationship was always cordial, if nothing more, but then again Gehrig wasn't effusive about anything. He had to enjoy the extra money Ruth put in his pocket, but one unpleasant incident did chill their relationship for several years. An offhand comment by Gehrig's mother about how well Ruth's daughter dressed stuck in the Babe's craw. He told Gehrig he never wanted to speak to him again. And he kept his word until the ceremony for Gehrig's retirement. After his famous farewell speech, the Babe walked up and gave his old partner a huge hug. All was forgiven.

The Yanks fell to second in 1933, as Babe and Lou tailed off to a mere 66 homers and 232 RBI between them. In 1934 Gehrig hit 49 homers, the most of his career, and drove in 165. With his .363 average also leading the league, he won his first Triple Crown. But the Yanks finished second, and Ruth's career was nearly over; after the season he was sent to the National League. Gehrig hit only 30 home runs in 1935, although he did bat .329.

The next year Joe DiMaggio arrived in a Yankee uniform, and the Yanks moved back to where they belonged—world champions. Gehrig clouted 49 home runs again, drove in 152, and led the league with 167 runs scored, his most ever. The Yankees dominated the Giants in a six-game Series, outscoring them by 20 runs. Gehrig's seven RBI tied him with Tony Lazzeri for the top slot. In 1937 Lou hit a dozen fewer homers, but he still collected 159 RBI, and the Yanks took only six games to beat John McGraw's Giants in the Series.

While Gehrig's statistics for the 1938 season would be marvelous for mere mortals, they were way below the level of performance he had established. He batted just .295, his lowest mark in 13 years. His 29 home runs and 114 RBI were the fewest he had since 1926. The Yankees swept the Series again, this time against the Cubs, but all Lou could manage were four singles in 14 at-bats. He was obviously losing his strength. Doctors diagnosed a gall bladder problem and put him on a bland diet, which only made him weaker. The end of his career had begun.

By spring training of 1939, teammates were noticing his unsteady, shuffling gait, quite different from his customary graceful walk. Few said anything. Most were too frightened. The 1939 season began with Gehrig where he had been for the past 13 years, at first base. But after just eight games, batting only .143 and obviously a shell of his former self, he took himself out of the lineup. When the batting order was announced with Babe Dahlgren at first base the next day, the crowd let out an audible gasp.

Gehrig was diagnosed by doctors at the Mayo Clinic with amyotrophic lateral sclerosis, the rare degenerative nerve disease that would later unofficially bear Gehrig's name. He would never play again. New York sportswriter Paul Gallico suggested that the team hold a day to honor him. They did so on July 4 of that year.

His farewell speech, although later edited and altered for the movies, was a monument to Gehrig's style as a person and a ballplayer. He began, not ended, the talk with, "Fans, for the past two weeks you have been reading about the bad break I

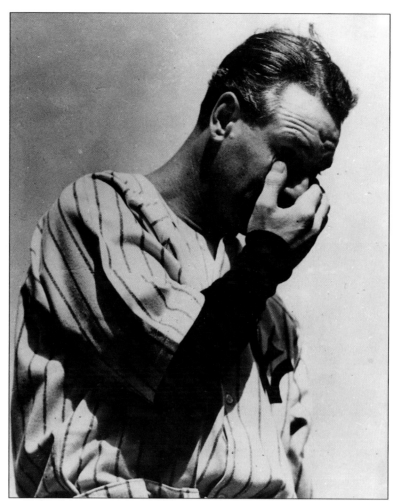

Gehrig finished his farewell speech on July 4, 1939, by saying, "I may have had a tough break, but I have an awful lot to live for." He died two years later, on June 2, 1941.

"Today I consider myself the luckiest man on the face of the earth."
—Gehrig, in his farewell speech

got. Yet today I consider myself the luckiest man on the face of the earth." Then he delivered a remarkable litany of why he considered himself so lucky, thanking first the fans, then listing people such as Yankees owners and executives; his former manager, Miller Huggins, and current one, Joe McCarthy; the New York Giants, "a team you would give your right arm to beat;" the groundskeepers; and his mother-in-law, parents, and wife. He concluded with words just as memorable as his opening remarks: "So I close in saying that I may have had a tough break, but I have an awful lot to live for."

The man sportswriter Jim Murray called "a symbol of indestructibility—a Gibraltar in cleats" was dead before his 38th birthday.

													BY THE NUMBERS		
Year	Team	G	AB	R	H	2B	3B	HR	HR%	RBI	BB	K	BA	SA	SB
1923	NY-A	13	26	6	11	4	1	1	3.8	9	2	5	.423	.769	0
1924	NY-A	10	12	2	6	1	0	0	0.0	5	1	3	.500	.583	0
1925	NY-A	126	437	73	129	23	10	20	4.6	68	46	49	.295	.531	6
1926	NY-A	155	572	135	179	47	20	16	2.8	112	105	73	.313	.549	6
1927	NY-A	155	584	149	218	52	18	47	8.0	175	109	84	.373	.765	10
1928	NY-A	154	562	139	210	47	13	27	4.8	142	95	69	.374	.648	4
1929	NY-A	154	553	127	166	32	10	35	6.3	126	122	68	.300	.584	4
1930	NY-A	154	581	143	220	42	17	41	7.1	174	101	63	.379	.721	12
1931	NY-A	155	619	163	211	31	15	46	7.4	184	117	56	.341	.662	17
1932	NY-A	156	596	138	208	42	9	34	5.7	151	108	38	.349	.621	4
1933	NY-A	152	593	138	198	41	12	32	5.4	139	92	42	.334	.605	9
1934	NY-A	154	579	128	210	40	6	49	8.5	165	109	31	.363	.706	9
1935	NY-A	149	535	125	176	26	10	30	5.6	119	132	38	.329	.583	8
1936	NY-A	155	579	167	205	37	7	49	8.5	152	130	46	.354	.696	3
1937	NY-A	157	569	138	200	37	9	37	6.5	159	127	49	.351	.643	4
1938	NY-A	157	576	115	170	32	6	29	5.0	114	107	75	.295	.523	6
1939	NY-A	8	28	2	4	0	0	0	0.0	1	5	1	.143	.143	0
Total	17	2164	8001	1888	2721	534	163	493	6.2	1995	1508	790	.340	.632	102

JOSH GIBSON

Josh Gibson's home runs were the stuff of legend. The sad part is, that's all they'll ever be. One of the greatest sluggers ever never got to play in the major leagues.

O F ALL THE GREAT ATHLETES denied a chance to play with their true peers because of the color of their skin, Josh Gibson may have been the one whom major-league baseball missed the most. "A big, beautiful man," as Buck O'Neil described him, Gibson may well have been the greatest slugger ever.

Some say Gibson hit 962 home runs in his career; others say 823. Some have claimed he hit 84 in one season; others say 75. The problem was, the Negro Leagues Josh played in weren't big on keeping stats. In a typical 50-game Negro League season, Josh would club a dozen or so homers and bat well over .300. To get to those incredible lifetime totals, you'd have to include all the games Josh played everywhere, against any and all competition. (By the same standards, Babe Ruth probably averaged a hundred home runs a year.)

But if the lifetime totals are bleary, it's not because Josh was lacking anything. In 17 years of Negro League ball, he led the league in homers 10 times. In 16 games against white big-leaguers, he batted near .430 and belted five homers.

With his short, quick stroke delivered by immense, bulging arm muscles and thick legs, Josh hit homers that went farther than anyone had ever seen. And his belts were screaming line drives, not looping arcs. Yes, some of the long-distance stories are apocryphal, such as the one in which he allegedly hit a ball all the way out of Yankee Stadium. (He didn't. He just cracked it 460 feet or so, six rows higher than the legendary Jimmie Foxx homer of 1932.) Satchel Paige

even claimed that Josh hit the top of the scoreboard clock at Wrigley Field, which would have made it a 700-foot homer. Sam Snead couldn't hit a golf ball that far with a three-iron. He tried.

But the ones that have been verified were nearly as remarkable. In *The Sporting News's Daguerreotypes,* reference is made to a homer he hit up the side of a mountain next to the ballpark in Welch, West Virginia. In Monessen, Pennsylvania, he hit one so far that the mayor got out the biggest tape measure he could find and declared that the ball had traveled 575 feet.

Gibson hit two over the left-field bleachers in Washington's huge Griffith Stadium. Mickey Mantle did it once. Eyewitnesses said Josh had the long-distance records for not only Yankee and Griffith, but also Forbes Field, Sportsman's Park, Crosley Field, and Cleveland's Municipal Stadium. They say he once hit a 375-foot homer in Indianapolis with just one hand.

Griffith was one of Josh's favorite parks. For several seasons his team played half of its home games there and half in Pittsburgh. One year he hit 10 home runs in Griffith (four in one game), something no major-leaguer who played 77 games a year there ever did. The outfield walls in Griffith were covered with advertising signs. Once Gibson hit a line drive that smashed off an ad showing hot dogs. "Paint and dust flew everywhere," tells William Brashler in his biography of Gibson. "A fan yelled, 'Josh sure knocked the mustard off that hot dog!'"

In his autobiography, *I Was Right on Time,* O'Neil tells the story of how, before the 1942 Negro League World Series, a smart-aleck rookie started poking fun at the aged (31!) Gibson. He found a bat that looked like it had been in Abner Doubleday's closet and said, "Josh, this must be your bat." Josh yanked out a piece of lumber that looked brand new except for a worn spot, the shape of a baseball, on the fat part of the barrel. Josh told the kid, "Son, I don't break 'em. I wear 'em out."

In his *Biographical Encyclopedia of the Negro Leagues,* Jim Riley tells a wonderful Gibson story. Supposedly Josh cracked a ball so far in Pittsburgh one day that it completely disappeared. The next day Gibson's team was playing in Philadelphia, and as he stepped to the plate a ball sailed out of

nowhere and was grabbed by the center fielder. "Yer out!" said the ump. "I mean, yesterday in Pittsburgh."

Josh joined other Negro League greats—and several to-be Hall of Famers—on the Homestead Grays in 1937, and together they won nine straight Negro National League pennants. His duels with pitcher Satchel Paige were also the stuff of legend.

A brain tumor took its toll on Gibson's health. He refused surgery, and painkillers along with his love of beer made him sick and angry, nothing like the jovial man he had been before. Although he led the league in homers again in 1946, he was a desperately sick man. He died on January 20, 1947, less than a month after his 36th birthday.

BY THE NUMBERS															
Year	Team	G	AB	R	H	2B	3B	HR	HR%	RBI	BB	K	BA	SA	SB
1930	Home	10	33	-	8	1	0	1	3.0	-	-	-	.242	.364	1
1931	Home	32	129	-	48	8	0	6	4.7	-	-	-	.372	.574	0
1932	Craw	46	147	-	42	3	5	7	4.8	-	-	-	.286	.517	1
1933	Home	34	116	-	42	8	1	6	5.2	-	-	-	.362	.603	1
1934	Craw	41	146	-	46	8	3	11	7.5	-	-	-	.315	.637	1
1935	Craw	37	129	-	43	7	1	11	8.5	-	-	-	.333	.659	3
1936	Craw	23	75	-	27	3	0	11	14.7	-	-	-	.360	.840	0
1937	Home	12	42	-	21	0	4	7	16.7	-	-	-	.500	1.190	0
1938	Home	19	74	-	23	1	0	4	5.4	-	-	-	.311	.486	1
1939	Wash	29	88	-	29	2	2	17	19.3	-	-	-	.330	.977	0
1940	Home	2	6	-	1	0	0	1	16.7	-	-	-	.167	.667	0
1942	Wash	51	158	-	53	8	1	15	9.5	-	-	-	.335	.684	3
1943	Home	57	209	-	108	23	8	16	7.7	-	-	-	.517	.933	0
1944	Home	28	97	-	35	3	3	6	6.2	-	-	-	.351	.639	0
1945	Home	31·	98	-	31	3	3	11	11.2	-	-	-	.316	.745	0
1946	Home	49	132	-	50	11	4	16	12.1	-	-	-	.379	.886	0
Total	16	501	1679	-	607	89	35	146	8.7	-	-	-	.361	.717	11

Before Gibson died at the young age of 36, few players in base-ball—of any color—enjoyed the game or the long ball as much as he did. In 16 games against major-leaguers, he batted close to .430 and rapped five home runs.

HANK GREENBERG

The original "Hammerin' Hank," Greenberg lost 4½ seasons to military duty. But when he was in the lineup, he was a potent slugger with a knack for clutch performances.

HANK GREENBERG AMASSED fewer than 10 full seasons of playing time in the major leagues, but no one got more out of that amount of time than he did.

Greenberg topped the .300 mark eight years in a row, and exceeded .335 four times. His career slugging percentage of .605 is the fifth highest ever. He is one of only four players to knock a homer into the center-field bleachers at old Comiskey Park in Chicago. In 1934 he slugged 63 doubles, a feat topped only three times in major-league history. He homered in all four of the World Series he played in. Perhaps most significantly, his lifetime average of .92 RBI per game ties Lou Gehrig and 19th-century slugger Sam Thompson as the highest ever.

Although Greenberg was blessed with height and a muscular build, he didn't have the speed or agility that many others did. He made up for what he lacked with hard work and dedication—and a healthy dose of street smarts. In 1948 Lefty Gomez was quoted in *The Sporting News* as telling Hank, "You used to say when I threw it from behind my ear nobody could hit it. So I'm flattered and throw from behind my ear— and you belt it. I didn't realize until later you were suckering me into giving away my curve."

Because he was a native New Yorker (of Romanian-Jewish immigrant background), both

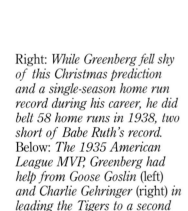

Right: *While Greenberg fell shy of this Christmas prediction and a single-season home run record during his career, he did belt 58 home runs in 1938, two short of Babe Ruth's record.* Below: *The 1935 American League MVP, Greenberg had help from Goose Goslin* (left) *and Charlie Gehringer* (right) *in leading the Tigers to a second straight pennant.*

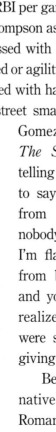

the Giants and the Yankees were interested in him. Giants manager John McGraw, however, felt the kid was too clumsy. A Yankee scout took Hank to a Yankee practice, and they watched a 26-year-old Lou Gehrig work out at first. "He's washed up," the scout allegedly told Hank. "You'll be there in a couple of years." Greenberg believed his eyes instead of the scout, and he signed with the Detroit Tigers.

In Greenberg's second full season, the Tigers won the pennant, scoring 150 more runs than any other club in the American League. Along with his 63 doubles that season, Hank homered 26 times and drove in 139 runs. The Tigers were stopped by St. Louis's "Gashouse Gang" in the Series. Hank hit .321 but stranded 16 baserunners.

The Tigers repeated in 1935, largely because of Greenberg. He hit 36 homers, drove in 170, and batted .328 to win the AL Most Valuable Player Award. But in the second game of the World Series against the Chicago Cubs, a pitch by Fabian Kowalik broke Hank's wrist. The next year he started out hot, with 16 RBI in his first dozen games, but in a collision with a baserunner he rebroke the wrist, and was out until 1937.

But what a comeback it was! Not only did Greenberg hit 49 doubles and 40 homers, he also drove in 183 runs, just one shy of Lou Gehrig's all-time AL mark. After nearly matching Gehrig, he then took on Babe Ruth in 1938. He set a record that year with 11 multihomer games, and with five games left in the season he had 58 home runs, two short of Ruth's mythical mark. But he "ran out of gas," as he said, and hit no more. He did set the major-league record that year with 39 homers at home.

In 1940 the Tigers hired notorious sign stealer Del Baker as their third base coach, and Hank showed what he could do when he knew what was coming. He led the league in doubles (50), homers (41), RBI (150), and slugging percentage (.670). The Tigers took the flag, and Hank won his second MVP crown. He batted .357 in that year's World Series, with six RBI and 10 hits, but the Tigers fell to the Cincinnati Reds.

Early in the 1941 season, Hank was drafted into the military. He was discharged on December 5, but two days later the Japanese attacked Pearl Harbor, and Hank re-enlisted. He didn't

return until July 1, 1945, but he returned in style, homering on his first day back for a Tiger win. In the last game of the year, Hank slugged a grand slam in the last of the 10th inning to win the pennant for the Tigers. He hit 13 homers and drove in 60 runs in his partial season. In the World Series his three-run homer in Game 2 was the winning margin.

In 1946 Greenberg hit 44 homers, but because he batted only .277, the Tigers released him. He was the first man ever to hit 40 long shots without batting .300. Until then sluggers had been great overall hitters; the man who could hit only home runs was rare.

The Pirates picked up Greenberg in 1947 for a huge salary and asked him to work with budding star Ralph Kiner. The Pirates moved in the left-field fence at Forbes Field, creating

"Greenberg Gardens," and Hank hit his last 25 homers. More importantly, he did what the Pirates asked. Second-year man Kiner hit 51 homers to lead the league.

Greenberg's 1938 season remains one of the best in Tigers history. In addition to his league-leading home run total of 58, he drove in 146 runs and scored 144.

BY THE NUMBERS															
Year	Team	G	AB	R	H	2B	3B	HR	HR%	RBI	BB	K	BA	SA	SB
1930	Det-A	1	1	0	0	0	0	0	0.0	0	0	0	.000	.000	0
1933	Det-A	117	449	59	135	33	3	12	2.7	87	46	78	.301	.468	6
1934	Det-A	153	593	118	201	**63**	7	26	4.4	139	63	93	.339	.600	9
1935	Det-A	152	619	121	203	46	16	**36**	5.8	**170**	87	91	.328	.628	4
1936	Det-A	12	46	10	16	6	2	1	2.2	16	9	6	.348	.630	1
1937	Det-A	154	594	137	200	49	14	40	6.7	**183**	102	101	.337	.668	8
1938	Det-A	155	556	**144**	175	23	4	**58**	**10.4**	146	**119**	92	.315	.683	7
1939	Det-A	138	500	112	156	42	7	33	6.6	112	91	95	.312	.622	8
1940	Det-A	148	573	129	195	**50**	8	**41**	7.2	**150**	93	75	.340	**.670**	6
1941	Det-A	19	67	12	18	5	1	2	3.0	12	16	12	.269	.463	1
1945	Det-A	78	270	47	84	20	2	13	4.8	60	42	40	.311	.544	3
1946	Det-A	142	523	91	145	29	5	**44**	8.4	**127**	80	88	.277	.604	5
1947	Pit-N	125	402	71	100	13	2	25	6.2	74	**104**	73	.249	.478	0
Total	13	1394	5193	1051	1628	379	71	331	6.4	1276	852	844	.313	.605	58

KEN GRIFFEY JR.

By coupling God-given talent with a constant striving for improvement, Ken Griffey Jr. is already carving himself a niche among the game's immortal batsmen.

Above right: A projected star before ever playing a big-league game, "Junior" has looked the hype straight in the eye. He could reach 400 career homers before turning 30. To do so, he needs to hit 50 in 1999. Below: More than just a slugger and offensive superstar, Griffey's heroics in the outfield have helped stamp him as one of baseball's best all-around players.

WHEN KEN GRIFFEY JR. WAS still a teenager, his name was being mentioned in the same sentence with Willie Mays and Mickey Mantle. How could he miss? He had good bloodlines; his dad, Ken Sr., played in the majors for 19 years. He was strong and fast. And he had that amazingly lovely swing, a positive work of art that enabled him to hit balls higher and farther than his slender body would indicate.

Not surprisingly, "Junior" was a gifted athlete at an early age. In fact, his mother had to take his birth certificate to Little League games to prove to angry parents that the boy striking their kids out and swatting all those home runs really was 10 years old. Ken starred in both baseball and football at Cincinnati's Moeller High. During his senior year he batted .478 and cracked seven homers in fewer than 30 games.

The Seattle Mariners chose Griffey with the first pick overall in the 1987 amateur draft. He spent just a season and a half in the minors, moving quickly to Double-A ball. The Mariners had ticketed him for Triple-A in 1989, but he never got there. His incredible spring training performance—.359, 33 hits, 21 RBI—earned him a shot at the bigs.

Griffey broke into the majors at age 19 and homered in his very first swing at his home park, Seattle's Kingdome. In a five-day stretch late in April, he smacked eight consecutive hits and reached base 11 times in a row. At the end of his first month in the majors, he was named American League Player of the Week. He was batting .300 with 13 home runs before the All-Star break, but a fall in the shower led to a broken finger that all but ended his season. He played in only 127 games and finished the season with 16 homers. Nevertheless, his graceful, often acrobatic defense in center field—which would lead to perennial Gold Gloves—wowed the locals. He even had a candy bar named after him.

The next season Griffey was Player of the Month for April, with a .385 batting average, five homers, and 17 RBI. He finished fourth in the league in total bases, knocked 22 homers, and tallied 80 RBI. In 1991, at just 21 years old, he upped his doubles total by 14, drilled 22 homers, drove in 100 runs, and rapped .327. He was also the first Mariner elected to the All-Star Game. In the first 20 years of their existence, he would be the only one.

In 1992 Griffey added five homers to his previous best and three more RBI. He batted .308 and finished fourth in slugging percentage. That season also saw Junior's first big-league grand slam; he added two more before the year was over to lead the league. Griffey ranked in the Top 10 in seven different offensive categories. He batted .358 against lefties, best in the league. In his third consecutive All-Star Game start, he was 3-for-3, including a homer, and won the game's MVP Award.

That said, 1993 was Junior's first great year. He homered in his first at-bat of the season. His .617 slugging percentage and 45 homers (just one behind Juan Gonzalez) were second in the league. His 359 total bases topped everyone. With his 109 RBI, he joined legends Joe DiMaggio, Ted Williams, Ty Cobb, and Mel Ott as the only men to have three consecutive 100-RBI seasons before the age of 24. On May 9 he tagged Minnesota's Scott Erickson for a homer that they're still talking about in Seattle. It rocketed off a speaker and still landed in the second deck.

With one of the sweetest swings in baseball, Griffey has led the American League in home runs three times despite missing significant time because of injuries.

But it was one stretch in July of '93 that turned everyone's heads. From the 20th through the 28th of that month, Griffey homered in eight consecutive games, tying the major-league record held by Dale Long and Don Mattingly. Six of those homers traveled distances of more than 400 feet. One was a grand slam. The last one, off Minnesota's Willie Banks, dented the facade in the third level of the Kingdome. In the next game he had two hits, including a double off the wall. "The Kid" had made his first step into the pantheon of great sluggers.

He followed it up in 1994 with a 40-homer season to lead the American League, although his team played only 112 games (70 percent of a season) because of the players' strike, robbing him of a chance to take a shot at Roger Maris's record 61 homers. After hitting seven 400-foot-plus shots in April, Junior swatted 15 more homers in May to set the record for the first two months of the season. Perhaps his biggest moment that year was when he took the breath away from millions of fans at the home run contest before the All-Star Game in Pittsburgh, when he knocked seven balls high into the upper

Above right: Griffey put on a power display before the 1994 All-Star Game in Pittsburgh, winning the home run contest while sending seven balls into the upper deck at Three Rivers.

deck at Three Rivers Stadium. His final homer that season was a grand slam, and he became the third youngest player to hit 150 homers.

In 1995 Griffey banged a three-run homer on Opening Day, but he totaled only six homers by May 26, when he broke his left wrist as he smashed into the Kingdome wall stealing an extra-base hit away from Kevin Bass. He returned in mid-August but was still weak until September. His team was in its first real pennant chase, and Junior wasn't about to rest. He came through in a big way, hitting seven home runs in September. The Mariners wore down the Oakland A's and tied them for the division crown. Junior's team took the playoff and then took on the New York Yankees.

In the Division Series Griffey was squarely in the middle of all the excitement. He hit two homers in a defeat in Game 1. His homer in the 12th inning of Game 2 gave the Mariners the lead, but they lost it in 15. In Game 4 he helped spark a victory with a homer, and scored three runs. In the final game Griffey homered in the eighth inning—his fifth of the series—against David Cone to ignite a Mariners comeback. Seattle was losing 5–4 in the 11th when a double by Edgar Martinez drove in Joey Cora with the tying run and Griffey with the winner. In the League Championship Series, the Mariners took Cleveland to six games before losing.

Griffey had another extraordinary year in '96, clubbing 49 homers (third in the league), driving in 140, and batting .303. Although he struggled at the beginning of the season, hitting just .215 after 17 games, he came on strong. The Mariners led baseball in runs scored, and Junior touched home 125 times himself, fifth best in the league. On May 21 that year, he hit his 200th home run. Only seven players in history have reached that milestone at a younger age, and six of them are in the Hall of Fame. And Griffey did all of that despite playing in pain half of the season with a broken bone in his right hand that required surgery. He missed 20 games. The Mariners also lost Edgar Martinez and Randy Johnson to injuries for much of that year, which is why they finished second.

KEN AND KEN

Ken Griffey Jr. and his father became the first father-son duo to play together in the major leagues. Ken Sr. joined his son's Seattle team in August 1990, having spent 17 years in the bigs with Cincinnati, the Yankees, and Atlanta. It was obvious they were comfortable together. Ken and Ken played together in 15 contests, with Pop hitting .400 in those games with three homers and 16 RBI. Son hit .312 with three homers and 11 RBI.

But the most magical event occurred on September 14. The story is told by Gaymon L. Bennett in David Porter's *African-American Sports Greats.* Ken Sr. homered off California Angel hurler Kirk McCaskill. As he crossed the plate, Ken Jr., the next batter, was there to shake his hand. Dad offered simple advice: "That's how you do it, son." Junior laughed out loud. But then the count on him reached 3-and-0.

"Manager Jim Lefebvre gave me the green light," Junior remembered. "I hit it solid and knew it was going out. I looked at Dad, and he couldn't believe it. I circled the bases, then trotted into the dugout and hugged him."

With 56 home runs in 1997, Griffey posted the best single-season long-ball total in the American League since Hank Greenberg slugged 58 homers in 1938.

The 1997 season was Griffey's first injury-free campaign in three years. And what a season he had! Starting with two homers on Opening Day against the Yanks, he set the major-league record for the most homers through April and May—24 (since broken by Mark McGwire). He had six dingers in his first eight games. He cooled off dramatically in June and July, swatting just eight long balls total in those two months, but a dozen homers each in August and September brought him within hollering distance of Maris, with 56. It was the most homers hit in one season in the American League since Maris, and the second most since Hank Greenberg's 58 in 1938. The Kid led the league in home run percentage for the second consecutive year. Griffey also drove in 147 runs. Only one man had driven in more AL runs in a season in 48 years. Junior also flirted with the magical 400 total-base mark, finishing with 393. That marked the highest number in a season in the American League in 19 years, and the second highest in 60. Not surprisingly, he also hit his longest homer ever that year—473 feet against the White Sox. He was named the league's MVP.

The 1998 season was definitely McGwire's and Sammy Sosa's year, but Junior was no slouch, either. He homered 56 more times, joining Babe Ruth and McGwire as the only men to top the 50 mark two years in a row. Only Griffey, McGwire, and Ruth have ever twice hit 56 or more home runs.

Through the 1998 season, Ken Griffey Jr., who won't turn 30 until November 1999, hit 350 home runs, drove in 1,018 runs, and batted an even .300. He averaged 49 home runs a year over his last five healthy seasons. Even more important, with the exception of injury years and labor disputes, he never hit fewer home runs in a season than he had the previous one. If he continues strong and healthy, the home run totals of Willie Mays (660), Ruth (714), and Hank Aaron (755) might well be within his reach.

Year	Team	G	AB	R	H	2B	3B	HR	HR%	RBI	BB	K	BA	SA	SB
1989	Sea-A	127	455	61	120	23	0	16	3.5	61	44	83	.264	.420	16
1990	Sea-A	155	597	91	179	28	7	22	3.7	80	63	81	.300	.481	16
1991	Sea-A	154	548	76	179	42	1	22	4.0	100	71	82	.327	.527	18
1992	Sea-A	142	565	83	174	39	4	27	4.8	103	44	67	.308	.535	10
1993	Sea-A	156	582	113	180	38	3	45	7.7	109	96	91	.309	.617	17
1994	Sea-A	111	433	94	140	24	4	40	9.2	90	56	73	.323	.674	11
1995	Sea-A	72	260	52	67	7	0	17	6.5	42	52	53	.258	.481	4
1996	Sea-A	140	545	125	165	26	2	49	9.0	140	78	104	.303	.628	16
1997	Sea-A	157	608	125	185	34	3	56	9.2	147	76	121	.304	.646	15
1998	Sea-A	161	633	120	180	33	3	56	8.8	146	76	121	.284	.611	20
Total	10	1375	5226	940	1569	294	27	350	6.7	1018	656	876	.300	.568	143

REGGIE JACKSON

The swaggering braggadocio of Reggie Jackson offended many people. But he backed up his big words with exceptional feats, particularly in the playoffs and World Series.

Above right: *Jackson altered his stance for the 1968 season, his first full big-league campaign and the Athletics' first year in Oakland. The result was a 29-homer performance. Below: It's no wonder Jackson was a fan favorite in 1969. He clobbered 45 homers by September 1, although he hit just two more the rest of the way.*

N HIS 1975 AUTOBIOGRAPHY, cowritten with Bill Libby, Reggie Jackson said, without a hint of modesty, "I am the best in baseball. . . . I can do it all and I create an excitement when I walk on the field." And that was two years before he became a New York Yankee.

Jackson could talk the talk as well as anyone. In Paul Dickson's *Baseball's Greatest Quotations,* there are 4½ pages of "Reggiespeak." Sportswriters loved him for it. The fans, though, loved him for what he did on the field.

Along with his 563 home runs, sixth best all time, he also drove in 1,702 runs, 17th best ever. Reggie was a true slugger: His 2,597 strikeouts are an all-time record. He led the league in homers four times, RBI once, and slugging percentage three times. And he was a winner: In 21 big-league seasons, he played for 11 division winners, six pennant winners, and five World Series champs. Best of all, when he came to bat in the postseason, he delivered better than anyone ever did.

He hit six home runs in League Championship Series, plus one in the famous 1978 playoff with Boston. In the World Series he was nonpareil. In 27 games he belted 10 homers, drove in 24, and batted .357. His World Series lifetime slugging percentage of .755 is the best ever. His five homers and 25 total bases in the 1977 World Series are also records.

Reggie began his slugging feats at Arizona State, where he was the first college player to hit a ball out of Phoenix Stadium. He was the second pick overall in the 1966 amateur draft by the Kansas City Athletics; the Mets, for some reason, picked catcher Steve Chilcott ahead of him. Jackson made his big-league debut in June 1967 and homered once in 35 games that year.

In 1968 the A's moved to Oakland. When Reggie adjusted his batting stance to get his hips into the ball sooner, it paid off immediately. He slugged 29 home runs. Oakland was beginning to build a team that would be a '70s powerhouse.

In 1969 Reggie lit up the world with an incredible slugging spree. In a June series against the Red Sox, he batted 14 times and drove in 15 runs. On July 2 he hit three homers. By July 29 he had 40. He was on pace to break Roger Maris's record of 61, and baseball was on fire about it. But Reggie inexplicably cooled off. Sitting on 45 homers on September 1, he hit only two more to finish with 47, one behind Frank Howard. Nevertheless, Jackson drove in 118 runs and led the league in slugging percentage and runs scored. Oakland finished second in the AL West.

Reggie's homer total fell off to just 23 in 1970, although that year he shocked baseball by clubbing a Dock Ellis pitch off the light tower on the right-field roof in Tiger Stadium. Meanwhile, Jackson's team was coming into its own. They took the AL West in 1971, aided by Reggie's 32 homers, only to lose in the League Championship Series to Baltimore.

In 1972 Jackson's homer, RBI, and batting totals were all down, but the red-hot A's knocked off Detroit in the ALCS and

headed toward the World Series. Reggie, though, wasn't able to play. He had torn a hamstring scoring a crucial run in the final game of the LCS. He had to watch from the bench as his team won its first of three consecutive World Series.

Jackson took the Most Valuable Player Award in 1973, leading the league with 32 homers and 117 RBI. He also was tops in runs scored and slugging. That year he had his first great October. Although he was only 3-for-21 in the LCS, he exploded in the Series. In Game 6 he drove in two runs and scored the third in a 3–1 A's victory. In Game 7 he hit his first Series homer, and it proved to be the clincher in the deciding game. Overall, he batted .310, led all batters with six RBI, and was named the Series MVP.

In 1974 Reggie was second in the league in home runs and slugging percentage, and the A's did it again, winning the LCS over Baltimore and the World Series over Los Angeles. No team without "Yankees" on their jerseys had ever won three straight world titles. And no team has since.

The 1975 season was more of the same, at least for a while. Reggie tied for the league lead with 36 homers and was third in total bases and fourth in RBI. The A's again won the AL West but were unseated from their championship throne when the Red Sox beat them in three straight in the ALCS, even though Jackson batted .417.

Meanwhile, the winds of change were blowing through the game. A landmark arbitrator's ruling stated that players could become free agents after playing out an option year and sign with whomever they chose. Tightfisted A's owner Charlie Finley didn't want to see his stars jump without getting something for himself in return, so he traded Reggie to Baltimore for

The 1977 World Series established Jackson as "Mr. October." He homered against the L.A. Dodgers three times in Game 6 and once each in Games 4 and 5.

the 1976 season. Reggie swatted 27 homers and drove in 91, but he had his mind set on a different team, preferably one with the big bucks to pay.

Reggie joined the Yankees, once the greatest team of all but one that had not played in the postseason for 13 years. He signed the biggest contract among the first crop of free agents—the then unheard-of sum of $3 million over five years. Fans gasped. Owners wailed.

Years earlier Reggie had said, "If I played in New York, they'd name a candy bar after me." He was right. Before he even joined the team, he angered some teammates-to-be by announcing in a pre-season interview in *Sport* magazine, "I'm the straw that stirs the drink." To no one's surprise, Reggie's seasons in New York would be tempestuous, even tumultuous. There were other strong personalities in the

Jackson and Billy Martin (right) *had their share of run-ins, but over the years no manager-slugger combination brought more flavor to baseball than they did.*

Bronx he would have to contend with: Thurman Munson, manager Billy Martin, and owner George Steinbrenner. But Reggie never doubted himself; it's unlikely many others did, either.

During his first season in pinstripes, 1977, Jackson hit 32 homers and drove in 110 runs, but his run-ins with Martin often took the headlines instead. The Yankees, racked with dissension, beat the Orioles in the AL East by 2½ games. That year's LCS was a noisy one. There were two bench-clearing brawls. Jackson, only 1-for-14 in the first four games, was benched by Martin for the finale, in what *The Sporting News* called "typical Yankee high drama." However, he returned to pinch-hit and knocked in the run that got the Yankees' comeback rolling. They topped the Royals 5–3, scoring four runs in the last two innings.

JACKSON VS. WELCH

Sometimes when a slugger fails, it can be even more dramatic than when he succeeds. There was no more dramatic at-bat in World Series history than the confrontation between Jackson and Dodger rookie fireballer Bob Welch in Game 2 of the 1978 Series.

Jackson, who had ended the 1977 Series with homers on his last four swings, picked up where he left off in 1978. He singled twice and homered in Game 1, although the Yanks were beaten 11–5. Jackson came to the plate in the ninth inning of Game 2 with two on and two out and L.A. up 4–3. All Reggie needed was a single, but he was swinging for the downs. It was as intense as baseball can be.

Jackson fell behind in the count 1–2. He then fouled off two pitches, took one for a ball, fouled off another, and took a ball that filled the count. Welch wanted to throw nothing but heat, and that was fine with Reggie. People watching on television were on the edge of their sofas.

Jackson's full-bore cuts, according to author Roger Angell, "resemble a dangerously defective drilling machine." Receiving one more high fastball, Jackson cranked a swing again—and missed. Strikeout. Game over. Jackson was uncharacteristically humble afterward. "The kid beat me," he said.

The Dodgers' 2–0 lead in Series games didn't last long. The Yanks took the next four, and Reggie got his revenge, towering a two-run homer on the first pitch he saw from Welch in the seventh inning of the final game to seal the Yankee victory.

Back in the Yankee cleanup spot in 1978, Jackson was poised to drive in such notables as (from left) *Mickey Rivers, Chris Chambliss, and Thurman Munson.*

In that year's World Series against Los Angeles, it was Reggie who provided all the drama. He had come into the Series as a .317 lifetime batsman in fall classics. After doubling and scoring early in Game 4, he came to bat in the sixth inning and homered for an insurance run in the Yanks' 4–2 win. The Dodgers won Game 5 to cut the Yankee lead in games to 3–2. Reggie homered in his final at-bat.

Game 6 was the legend. Reggie walked his first time up. In the fourth inning, with his team down 3–2 and Munson on base, Jackson homered on the first pitch from Burt Hooton to give the Bronxmen the lead. The Yankee Stadium faithful went mad; they smelled a return to glory. In the fifth inning, Jackson again saw one pitch, this time from Elias Sosa, and he deposited that one into the stands, too. The crowd was really charged now. In the eighth Reggie stepped to the plate once more. Hurler Charlie Hough threw one of his famous knuckle-curves. But it did neither. Reggie creamed that one, too. On four consecutive swings in the pressure cooker of the World Series, Reggie Jackson had hit four home runs. He *was* "Mr. October."

The 1978 season brought another Yankee championship—in some ways different, in some the same. More battles with Jackson and Steinbrenner got Martin fired. Jackson, who had been moved out of his familiar cleanup spot by Martin, returned to where he belonged. A huge Red Sox lead was burned away by the searing New Yorkers. When they finished the season in a dead heat, they met for a one-game playoff.

Jackson homered in the game, but it was atypical slugger Bucky Dent who delivered the big Yankee blow. In that year's ALCS Jackson hit .462 with two homers and six RBI in a four-game win over Kansas City. When the Yanks blew away the Dodgers again in six games in that year's World Series, Reggie led all batters with eight RBI and a .696 slugging average to go along with his two homers.

Reggie's 41 homers tied for the league lead in 1980. But Kansas City, having been beaten by the Yanks in the LCS in 1976, '77, and '78, got its revenge in a three-game sweep. In the weird strike-induced split season of 1981, Jackson played just 94 games. He had his lowest home run and RBI totals since he played in 35 games in 1967. Most people felt Reggie's career was over. They were wrong.

A big-money player in his day, Jackson joined the Angels in 1982 when owner Gene Autry offered him a one-year pact worth $700,000. That year Jackson powered a loop-high 39 homers and California won its division.

**"I'm the straw that stirs the drink."
—Jackson**

He became a free agent again for the 1982 season and signed with the California Angels. When Angel owner Gene Autry offered Jackson a one-year deal for $700,000, even Reggie was amazed. "I guess he likes me," he told *Sports Illustrated*. All Jackson did that year was belt 39 homers and drive in 101 runs to help Autry's team to the Western Division title. But time was passing Reggie by. It seemed to be an omen when in the fifth and deciding game of the League Championship Series (Reggie had homered once in the series), with Milwaukee up by a run, Mr. October was stuck in the on-deck circle as the Brewers closed out the game.

Jackson played five more seasons, adding 99 homers to his career total. He hit two doubles in the 1986 LCS for the Angels. He finished his bombastic career back where he had seen his first glory, in Oakland.

BY THE NUMBERS															
Year	Team	G	AB	R	H	2B	3B	HR	HR%	RBI	BB	K	BA	SA	SB
1967	KC-A	35	118	13	21	4	4	1	0.8	6	10	46	.178	.305	1
1968	Oak-A	154	553	82	138	13	6	29	5.2	74	50	171	.250	.452	14
1969	Oak-A	152	549	123	151	36	3	47	8.6	118	114	142	.275	**.608**	13
1970	Oak-A	149	426	57	101	21	2	23	5.4	66	75	135	.237	.458	26
1971	Oak-A	150	567	87	157	29	3	32	5.6	80	63	161	.277	.508	16
1972	Oak-A	135	499	72	132	25	2	25	5.0	75	59	125	.265	.473	9
1973	Oak-A	151	539	99	158	28	2	**32**	5.9	**117**	76	111	.293	**.531**	22
1974	Oak-A	148	506	90	146	25	1	29	5.7	93	86	105	.289	.514	25
1975	Oak-A	157	593	91	150	39	3	**36**	6.1	104	67	133	.253	.511	17
1976	Bal-A	134	498	84	138	27	2	27	5.4	91	54	108	.277	**.502**	28
1977	NY-A	146	525	93	150	39	2	32	6.1	110	74	129	.286	.550	17
1978	NY-A	139	511	82	140	13	5	27	5.3	97	58	133	.274	.477	14
1979	NY-A	131	465	78	138	24	2	29	6.2	89	65	107	.297	.544	9
1980	NY-A	143	514	94	154	22	4	**41**	8.0	111	83	122	.300	.597	1
1981	NY-A	94	334	33	79	17	1	15	4.5	54	46	82	.237	.428	0
1982	Cal-A	153	530	92	146	17	1	**39**	7.4	101	85	156	.275	.532	4
1983	Cal-A	116	397	43	77	14	1	14	3.5	49	52	140	.194	.340	0
1984	Cal-A	143	525	67	117	17	2	25	4.8	81	55	141	.223	.406	8
1985	Cal-A	143	460	64	116	27	0	27	5.9	85	78	138	.252	.487	1
1986	Cal-A	132	419	65	101	12	2	18	4.3	58	92	115	.241	.408	1
1987	Oak-A	115	336	42	74	14	1	15	4.5	43	33	97	.220	.402	2
Total	21	2820	9864	1551	2584	463	49	563	5.7	1702	1375	2597	.262	.490	228

HARMON KILLEBREW

The purest of sluggers—home runs were the be-all and end-all of his game—Harmon Killebrew had many people believing he would be the man to threaten Babe Ruth's lifetime record.

THE TOP RIGHT-HANDED home run hitter in American League history, and the fifth best overall with 573, Harmon Killebrew was built for the long ball, with his powerful upper body and tree-trunk legs. Eight times he hit 40 home runs or more in a season, as many as Hank Aaron. Harmon's lifetime homer ratio is securely in the Ruth-McGwire stratosphere.

Nine times Killebrew drove in more than 100 runs in a season. And like the other true sluggers of the game, he knew how to wait for his pitch: He was walked 90 times or more in 10 different seasons. In fact, one year in which he hit 49 home runs, he led the league in on-base percentage. Killebrew could hit no matter where he played. He was an All-Star 11 times, at three different positions.

Above right: In 1971 Killebrew became the 10th big-league player to surpass the 500 barrier in career home runs. Nos. 500 and 501 came off Baltimore's Mike Cuellar. Below: Many figured Killebrew for the man who would break the single-season record of 61 homers set by Roger Maris (left). Killebrew reached the 40s eight times.

Harmon's muscles were a combination of good genes and hard work. His grandfather was said to be the strongest man in the Union Army in the Civil War. Harmon's dad picked up spare change as a professional wrestler (long before that became showbiz). And like Jimmie Foxx, Harmon built his strength as a kid doing farm chores. His muscles weren't put on in a weight room with steroids. Harmon was a quiet, gentlemanly sort. It was only at the plate that he earned the nickname "Killer."

Killebrew was spotted playing semipro baseball in Idaho by Washington Senators scout Ossie Bluege. Bluege saw the youngster play four games, in which he hit four homers and three triples and had four other hits. One of the homers went over 425 feet. Bluege's wire to Washington offered this terse evaluation: "The sky's the limit." It's been said that the Boston Red Sox were interested in Harmon, too. Who knows what kind of slugging totals he would have put together with the Green Monster as his friend?

Killebrew signed as a "bonus baby," so under the rules of the time he had to stay with the big-league club for two years. He played in just 47 games with Washington in 1954 and '55, hitting four homers, before he was sent down.

In his first season as a big-league regular, which wasn't until 1959, he belted 42 home runs, tying Rocky Colavito for the league lead. He also drove in 105 for the last-place Senators. In one stretch of 17 games, he slugged two homers in a game five times. But that was just the beginning. In his career he wound up with 46 multihomer games, tied for eighth all-time with Mickey Mantle.

After hitting 31 homers in 1960, Killebrew and his teammates moved to Minnesota to become the Twins. Farm boy Harmon took to the Minnesota air and ballpark, and the fans took to him in a big way. He began a slugging spree that few would ever match. In 1961, the year Roger Maris swatted

61 homers, Killebrew belted 46. Then Harmon hit 48, 45, and 49 the next three years, leading the league every year, and drove in 455 over the four seasons.

On July 18, 1962, Killebrew and teammate Bob Allison each hit a grand slam in the same inning against Cleveland—the first time that had been done since 1890. Harmon finished his career with 11 grand slams. In 1963 he hit four homers in a doubleheader, setting an American League record. In 1964 he had 30 by the All-Star break.

In 1965 Harmon suffered a sore elbow and played in only 113 games. He managed just 25 homers and 75 RBI. One of those homers was a clutch two-run game-winner in the ninth inning in July. His Twins put together a great year, going to the World Series before losing to the Dodgers. Killebrew homered once in the Series.

Two years later Harmon led the league in home runs again with 44. For the second time he led the league in walks. After he tore a hamstring stretching for a throw at the 1968 All-Star Game, many baseball pundits felt his grand career was over.

Boy, were they wrong. He returned in 1969 with his greatest season ever: 49 homers, 140 RBI, and the MVP Award. The Twins took the AL West before losing to Baltimore in three games. The Orioles pitched around Harmon; he had just eight at-bats in the three games. In 1970 Killebrew belted 41 homers and drove in 113, but the Twins' LCS rematch with the Orioles had the same result, even though Harmon's three hits included two homers.

Killebrew's homer total fell to 28 in 1971, although he led the league in RBI and walks again. The pounding of artificial turf was wearing out his knees. He ended his 22-year career in 1975 with Kansas City.

No right-hander in American League history can rival Killebrew in the home run department. The muscular slugger finished his career with 573.

BY THE NUMBERS															
Year	Team	G	AB	R	H	2B	3B	HR	HR%	RBI	BB	K	BA	SA	SB
1954	Was-A	9	13	1	4	1	0	0	0.0	3	2	3	.308	.385	0
1955	Was-A	38	80	12	16	1	0	4	5.0	7	9	31	.200	.363	0
1956	Was-A	44	99	10	22	2	0	5	5.1	13	10	39	.222	.394	0
1957	Was-A	9	31	4	9	2	0	2	6.5	5	2	8	.290	.548	0
1958	Was-A	13	31	2	6	0	0	0	0.0	2	0	12	.194	.194	0
1959	Was-A	153	546	98	132	20	2	42	7.7	105	90	116	.242	.516	3
1960	Was-A	124	442	84	122	19	1	31	7.0	80	71	106	.276	.534	1
1961	Min-A	150	541	94	156	20	7	46	8.5	122	107	109	.288	.606	1
1962	Min-A	155	552	85	134	21	1	48	8.7	126	106	142	.243	.545	1
1963	Min-A	142	515	88	133	18	0	45	8.7	96	72	105	.258	.555	0
1964	Min-A	158	577	95	156	11	1	49	8.5	111	93	135	.270	.548	0
1965	Min-A	113	401	78	108	16	1	25	6.2	75	72	69	.269	.501	0
1966	Min-A	162	569	89	160	27	1	39	6.9	110	103	98	.281	.538	0
1967	Min-A	163	547	105	147	24	1	44	8.0	113	131	111	.269	.558	1
1968	Min-A	100	295	40	62	7	2	17	5.8	40	70	70	.210	.420	0
1969	Min-A	162	555	106	153	20	2	49	8.8	140	145	84	.276	.584	8
1970	Min-A	157	527	96	143	20	1	41	7.8	113	128	84	.271	.546	0
1971	Min-A	147	500	61	127	19	1	28	5.6	119	114	96	.254	.464	3
1972	Min-A	139	433	53	100	13	2	26	6.0	74	94	91	.231	.450	0
1973	Min-A	69	248	29	60	9	1	5	2.0	32	41	59	.242	.347	0
1974	Min-A	122	333	28	74	7	0	13	3.9	54	45	61	.222	.360	0
1975	KC-A	106	312	25	62	13	0	14	4.5	44	54	70	.199	.375	1
Total	22	2435	8147	1283	2086	290	24	573	7.0	1584	1559	1699	.256	.509	19

RALPH KINER

Early in his career, Ralph Kiner obtained a film of Babe Ruth hitting a home run. Kiner studied it frame by frame, and made Ruth's swing his own. It paid off.

O F ALL THE HOME RUN FEATS in big-league history, the one set by Ralph Kiner is truly unbelievable. In his first seven seasons in the majors, Kiner led or tied for the home run lead seven times. His lifetime home run ratio is third behind Mark McGwire's and Babe Ruth's.

Kiner could hit the ball far, but he could hit for average, too. In his brief 10-year career, he topped the .300 mark three times. His lifetime average is a not-too-shabby .279. With a great batting eye, he walked 100 times or more six straight seasons, and he scored 100 or more runs six times. His lifetime on-base percentage is a fine .398.

But Kiner played most of his career in Pittsburgh, and his team, headed by general manager Branch Rickey, wasn't called "The Rickey Dinks" for nothing. The woeful Bucs still set attendance records, almost solely because of Kiner. It was a common sight to see the Forbes Field stands emptying early in another

Above right: The powerful and prolific Kiner made a name for himself quickly despite playing most of his career with woeful Pittsburgh teams. Below: Kiner and Johnny Mize (left) shared the National League home run crown with 51 apiece in 1947. Kiner topped that with 54 round-trippers two years later.

Pirate loss—but only if Kiner wasn't going to bat again.

After 1952, Kiner's seventh consecutive season of hitting as many homers as anyone in the National League, Rickey tried to cut his salary by 25 percent. "We could have finished last without you," Rickey rationalized. Early in the next season, Kiner was dealt to the Cubs in a huge 10-player swap (Kiner and three Bucs went to Chicago for six Cubs and $150,000). It is a date still celebrated in infamy by older Pirates fans.

Kiner might have signed with the Yankees in the early 1940s, but with their loaded minor-league rosters they wanted to start him at Class-D, the lowest rung on the ladder. Kiner figured it could take him seven years to make the bigs. Instead, the Pirates offered him a chance to begin his career at Class-A. Ralph calculated he could be hitting major-league homers in four years. With the exception of three years in the military (1943 to 1945), he did it in three.

In his first two big-league spring training at-bats, he homered twice. During his term in the service, he bulked up and, although he was supposed to return to the minors for the 1946 season, he belted a dozen homers in the spring that year to win the roster spot. His 23 home runs were tops in the National League.

Perhaps the biggest break Kiner got in his career happened the next year. The Pirates enticed "Hammerin' Hank" Greenberg out of retirement with the biggest contract ever paid a major-leaguer—$100,000 for one season—plus every perk Greenberg could think of. They wanted Hank to train Ralph. To sweeten the pot for everybody, they added a bullpen in left-center field at Forbes, creating a shorter porch that was christened "Greenberg Gardens."

Hank's greatest value to the Pirates was his education of the young Kiner. After striking out 109 times to lead the league in 1946, Ralph slashed his whiffs to 81 with Greenberg around—and would never fan more than 90 times in a season again. Greenberg also taught Kiner how to dress and behave. They were lessons Ralph never forgot.

It took a while, though. Off to a horrible start, with just three homers by Memorial Day, 1947, Kiner was slated to be sent down. Greenberg talked management into changing their minds. Kiner walloped 48 more homers that season; his 51 placed him alongside Hack Wilson as the only two men ever to hit 50 in the NL. In a four-game stretch from September 10 through 12, Kiner cracked four home runs. His batting average was .313 that year, and his .639 slugging average led the league.

In 1948 Ralph tagged 40 more long balls. In 1949 he went on a tear in September, slugging 16 homers that month to finish just two behind Wilson's NL record of 56. Kiner's 127 RBI led the loop.

In 1950 Kiner's 47 homers earned him the award as *The Sporting News* Player of the Year. In that year's All-Star Game, he homered in the ninth inning to tie the game, and the Nationals won in 14. Kiner hit 42 and 37 homers in 1951 and

1952, but the Pirates were abysmal, and he was sent to the Cubs early the next year.

The back problems that had bothered Ralph for several years worsened in the Windy City. He hit 50 homers for the Cubs in two years, and in November 1954 his old pal Greenberg traded to bring him to Cleveland, where Greenberg was general manager. The chronic sciatica didn't improve; it was Kiner's last season. He retired at age 32.

Kiner hit 13 grand slams in his career, and four times hit three homers in one game. Kiner and Willie Mays are the only National Leaguers in history with two 50-homer seasons.

It wasn't until Kiner's eighth summer in the majors that he failed to earn at least a share of the league lead in home runs. He posted two seasons of 50-plus.

BY THE NUMBERS

Year	Team	G	AB	R	H	2B	3B	HR	HR%	RBI	BB	K	BA	SA	SB
1946	Pit-N	144	502	63	124	17	3	**23**	4.6	81	74	109	.247	.430	3
1947	Pit-N	152	565	118	177	23	4	**51**	**9.0**	127	98	81	.313	**.639**	1
1948	Pit-N	156	555	104	147	19	5	**40**	7.2	123	112	61	.265	.533	1
1949	Pit-N	152	549	116	170	19	5	**54**	9.8	127	**117**	61	.310	**.658**	6
1950	Pit-N	150	547	112	149	21	6	**47**	8.6	118	122	79	.272	.590	2
1951	Pit-N	151	531	**124**	164	31	6	**42**	7.9	109	**137**	57	.309	**.627**	2
1952	Pit-N	149	516	90	126	17	2	**37**	7.2	87	**110**	77	.244	.500	3
1953	Pit-N	41	148	27	40	6	1	7	4.7	29	25	21	.270	.466	1
	Chi-N	117	414	73	117	14	2	28	6.8	87	75	67	.283	.529	1
	Yr	158	562	100	157	20	3	35	6.2	116	100	88	.279	.512	2
1954	Chi-N	147	557	88	159	36	5	22	3.9	73	76	90	.285	.487	2
1955	Cle-A	113	321	56	78	13	0	18	5.6	54	65	46	.243	.452	0
Total	10	1472	5205	971	1451	216	39	369	7.1	1015	1011	749	.279	.548	22

DAVE KINGMAN

Dave Kingman's absolutely singular status as "slugger and nothing but" guaranteed him a unique place in baseball history— the man who hit more home runs than anyone not in the Hall of Fame.

Thousands of major-leaguers exceeded Kingman's .236 career average, but only eight have posted a better home run percentage.

D AVE KINGMAN'S TALL (6'6"), muscular frame and devastating uppercut batting stroke resulted in tape-measure home runs. He retired with 442 home runs. Unfortunately, he also had the worst strikeout-to-homer ratio of anyone who hit more than 300 homers. And seldom did he do anything else. In 15 full seasons he hit more than .270 only twice. He was an embarrassment no matter what position he played in the field. And he wasn't the most likable sort, either. He particularly disdained sportswriters. He once presented a female writer with a rat.

Kingman was a great pitcher in college at Southern California. But it was the power in his bat that led manager Rod Dedeaux to take him off the mound and install him in the outfield. Called up to the San Francisco Giants late in the 1971 season, "King Kong's" homer against San Diego (one of six he hit in 111 games) clinched the National League West title. In that year's League Championship Series, he managed just one single in nine at-bats. It was his last appearance in post-season play.

In 1972 "Kong" belted 29 homers, the first of a dozen 20-homer seasons. The next two years he hit a total of 42 home runs, but the Giants were going nowhere and they sold him to the New York Mets, who were desperate for power to augment their stellar pitching. In 1975 Kingman knocked 36 balls out of the park, just two behind league leader Mike Schmidt, but he drove in just 88 because he batted .231. The Mets finished third. The next season was almost an exact duplicate. Kingman hit 37 homers, only one behind Schmidt, but knocked in just 86. Again, the Mets finished third.

Going nowhere in 1977, New York dealt Kingman to San Diego after he hit just nine homers in 58 games. Kong was on his way to a unique one-season baseball odyssey. That year he played for four different teams, one in each of the game's four divisions, and homered for every one of them. After San Diego he was sold to the California Angels and then to the New York Yankees. His season totals were 26 homers and 78 RBI. No ostensibly quality player has ever seen so much travel time in one year.

After all that, Kingman decided to test the waters of free agency and signed with the Chicago Cubs, which turned out to be a good choice. His first year there, 1978, he had a typical Kingman season: 28 homers and 79 RBI. The next year he realized that with the Wrigley Field wind helping out, he could cut down on his stroke. He wound up having a year that ranks with many Hall of Famers. He batted .288, his career high, and led the National League with 48 homers. He also topped the league in slugging average and finished just three RBI behind leader Dave Winfield, with 115. He also played a huge role in one of the wackiest home run orgies in baseball history.

The date was May 17, 1979, Cubs against Philadelphia on an extra-windy day at Wrigley. By the end of the first inning,

George Foster high-fives King Kong after Kingman's three-run homer at L.A. on July 17, 1982. With his enormous upper-cut swing, Kingman skied 'em to the clouds.

Kingman towers one into the Shea Stadium parking lot on April 20, 1981. "It felt good," he said afterward.

the Phils were clinging to a 7–6 lead. By the middle of the third, they were up 15–6. In Kingman's first at-bat, he hit a home run that almost cleared a building on the far side of Waveland Avenue. In Kingman's next at-bat, Phils hurler Doug Bird threw the first pitch high and tight. Kingman shrugged it off, then deposited another homer onto Waveland. Kingman's third home run of the day was the longest—it bounced off a porch on the fourth house along the avenue.

All in all that day, players slugged 11 homers and 50 hits—24 of them for extra bases. Kingman scored four runs to go with his six RBI. But in the last of the 10th, with the Phillies having taken the lead 23–22 on Mike Schmidt's homer, Kingman struck out, and his Cubs lost a slugfest for the ages.

Dealt back to the Mets before the 1981 season, Kingman won the home run title in 1982 with 37. But he managed just nine doubles and one triple and batted .204, lowest for any home run titlist ever. He also tied a major-league record that

season by fanning five times in a nine-inning game. The following season he slumped to .198, with only 13 homers. He played in just 100 games, as the Mets welcomed a kid named Darryl Strawberry.

Kingman joined Oakland in 1984 and earned the Comeback Player of the Year Award, batting .268 with 35 homers and 118 RBI. But his relations with the press and teammates were getting nastier. After hitting 35 homers in 1986, he became a free agent again. No one made him an offer.

Year	Team	G	AB	R	H	2B	3B	HR	HR%	RBI	BB	K	BA	SA	SB
1971	SF-N	41	115	17	32	10	2	6	5.2	24	9	35	.278	.557	5
1972	SF-N	135	472	65	106	17	4	29	6.1	83	51	140	.225	.462	16
1973	SF-N	112	305	54	62	10	1	24	7.9	55	41	122	.203	.479	8
1974	SF-N	121	350	41	78	18	2	18	5.1	55	37	125	.223	.440	8
1975	NY-N	134	502	65	116	22	1	36	7.2	88	34	153	.231	.494	7
1976	NY-N	123	474	70	113	14	1	37	7.8	86	28	135	.238	.506	7
1977	NY-N	58	211	22	44	7	0	9	4.3	28	13	66	.209	.370	3
	SD-N	56	168	16	40	9	0	11	6.5	39	12	48	.238	.488	2
	Yr	114	379	38	84	16	0	20	5.3	67	25	114	.222	.422	5
	Cal-A	10	36	4	7	2	0	2	5.6	4	1	16	.194	.417	0
	NY-A	8	24	5	6	2	0	4	16.7	7	2	13	.250	.833	0
	Yr	18	60	9	13	4	0	6	10.0	11	3	29	.217	.583	0
1978	Chi-N	119	395	65	105	17	4	28	7.1	79	39	111	.266	.542	3
1979	Chi-N	145	532	97	153	19	5	48	9.0	115	45	131	.288	.613	4
1980	Chi-N	81	255	31	71	8	0	18	7.1	57	21	44	.278	.522	2
1981	NY-N	100	353	40	78	11	3	22	6.2	59	55	105	.221	.456	6
1982	NY-N	149	535	80	109	9	1	37	6.9	99	59	156	.204	.432	4
1983	NY-N	100	248	25	49	7	0	13	5.2	29	22	57	.198	.383	2
1984	Oak-A	147	549	68	147	23	1	35	6.4	118	44	119	.268	.505	2
1985	Oak-A	158	592	66	141	16	0	30	5.1	91	62	114	.238	.417	3
1986	Oak-A	144	561	70	118	19	0	35	6.2	94	33	126	.210	.431	3
Total	16	1941	6677	901	1575	240	25	442	6.6	1210	608	1816	.236	.478	85

MICKEY MANTLE

Baseball had never seen a man with the blistering speed and immense power of Mickey Mantle. Belting shots 500 feet or more, he virtually invented the term "tape-measure home run."

Above right: *An idol from his early playing days, Mantle captured the hearts of millions with his awesome power and the gutsy way he approached the game.* Below: *Mantle stood out even in a gathering that featured sluggers* (from left) *Roger Maris, Rocky Colavito, and Norm Cash.*

I N *SPORT* MAGAZINE IN 1957, writer Tom Meany said this of Mickey Mantle: "Always within Mantle is the knowledge that any game he plays could be his last—one throw, one swing, one slide could write the end of his major-league career. Yet Mick plays every game to the hilt, a tremendous tribute to his courage."

Mantle was the greatest player on the greatest team in the nation's biggest city—the true successor to Yankee legends Babe Ruth and Joe DiMaggio. What made the Mick extra special, and so beloved by a whole generation of baseball fans, was the way he gutted through constant, nagging pain while also remaining a lovable, fun-loving character.

A talented athlete as a child, and driven by a desire to please his father, "Mutt," an Oklahoma miner, Mantle was learning to switch-hit by the time he was five. But his physical

problems also began at an early age. Kicked in the shin during football practice at age 14, he developed osteomyelitis, an inflammation of the bone. Doctors were considering amputation but opted instead for huge doses of the new wonder drug penicillin. It saved his leg, though the problem and the pain stayed with him for many years.

At shortstop in the New York Yankees' farm system, Mantle's fielding was abysmal but his hitting was amazing. In his first full minor-league season, 1950, he led the Western Association in runs, hits, and batting average (.383) while hitting 26 homers and driving in 136 runs. In 1951 his performance in spring training, which included two 500-foot home runs from opposite sides of the plate in the same game, earned him a shot at the bigs.

Playing right field while DiMaggio patrolled center, Mantle hit his first home run as a Yankee off White Sox Randy Gumpert on May 1. The distance was calculated at 450 feet. But Mantle seemed confused by major-league pitching and was sent down to Kansas City. He returned later in the season to finish with 13 homers and a .267 batting average.

In 1952 DiMaggio was gone and Mantle was the Yank center fielder. And he was on his way to making history. During his 18-year career as a Yankee, Mickey scored 1,677 runs, collected 2,415 hits, swatted 344 doubles, knocked in 1,509 runs, and batted .298. His 536 home runs are the eighth most of all time. He topped the American League in runs six times, walks five times, homers four times, and slugging percentage four times. Ten times he received more than 100 walks in a season. From 1955 through 1962 he averaged 40 homers and 101 RBI while batting .315.

Mantle played in 20 All-Star Games, and he hit better than .300 10 times. On 10 occasions he homered from both sides of the plate in the same game. Of the top six seasons of home runs by a switch-hitter, five are Mickey's.

Mantle took the American League MVP crown three times, the first in 1956 when he won the Triple Crown. He led the league with a .353 average, 52 homers, 130 RBI, 132 runs scored, and a .705 slugging average. He became the first American Leaguer to hit more than 50 dingers since Hank Greenberg, and only the sixth person to hit 50 ever. He was also second in walks and on-base percentage. In doing all that, he

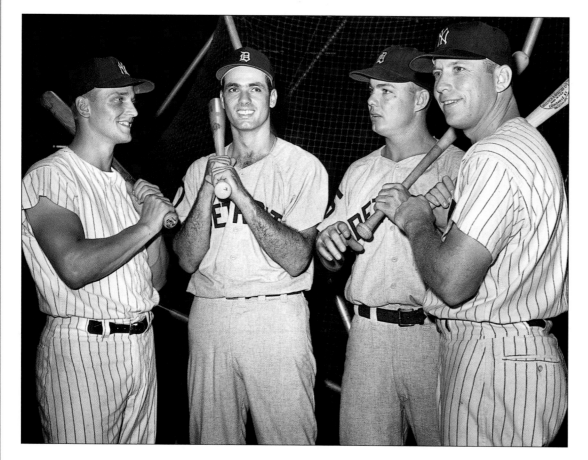

became the only player in baseball history besides Jimmie Foxx to hit 50 homers and win a batting title the same season. To cap off that remarkable year, Mantle hit a home run to help win the Don Larsen perfect game in the World Series—and made a sparkling running catch to preserve the masterpiece.

The Mick's second MVP Award came in 1957, when he batted .365, led the league in runs scored, hit 34 homers, and drove in 94 runs. He was in the top five in every batting category except doubles and triples. In 1962 he took his third MVP trophy when he batted .321 with 30 homers and 89 RBI. None of those stats led the league, but Yankee publicist Jackie Farrell,

as quoted in Paul Dickson's *Baseball's Greatest Quotations,* had a reply: "What did he lead the league in? He led the league in manhood, that's what."

Mantle's speed, before injuries took their toll, was legendary. Timed to first base in just 3.1 seconds, he was probably the fastest man in the game at that time. His positively lethal drag bunts gave opposing third basemen gray hairs. Mantle actually scored more runs than he drove in during his career, which is a rarity for power hitters.

The Yanks played in a dozen World Series with Mantle on the team. They won seven world championships. And Mickey

This 1958 World Series home run was one of a record 18 fall classic dingers for the most popular player on his sport's most popular team.

> "He has more speed than any slugger and more slug than any speedster—and nobody has ever had more of them together."
> —Casey Stengel

MICK AND MUTT

By naming his son after superstar Mickey Cochrane, and turning him into a switch-hitter at age five, Mutt Mantle made it clear that he had high hopes for his son's athletic success. But one incident between the two really set Mickey on the path to stardom.

After performing poorly as a Yankee rookie early in the 1951 season, Mantle was shipped back to Triple-A Kansas City, but his hitting problems didn't stop. The story is told that Mantle called his father back in Oklahoma thoroughly discouraged. "I don't think I can play baseball anymore," Mickey said.

The next day his father appeared at the youngster's hotel room. He began grabbing Mickey's clothes and throwing them into a suitcase. "What are you doing?" asked Mickey. "Packing," his dad replied. "If you're giving up, you can come home with me. We'll work in the mines together."

His dad's attitude snapped Mickey out of his doldrums. By the time he was recalled to the Yankees late in August, he had hit .361 in his 40 Kansas City games while swatting 11 homers and driving in 50 runs.

That October, the day after Mantle injured his ankle tripping over a Yankee Stadium drain, his father was admitted to the hospital and diagnosed with Hodgkin's disease. He died a year later.

had plenty to do with their success. He holds lifetime World Series records with 18 home runs, 42 runs scored, 40 RBI, 123 total bases, 26 extra-base hits, and 43 walks.

In Game 6 of the 1952 Series, his eighth-inning smash rescued the Yankees from Series defeat. And in Game 7 he hit the home run that provided the margin of victory in a 4–1 Yankee win. In Game 5 of the 1953 Series, he belted a grand slam.

In 1964, Mickey's last World Series, he led off the bottom of the ninth with the score tied at one and slugged the first pitch deep into the right-field stands to win the game. He scored eight runs and drove in eight to lead all Series batsmen that year. His third homer in that Series broke Ruth's record for lifetime Series homers.

Mantle's clouts were not only frequent; they were far. He was incredibly strong. Outfielder Jim Busby, interviewed in *The Sporting News* in March 1955, said Mantle "is the strongest man in baseball. He hits the ball so hard, he knocks the spin off it." Mickey often hit homers on balls he thought he had missed. Teammate Tony Kubek recalls in Danny Peary's *Cult Baseball Players* that at least three times he saw Mantle slam his bat to the ground, snapping it in two because he thought he hadn't hit the ball well, only to see it leave the park.

Mantle pretty much invented the idea of the tape-measure home run—or at least Yankee publicist Red Patterson did. In 1953 Mantle, using the bat of the great-named but little used Yankee sub Loren Babe, knocked a ball clear out of immense Griffith Stadium in Washington, D.C. Patterson tracked down the kid who had picked it up and announced to the world that Mantle's blast off Chuck Stobbs had gone 565 feet. Yankee reliever Bob Kuzava quipped, "You could have chopped it up into 15 singles."

On May 13, 1955, Mantle hit three homers into the Yankee Stadium bleachers, each one over the 461-foot sign. In his career he belted balls off the facade that hung from Yankee Stadium's right-field roof five times. In May 1963 it was estimated that one of those homers would have gone 601 feet if the roof hadn't been in the way.

Mantle played a vital role in teammate Roger Maris's assault on Ruth's "unreachable"

Mantle became just the seventh major-leaguer to blast 400 balls out of the park when he took Detroit deep in September 1962. He was only 30 years old.

60-homer season mark. Batting ahead of Mantle, Maris was not intentionally walked all year. For much of the season, the two carried on a friendly rivalry as they chased the record together. In fact, they were roommates on the road and shared an apartment in Queens while at home.

When a flu infection struck Mantle in September, he went to see an eccentric doctor, who injected him with something unusual in the hip. Mantle's side abscessed, and he missed a chance to match homers with Maris. The Mick finished with 54, thereby setting with Maris an all-time record for homers by teammates in the same season: 115. Mantle led the league with a .687 slugging percentage and 126 walks that year. He tied Maris with 132 runs scored.

Quoted in the *Boston Post,* teammate Clete Boyer said Mantle was "a celebrity in his own clubhouse. He is the kind of man we all want to be." No one loved Mickey more than his cantankerous manager, Casey Stengel. Casey was quoted in *Baseball Stars of 1963* as saying, "He has more speed than any slugger and more slug than any speedster—and nobody has ever had more of them together."

The story was told in the *San Francisco Examiner* that before the 1952 World Series, Stengel, the "Ole Perfesser," gave Mantle a private lesson in playing the tricky hops off the outfield wall in Ebbets Field. Casey, of course, had played there back in the 1910s. Mantle was astounded at his aged manager's understanding. Casey replied, "What do ya think, I was born old?"

Mantle liked the late nights and bright lights of Manhattan. Joining Mickey as the top Yankee carousers were Billy Martin and Whitey Ford. One night in 1957 a fight broke out in New York's legendary Copacabana nightclub. To protect Mantle from more carousing, Martin was traded away. Mantle believed that like his father and grandfather, who had both died from Hodgkin's disease, he was destined for an early death. At age 46 he uttered the famous line, "If I knew I was going to live this long, I would have taken better care of myself."

The litany of Mantle's injuries is remarkable. In addition to the bone infection, he tore cartilage in his right knee tripping over an exposed drain in the Yankee Stadium outfield during the 1951 World Series. In the 1957 World Series, the Braves' Red Schoendienst fell hard on Mantle's right shoulder, and the pain bothered him for years. In 1963 he broke an ankle and was out of the lineup for two months. Of course, in true Mantle fashion, he proved heroic in his first at-bat back: He belted a game-tying, two-out pinch homer in the ninth. The recurrent damage to his body from the mishaps forced him to spend his final two seasons playing first base.

After the consistent pain led him to retire, Mantle's fame only grew. He came to grips with his alcoholism in a way that won the admiration of a new generation of baseball fans. And he was a leader in the fight for organ donors, as he himself received a transplanted liver the year before his death in 1995.

Above: *Willie Mays* (left) *and Mantle shared All-Star lineup cards in 1958. Debates raged for years as to which New York center fielder was better: Willie or Mickey.* Left: *No baseball fan of his era is likely to forget the Mick, the hard-living legend who died in 1995 with 536 home runs and more than 1,500 RBI.*

BY THE NUMBERS															
Year	Team	G	AB	R	H	2B	3B	HR	HR%	RBI	BB	K	BA	SA	SB
1951	NY-A	96	341	61	91	11	5	13	3.8	65	43	74	.267	.443	8
1952	NY-A	142	549	94	171	37	7	23	4.2	87	75	111	.311	.530	4
1953	NY-A	127	461	105	136	24	3	21	4.6	92	79	90	.295	.497	8
1954	NY-A	146	543	129	163	17	12	27	5.0	102	102	107	.300	.525	5
1955	NY-A	147	517	121	158	25	11	37	7.2	99	113	97	.306	.611	8
1956	NY-A	150	533	132	188	22	5	52	9.8	130	112	99	.353	.705	10
1957	NY-A	144	474	121	173	28	6	34	7.2	94	146	75	.365	.665	16
1958	NY-A	150	519	127	158	21	1	42	8.1	97	129	120	.304	.592	18
1959	NY-A	144	541	104	154	23	4	31	5.7	75	93	126	.285	.514	21
1960	NY-A	153	527	119	145	17	6	40	7.6	94	111	125	.275	.558	14
1961	NY-A	153	514	132	163	16	6	54	10.5	128	126	112	.317	.687	12
1962	NY-A	123	377	96	121	15	1	30	8.0	89	122	78	.321	.605	9
1963	NY-A	65	172	40	54	8	0	15	8.7	35	40	32	.314	.622	2
1964	NY-A	143	465	92	141	25	2	35	7.5	111	99	102	.303	.591	6
1965	NY-A	122	361	44	92	12	1	19	5.3	46	73	76	.255	.452	4
1966	NY-A	108	333	40	96	12	1	23	6.9	56	57	76	.288	.538	1
1967	NY-A	144	440	63	108	17	0	22	5.0	55	107	113	.245	.434	1
1968	NY-A	144	435	57	103	14	1	18	4.1	54	106	97	.237	.398	6
Total	18	2401	8102	1677	2415	344	72	536	6.6	1509	1733	1710	.298	.557	153

ROGER MARIS

It took Mark McGwire's generosity toward Maris's family in 1998 to resurrect the memory of Roger's great achievement, which brought him pain and travail, not glory and adulation.

Above right: *Maris and Mickey Mantle* (right) *helped carry on a tradition of Yankee power started by the Babe, whose widow took part in this 1961 Babe Ruth League ceremony.* Below: *Who else in 1961? After hitting a then-record 61 home runs, Maris accepted the American League MVP trophy from AL President Joe Cronin.*

R OGER MARIS'S BIGGEST PROBLEM was that he wasn't Babe Ruth. But who ever was? During his assault on the Ruthian 60-homer record in 1961, Maris was tortured. The effort of the feat was shoved aside by critics who claimed he was lazy, surly, and arrogant.

Worse yet, New York Yankees fans never warmed to him as they had to Mickey Mantle. (Although history does tell that the opposing pitcher was booed for throwing wide ones to him on the last day of the record 1961 season.) With the McGwire/Sosa 1998 lovefest season fresh in people's minds, it's almost impossible to comprehend the torment that Maris's accomplishment caused him. Besieged daily by hounding media types, the quiet, reclusive Maris felt the pressure. His hair began falling out in clumps. He said afterwards, "As a ballplayer I would be delighted to do it again. As an individual I doubt if I could possibly go through it again."

Adding to the furor surrounding Maris was Commissioner Ford Frick's "asterisk" remark, in which he stated that if Maris broke Ruth's record in more than 154 games (1961 was the first season of expansion and the first of more than 154 games), Maris's achievement would have an asterisk next to it in the record books. Maris's comment? "A season is a season."

Maris began demonstrating that he had the stuff of a slugger in 1954, his second pro season, with Keokuk of the Three-I League. He homered 32 times, drove in 111 runs, and batted .315. The following season he hit 20 homers while playing for Tulsa and Reading. After a 17-homer campaign with Triple-A Reading, the Cleveland Indians called him up to begin the 1957 season. The day after the opener, he went 3-for-5 and hit his first big-league homer—a grand slam to win the game. For a while he was leading the league in homers and RBI, but he broke a rib on a headfirst slide and ended the year with 14 homers. The next year, traded to Kansas City in midseason, he finished with 28 homers. But he belted just 16 the following year.

But then the Yankees beckoned. New York, having finished third in 1959—their lowest finish in 11 years—swung a huge trade with Kansas City. The A's got 38-year-old former star Hank Bauer, plus Norm Siebern, Marv Throneberry, and Don Larsen. New York received Maris, Joe DeMaestri, and Kent Hadley.

Maris's compact swing was perfect for the short porch down Yankee Stadium's right-field line. In his first game as a Yankee, in 1960, he swatted two homers, a double, and a single. That year he led the league in slugging average and RBI. His 39 homers were just one behind teammate Mickey Mantle, and he also finished second to Mantle in total bases and runs scored. The Yankees were back where they belonged—in the World Series—and Maris was named American League Most Valuable Player. He hit two solo homers in the Yankees' unforgettable World Series loss to the Pittsburgh Pirates.

Breaking Ruth's record in 1961 was an incredible feat. Said Maris, in typical fashion: "Maybe I'm not a great man, but I damn sure want to break the record." For most of the year, he and Mickey performed a 1–2 punch that brought back to mind the Ruth-Gehrig days. When Mantle fell ill in September, Roger passed him by. Maris belted homer No. 59 in the season's 155th game, giving him more in a season than anyone not named Ruth.

Maris swatted the 60th in Game 159, and the 61st in what was actually the Yankees' 163rd game of the season (they had one tie, in which players' records were kept even though the game's result wasn't reflected in the standings). The shy Maris had to be forced by his teammates to leave the dugout for a curtain call by the Yankee faithful.

In that remarkable year Maris also led the AL in RBI with 142 and in total bases with 366; he tied Mantle for runs scored with 132. Maris knocked seven homers in six consecutive games from August 11 through 16. And he tied the American League record for homers in a doubleheader, with four on July 25.

The following year, according to John Holway in *The Sluggers,* Maris claimed he was hitting the ball an eighth of an inch higher than the previous year. He wound up with "only" 33 homers. Injuries curtailed his effectiveness in 1963 and 1965.

Traded to St. Louis for the 1967 season, his sterling defensive work (he had always been an underappreciated outfielder) helped the Cardinals to two consecutive world titles. That gave Roger another honor: He appeared in more World Series in the 1960s than any other player.

The swing that broke Ruth's longstanding single-season record came on the last day of the 1961 campaign, before a less-than-capacity Yankee Stadium crowd.

BY THE NUMBERS															
Year	Team	G	AB	R	H	2B	3B	HR	HR%	RBI	BB	K	BA	SA	SB
1957	Cle-A	116	358	61	84	9	5	14	3.9	51	60	79	.235	.405	8
1958	Cle-A	51	182	26	41	5	1	9	4.9	27	17	33	.225	.412	4
	KC-A	99	401	61	99	14	3	19	4.7	53	28	52	.247	.439	0
	Yr	150	583	87	140	19	4	28	4.8	80	45	85	.240	.431	4
1959	KC-A	122	433	69	118	21	7	16	3.7	72	58	53	.273	.464	2
1960	NY-A	136	499	98	141	18	7	39	**7.8**	**112**	70	65	.283	**.581**	2
1961	NY-A	161	590	**132**	159	16	4	**61**	10.3	**142**	94	67	.269	.620	0
1962	NY-A	157	590	92	151	34	1	33	5.6	100	87	78	.256	.485	1
1963	NY-A	90	312	53	84	14	1	23	7.4	53	35	40	.269	.542	1
1964	NY-A	141	513	86	144	12	2	26	5.1	71	62	78	.281	.464	3
1965	NY-A	46	155	22	37	7	0	8	5.2	27	29	29	.239	.439	0
1966	NY-A	119	348	37	81	9	2	13	3.7	43	36	60	.233	.382	0
1967	StL-N	125	410	64	107	18	7	9	2.2	55	52	61	.261	.405	0
1968	StL-N	100	310	25	79	18	2	5	1.6	45	24	38	.255	.374	0
Total	12	1463	5101	826	1325	195	42	275	5.4	851	652	733	.260	.476	21

EDDIE MATHEWS

Until Mike Schmidt came along, Eddie Mathews was the greatest slugger ever to play third base—a position that up until then was strictly a spot for glovemen and singles hitters, not sluggers.

N HIS HALL OF FAME induction speech, Eddie Mathews explained the origin of his batting style. "My mother used to pitch to me and my dad would shag balls," he said. "If I hit one up the middle, close to my mother, I'd have some extra chores to do. So Mom was instrumental in making me a pull hitter."

Mathews helped redefine the third base position. A few power hitters had played the position before, but for the most part third base was seen as a defensive slot—a second shortstop, as it were. Mathews was a fine fielder, but he brought the long ball to third base. He proved that a man with muscle could still handle the defensive demands of the slot. After Mathews came a host of hard-hitting third sackers—Ron Santo, Ron Cey, Mike Schmidt, Matt Williams. Eddie slugged 512 home runs. If his career had not been shortened by injury, who knows where he might have finished.

Hank Aaron and Mathews were the most prolific slugging teammate duo ever—better than Ruth/Gehrig, better than Mays/McCovey. Aaron and Mathews combined for the remarkable total of 863 home runs and 2,633 RBI in the 13 seasons they played together. They both homered in the same game 75 times, another record.

The key to Mathews's power was his quick swing, which generated incredible bat speed. Carl Erskine, in *The Ballplayers,* said, "He swings the bat faster than anyone I ever saw." Even the legendary Ty Cobb said of Mathews, "I've only known three or four perfect swings in my time. This lad has one of them."

Mathews set his sights on the majors when he was just a teenager. Before he graduated from high school, he and his father studied the major-league rosters, looking for the team most likely to need a third baseman soon. Their verdict? The Boston Braves, since their third sacker, Bob Elliott, was 33. Eddie indeed signed with the Braves. Mathews also refused the extra money he would get as a "bonus baby," because by rule it meant he would spend (i.e., waste) his first two years sitting on the major-league bench.

At age 17 Mathews became a Brave farmhand in North Carolina. He hit .363 with 17 home runs his first year. Interestingly, his next three years in the minors were in Atlanta and Milwaukee, two towns in which he would also play big-league ball. (He would become the only Brave to play in Boston, Milwaukee, and Atlanta.) In fact, in his first at-bat with the Milwaukee Brewers of the American Association, he belted a grand slam.

By 1952 Mathews was ready for the majors, even though he was just 20 years old. He clubbed 25 homers as a rookie, including some tape-measure jobs in Philadelphia, St. Louis, and Cincinnati. When the team moved to Milwaukee in 1953, Eddie bloomed. And boomed. He slugged 47 homers to lead the National League and also drove in 135 runs. He followed that up with 40 homers the next year and 41 the year after that, and in both seasons he knocked in more than 100 runs. After his first five seasons, his 190 homers were way ahead of Babe Ruth's 714-homer pace.

With Mathews and Aaron, the Braves were a powerhouse. In the 1957 World Series, they took on the vaunted Yankees. In Game 4 Mathews hit the game-winning homer. In Game 5 his infield single plated the winning run. Milwaukee upset New York in seven.

The Braves repeated as National League champs in 1958, then lost to the Yankees in the Series. They lost a three-game playoff with the Dodgers in 1959, though it wasn't Eddie's fault. He hit 46 homers that year, plus one in the second game of the playoffs. For the decade of the '50s, Mathews hit 299 homers—more than all but two men—and Eddie hadn't come up until '52.

Eddie just missed the 40-homer mark in 1960, with 39. When he hit 32 in 1961, he became the only man to hit

Mathews's days as a pull hitter started long before he became a pro baseball player. Hitting one up the middle meant extra chores from Mom.

30 homers or more in nine consecutive seasons. After 10 years in the majors, he was averaging 37 homers a year.

But torn ligaments in his shoulder in 1962 were slow to heal. Mathews didn't hit 30 again until 1965, and his career was over just three years later, at the age of 37. Mathews had homered in 24 different ballparks in his career, and he had taken 199 different pitchers deep. His 512 home runs stood as the record for third basemen until Schmidt.

Despite his memorable slugging career, Mathews's fondest baseball memory was of the superb defensive play he made in the 1957 World Series. He snared a screaming shot by Moose Skowron with the bases loaded to stifle a Yankee rally and end the Series.

		BY THE NUMBERS													
Year	Team	G	AB	R	H	2B	3B	HR	HR%	RBI	BB	K	BA	SA	SB
1952	Bos-N	145	528	80	128	23	5	25	4.7	58	59	115	.242	.447	6
1953	Mil-N	157	579	110	175	31	8	**47**	**8.1**	135	99	83	.302	.627	1
1954	Mil-N	138	476	96	138	21	4	40	8.4	103	113	61	.290	.603	10
1955	Mil-N	141	499	108	144	23	5	41	8.2	101	**109**	98	.289	.601	3
1956	Mil-N	151	552	103	150	21	2	37	6.7	95	91	86	.272	.518	6
1957	Mil-N	148	572	109	167	28	9	32	5.6	94	90	79	.292	.540	3
1958	Mil-N	149	546	97	137	18	1	31	5.7	77	85	85	.251	.458	5
1959	Mil-N	148	594	118	182	16	8	**46**	**7.7**	114	80	71	.306	.593	2
1960	Mil-N	153	548	108	152	19	7	39	7.1	124	111	113	.277	.551	7
1961	Mil-N	152	572	103	175	23	6	32	5.6	91	**93**	95	.306	.535	12
1962	Mil-N	152	536	106	142	25	6	29	5.4	90	**101**	90	.265	.496	4
1963	Mil-N	158	547	82	144	27	4	23	4.2	84	124	119	.263	.453	3
1964	Mil-N	141	502	83	117	19	1	23	4.6	74	85	100	.233	.412	2
1965	Mil-N	156	546	77	137	23	0	32	5.9	95	73	110	.251	.469	1
1966	Atl-N	134	452	72	113	21	4	16	3.5	53	63	82	.250	.420	1
1967	Hou-N	101	328	39	78	13	2	10	3.0	38	48	65	.238	.381	2
	Det-A	36	108	14	25	3	0	6	5.6	19	15	23	.231	.426	0
1968	Det-A	31	52	4	11	0	0	3	5.8	8	5	12	.212	.385	0
Total	17	2391	8537	1509	2315	354	72	512	6.0	1453	1444	1487	.271	.509	68

The 1957 Milwaukee Braves, powered by Mathews (pictured) *and Hank Aaron, upset the Yankees in seven games to win the World Series. Mathews tallied a homer, three doubles, and eight walks.*

WILLIE MAYS

The image many have of Willie Mays as an exuberantly soaring outfielder making miracle catches misses what may have been Mays's true greatness: a tremendous power hitter with near-Ruthian numbers.

TWENTY-YEAR-OLD Willie Mays was hitting .477 for Minneapolis in the American Association in May 1951 when the New York Giants called him to the big leagues. Mays was already such a fan favorite that the Giants ran an ad in a Minneapolis newspaper apologizing for removing this incredible young talent from them. Willie, however, failed to hit in his first dozen at-bats and asked to be sent back down.

"As long as I'm here, you're my center fielder," his manager, Leo Durocher, told him bluntly. The story goes that Willie homered on the next pitch he saw, from Warren Spahn. Later Spahn "apologized" to all the pitchers in the National League. "If I had got him out," Spahn said, "we might have been rid of him."

Mays finished the season hitting .274 with 20 homers and was named Rookie of the Year. This was the Giants team that made the incredible comeback to tie the Dodgers on the final day of the season and then won the three-game playoff on Bobby Thomson's three-run homer—the "Shot Heard 'Round the World."

For years Willie shared the New York spotlight with Yankee Mickey Mantle and Dodger Duke Snider as the game's best center fielders. Each had his unique style, but Willie's was definitely the most engaging. It was more than his awesome talents that endeared him to New York fans. His ebullience showed through in everything he did. Willie didn't just beat the opposition; he seemed to have the grand fun of a young kid doing it. As he told *The Sporting News* on July 25, 1970, "Baseball is a fun game, and I love it. I like to play happy."

Happy is what he made millions of fans in his career as they watched him hit, field, run, and throw better than almost anyone else ever had. Tallulah Bankhead, in *The Baseball Card Engagement Book,* was quoted as saying, "There have been only two authentic geniuses in the world, Willie Mays and William Shakespeare." Durocher also reached for stratospheric comparisons to describe Willie in George Plimpton's *Out of My League:* "Joe Louis, Jascha Heifetz, Sammy Davis and Nashua [the racehorse] rolled into one."

Mays's batting stats are simply awe-inspiring. His 660 homers are the third most of all time. And Willie spent most of 1952 and all of 1953 in the military. He also hit 523 doubles and 140 triples. He is fourth all time in extra-base hits (1,323), fifth in runs scored (2,062), seventh in RBI (1,903), and 10th in slugging average. He led the league in home runs and stolen bases four times each, in slugging five times, and in triples three times. He was the first man to hit 50 homers in the same season in which he stole 20 bases.

In 1954 Mays won his only batting title, hitting .345. But he finished second in batting three times and third twice. From 1961 through 1967, he averaged 44 homers a year. He hit 51 homers in 1955, and then 10 years later hit 52. Once he hit four homers in a single game. He holds the National League record for most games with two or more homers: 63. Twenty-two of his long shots came in extra innings, six more than Babe Ruth, who's second on the list.

Mays had 300 or more total bases in 13 consecutive seasons. That's as many as Lou Gehrig; only Ruth had more. And he played in 150 games or more for 13 years in a row—especially impressive when you consider his team played only 154 for the first eight of those years. At age 40 he led the league in walks, hit 18 home runs, and was 23 of 26 in stolen base attempts. In August 1965 he hit 17 homers in one month; until 1998, only one man had ever hit more. And, by the way, Mays has more putouts than any other outfielder in history.

When Willie returned to baseball after military duty in 1954, he did more than just improve on his solid rookie numbers. His

Above right: *At age 34, Mays won his second National League MVP trophy in 1965. He led the league with 52 home runs and a slugging average of .645.* Below: *Mays took a back seat to no one in baseball when it came to stardom, not even All-Stars Roberto Clemente* (left) *or Hank Aaron* (right).

Mays belted 37 home runs for the Giants during the summer of 1966, the last season in which the "Say Hey Kid" hit more than 30.

> ## "Baseball is a fun game, and I love it. I like to play happy."
> ### —Mays

stats went completely through the roof. His .345 average was the best in the National League. So were his 13 triples and .667 slugging percentage. His 41 homers were fourth best. He finished with 377 total bases, just one behind Duke Snider's league-leading number. He was also in the top five in on-base percentage and runs scored. He drove in 110 runs. Of course, he was the National League Most Valuable Player, which began a string of a dozen years in which he was lower than sixth in the MVP voting only once. His Giants won the pennant again, and it was Willie's two incredible defensive plays in center in Game 1 that shattered the confidence of the 111-game winning Cleveland Indians and led to a Giant Series sweep.

So what did Willie do for an encore in 1955? He hit 13 triples to lead the league again, and he upped his homer total by 10. His 51 circuit clouts put him in the company of Hack Wilson, Johnny Mize, and Ralph Kiner as the only National Leaguers to record half a hundred in one season. His Giants, though, finished third behind the Dodgers, then fell to sixth two years in a row. Willie "slumped" to 35 and 36 homers, although he did lead the National League in 1957 in slugging percentage and triples, with 20. That year he reached the 20 figure in doubles, triples, homers, and stolen bases—the first time that had ever been done.

The Giants packed up for the West Coast following the 1957 season, and Willie, who loved playing stickball with kids on the streets of Harlem, begrudgingly became a Californian. In San Francisco the fans didn't develop the instant passion for Mays that their counterparts in the Big Apple had, and Willie's performance indicated that he sensed it. In his first year on the Coast, he hit just 29 homers, the fewest since his rookie season. The next two years he followed up with 34 and 29 again; the Giants were much improved, though they still were not bona fide contenders.

THE STAR OF STARS

For years in the late 1950s and early '60s, Willie Mays made baseball's annual All-Star Game his own personal show. Often batting leadoff, he was the man you wanted to watch. If something was going to happen, there was a good chance Willie would be at the center of it. And remember, this was in the era of Roberto Clemente, Hank Aaron, and Frank Robinson.

In the '55 midsummer classic, Willie's two hits helped the National League rally for a 6–5 win. In the 1956 game he swatted a two-run homer. In 1957 he had two hits, one a vital triple. In the first game of 1959, his ninth-inning triple knocked home the winning run. In the first of the 1960 games, he started the game with a triple and later added a double and single to his hit collection. In the second game that year, he had three more hits, one of them a homer.

In the first game of 1961, Willie drove in the tying run in the bottom of the 10th inning with a double and then scored the winner shortly thereafter. In 1963 he drove in two runs, scored two more, stole two bases, and capped it off with a lovely defensive play in the outfield. In 1965 he homered, walked twice, and scored the winning run. In 1968 he started the game with a single. His dance off first rattled Luis Tiant, who threw wildly in a pickoff attempt that advanced him to second. Later that inning he scored the only run of the game.

A young Mays, bats in hand, was called up with great expectations by the New York Giants in 1951. With 20 home runs, he was named Rookie of the Year.

In 1961 Willie shook off any remaining nostalgia he had for New York and started another amazing string of offensive greatness. That year he hit 40 homers, second in the league behind teammate Orlando Cepeda, and led the league in runs scored. In 1962 his 49 homers led the league, as did his 382 total bases. He was second in runs, doubles, and RBI. Even better, his final homer of the season gave the Giants a 2–1 win over Houston, which meant Willie's team had tied the Los Angeles Dodgers for the National League flag.

In the best-of-three playoff, Mays rose to the occasion. He belted two homers in Game 1 to help the Giants to an 8–0 victory. In Game 3 San Francisco was down 4–2 entering the ninth inning. But Willie slashed a single off the body of Dodger reliever Ed Roebuck that keyed a four-run rally, and the Giants returned to the World Series for the first time in eight years.

Mays batted just .250 in the Series, and the Giants lost in seven games to the Yankees. In the ninth inning

In 1958 Mays's Giants went from New York to San Francisco, while Duke Snider (right) and the Dodgers moved from Brooklyn to Los Angeles.

New Yorkers celebrated Willie Mays Day in 1963, 10 years before Mays finished his Hall of Fame career with 660 home runs.

of the final game, with his team down 1–0, Willie lined a two-out double into right field. Roger Maris made a stellar grab and throw, which forced Matty Alou to hold at third. Willie McCovey's liner to Bobby Richardson ended one of the great Series games of all time.

In 1963 Mays belted 38 home runs, but one of them ranked with the most dramatic of all time. It came in the 16th inning of an amazing pitcher's duel between Warren Spahn and Juan Marichal. Neither pitcher had allowed a single run; both had gone the distance when Willie took Warren deep to provide the winning margin.

Mays was still at the top of his form in 1964, when his 47 homers and .607 slugging percentage led the league. He was second in runs and total bases and third in RBI. In 1965, at age 34, Willie won his second MVP title with a season for the record books, perhaps his best hitting season ever. Not only did he club 52 homers, joining just a handful of men to slug 50 twice, but he hit .317 (third best in the NL). He led the league in total bases, on-base percentage, and slugging average, and finished second in runs and third in RBI. The Dodgers edged out the Giants for the NL pennant by just two games.

Mays's last year of more than 30 homers was 1966, when he hit 37. He came back with a 28-homer season in 1970, at the age of 39. Early in the 1972 season, Willie was traded back to New York, this time to the Mets, as they tried to resurrect some of the ancient glory. For a while Willie did what New York fans expected, and the old magic returned. In his first game in a Mets uniform, he homered to help beat—who else?—the Giants. In his next game he walked and then scored on a triple when he knocked the ball out of the catcher's glove. Two days later he belted a two-run homer for another Met win.

With Willie's inspirational play and a stellar young pitching staff, the Mets squeaked to the 1973 National League East title and went the distance of five games to beat the Reds in the League Championship Series. In the final-game victory, Willie knocked in a run. The aged Mays ended his career by appearing in just three games of the World Series, as the Mets fell to the A's in seven games.

In his 22-year career, Willie was named to the All-Star team 20 times and played in 24 games (for several seasons there were two All-Star Games a year). He holds or shares All-Star lifetime records for at-bats, hits, runs, triples, extra-base hits, and stolen bases. If there ever was an All-Star, it was Willie Mays.

BY THE NUMBERS

Year	Team	G	AB	R	H	2B	3B	HR	HR%	RBI	BB	K	BA	SA	SB
1951	NY-N	121	464	59	127	22	5	20	4.3	68	57	60	.274	.472	7
1952	NY-N	34	127	17	30	2	4	4	3.1	23	16	17	.236	.409	4
1954	NY-N	151	565	119	195	33	13	41	7.3	110	66	57	.345	.667	8
1955	NY-N	152	580	123	185	18	13	51	8.8	127	79	60	.319	.659	24
1956	NY-N	152	578	101	171	27	8	36	6.2	84	68	65	.296	.557	40
1957	NY-N	152	585	112	195	26	20	35	6.0	97	76	62	.333	.626	38
1958	SF-N	152	600	121	208	33	11	29	4.8	96	78	56	.347	.583	31
1959	SF-N	151	575	125	180	43	5	34	5.9	104	65	58	.313	.583	27
1960	SF-N	153	595	107	190	29	12	29	4.9	103	61	70	.319	.555	25
1961	SF-N	154	572	129	176	32	3	40	7.0	123	81	77	.308	.584	18
1962	SF-N	162	621	130	189	36	5	49	7.9	141	78	85	.304	.615	18
1963	SF-N	157	596	115	187	32	7	38	6.4	103	66	83	.314	.582	8
1964	SF-N	157	578	121	171	21	9	47	8.1	111	82	72	.296	.607	19
1965	SF-N	157	558	118	177	21	3	52	9.3	112	76	71	.317	.645	9
1966	SF-N	152	552	99	159	29	4	37	6.7	103	70	81	.288	.556	5
1967	SF-N	141	486	83	128	22	2	22	4.5	70	51	92	.263	.453	6
1968	SF-N	148	498	84	144	20	5	23	4.6	79	67	81	.289	.488	12
1969	SF-N	117	403	64	114	17	3	13	3.2	58	49	71	.283	.437	6
1970	SF-N	139	478	94	139	15	2	28	5.9	83	79	90	.291	.506	5
1971	SF-N	136	417	82	113	24	5	18	4.3	61	112	123	.271	.482	23
1972	SF-N	19	49	8	9	2	0	0	0.0	3	17	5	.184	.224	3
	NY-N	69	195	27	52	9	1	8	4.1	19	43	43	.267	.446	1
Yr		88	244	35	61	11	1	8	3.3	22	60	48	.250	.402	4
1973	NY-N	66	209	24	44	10	0	6	2.9	25	27	47	.211	.344	1
Total	22	2992	10881	2062	3283	523	140	660	6.1	1903	1464	1526	.302	.557	338

WILLIE McCOVEY

At first his nickname was "Stretch." When he joined Ray Kroc's Padres, he became "Big Mac." But regardless of what they called him, Willie McCovey hit more home runs than any other National League first baseman ever.

L IKE MANY HOME RUN wallopers, Willie McCovey's very batting stance was enough to instill terror into the hearts of pitchers. But McCovey didn't do it with rippling muscles or a broad, intimidating stance. The 6'4" "Stretch" seemed to be coiled like a huge snake, ready to strike with instantaneous force. The overall effect was one of calculated, poised menace.

On the day of McCovey's election to the Hall of Fame, Nick Peters of *The Oakland Tribune* wrote: "He did it all despite arthritic knees, a troublesome hip, aching feet and assorted other ailments. He did it in the Candlestick Park cold and despite more intentional walks than any player of his era."

Playing in the Pacific Coast League in 1959 at age 21, McCovey belted 29 home runs in three months, and the Giants brought him to the big leagues. McCovey's debut was something exceptional. In his very first game, batting against Hall of Famer-to-be Robin Roberts, McCovey smashed two triples and two singles. He appeared in only 52 big-league games that year, but he hit 13 homers and five triples and batted .354. He even had a 23-game hitting streak. He was the Rookie of the Year. Unanimously.

Although an early-season slump sent him back to the minors in 1960, he was back in time to finish with 13 more home runs in 101 games. The problem was, San Francisco had Orlando Cepeda (who had been Rookie of the Year in 1958) at first base, and Willie found himself platooned in the outfield. He appeared in just 106 games in 1961 and only 91 in 1962, although he hit 18 and 20 homers in his limited duty.

In the 1962 World Series, McCovey appeared in just four games. His three hits included a triple and a homer. But it was the one he didn't get in Game 7 that has gone down in history. With the Giants losing 1–0 and men on second and third with two outs in the last of the ninth, McCovey ripped a line drive that New York second sacker Bobby Richardson snagged to end the Series. His almost-hit became a recurring theme in the Peanuts comic strip—and in the hearts of Giants fans and Yankee haters everywhere.

In 1963 McCovey got the nod as the Giants' full-time left fielder, appearing in 135 games there and 23 at first. He responded in a big way, hitting 44 homers to lead the league. Of his first five big-league seasons, it was the only one in which he would get more than 365 at-bats. McCovey slumped in '64 while Cepeda was traded away. McCovey hit 39 homers in 1965, second in the league to Willie Mays. But McCovey's best years were yet to come.

After 36 homers in 1966 and 31 in 1967, he topped all National League hitters with 36 homers and 105 RBI in 1968. In 1969 he led the league again with 45 long balls (homering in an amazing 9.2 percent of his at-bats), and also was tops in seven other offensive departments, including RBI, on-base percentage, and slugging. He received a record 45 intentional walks, and was fifth in the league in batting average. Not surprisingly, he was voted the NL's MVP. In that year's All-Star Game, he hit two homers to key the NL win and was named the MVP of that game, too.

For four consecutive seasons, 1967 through 1970, Stretch led the National League in home run percentage. In 1970 Willie homered in all 12 NL parks, a rare accomplishment, as he swatted a total of 39.

In 1971 a knee injury held Willie to just 105 appearances. In that year's National League Championship Series against Pittsburgh, he hit .429 and slugged two homers, although the

Above right: In a playing career that touched four different decades, McCovey led the league in home runs three times, including twice with 40-plus dingers. Below: Mays, Kirkland, and McCovey (left to right) formed a Giants trio that gave the opposition the Willies in the late 1950s. Mays and McCovey homered 800 times as teammates.

Giants couldn't defeat the eventual world champs. With Mays dealt to the Mets in early 1972, the two Willies finished their career together as the second greatest slugging duo in history: They belted exactly 800 home runs as teammates.

In 1973 McCovey homered twice in one inning. Then in 1977 he did it again, and one was a grand slam. McCovey's 18 grand slams are third only to Lou Gehrig and Eddie Murray in baseball history. His three pinch-hit grannies are tied for the major-league record.

When he retired after three years with San Diego and a four-year return engagement in San Francisco, Willie had appeared as a player in four decades. He had led the league in home runs three times and RBI twice. His 521 home runs tie him with Ted Williams for the 10th highest total ever, and McCovey's total is the best of any NL left-handed batter. You have to wonder what his numbers would have been like if he hadn't been forced to platoon early in his career.

BY THE NUMBERS

Year	Team	G	AB	R	H	2B	3B	HR	HR%	RBI	BB	K	BA	SA	SB
1959	SF-N	52	192	32	68	9	5	13	6.8	38	22	35	.354	.656	2
1960	SF-N	101	260	37	62	15	3	13	5.0	51	45	53	.238	.469	1
1961	SF-N	106	328	59	89	12	3	18	5.5	50	37	60	.271	.491	1
1962	SF-N	91	229	41	67	6	1	20	8.7	54	29	35	.293	.590	3
1963	SF-N	152	564	103	158	19	5	44	7.8	102	50	119	.280	.566	1
1964	SF-N	130	364	55	80	14	1	18	4.9	54	61	73	.220	.412	2
1965	SF-N	160	540	93	149	17	4	39	7.2	92	88	118	.276	.539	0
1966	SF-N	150	502	85	148	26	6	36	7.2	96	76	100	.295	.586	2
1967	SF-N	135	456	73	126	17	4	31	6.8	91	71	110	.276	.535	3
1968	SF-N	148	523	81	153	16	4	36	6.9	105	72	71	.293	.545	4
1969	SF-N	149	491	101	157	26	2	45	9.2	126	121	66	.320	.656	0
1970	SF-N	152	495	98	143	39	2	39	7.9	126	137	75	.289	.612	0
1971	SF-N	105	329	45	91	13	0	18	5.5	70	64	57	.277	.480	0
1972	SF-N	81	263	30	56	8	0	14	5.3	35	38	45	.213	.403	0
1973	SF-N	130	383	52	102	14	3	29	7.6	75	105	78	.266	.546	1
1974	SD-N	128	344	53	87	19	1	22	6.4	63	96	76	.253	.506	1
1975	SD-N	122	413	43	104	17	0	23	5.6	68	57	80	.252	.460	1
1976	SD-N	71	202	20	41	9	0	7	3.5	36	21	39	.203	.351	0
	Oak-A	11	24	0	5	0	0	0	0.0	0	3	4	.208	.208	0
1977	SF-N	141	478	54	134	21	0	28	5.9	86	67	106	.280	.500	3
1978	SF-N	108	351	32	80	19	2	12	3.4	64	36	57	.228	.396	1
1979	SF-N	117	353	34	88	9	0	15	4.2	57	36	70	.249	.402	0
1980	SF-N	48	113	8	23	8	0	1	0.9	16	13	23	.204	.301	0
Total	22	2588	8197	1229	2211	353	46	521	6.4	1555	1345	1550	.270	.515	26

When McCovey uncoiled his 6'4" frame, the result spelled doom for opposing pitchers. Truly a slugger, Stretch blasted far more home runs (521) than doubles (353).

MARK McGWIRE

Baseball fans still revel in the excitement that Mark McGwire brought to the game in the incredible summer of 1998. Seventy home runs, and with a whole lot of class.

Above right: *At first, McGwire did not enjoy the extra attention merited by his home run pace. At the urging of others, he later adopted a more easygoing approach.* Below: *Matthew McGwire, a part-time batboy with the Cardinals, celebrated with the most famous dad in sports after home run No. 61 tied Roger Maris and surpassed the Babe.*

MARK McGWIRE WAS A MEMBER of the U.S. Olympic baseball team in 1984 when they visited Cooperstown. Mark remembers walking up to the front door of the Baseball Hall of Fame and Museum, then turning around to get some pizza. "I didn't appreciate history at the time," he told *Sports Illustrated* in 1998. But before long, Mark would firmly establish his place in Cooperstown with his unbelievable slugging feats. His uniform, in fact, is already there.

In his first full season with the Oakland A's in 1987, McGwire bashed 49 home runs, which smashed the previous rookie record by 11. He was voted American League Rookie of the Year unanimously. On June 27 and 28 that year, he slugged five homers to tie the all-time record for homers in consecutive games. By the All-Star break he had hit 33. Although he cooled off, he sent a strong message of what the future might hold. He and young, slugging teammate Jose Canseco were dubbed the "Bash Brothers."

Over the next five seasons, McGwire walloped 168 homers. In the last of those years, back problems kept him out of the lineup for 23 games, but he still smashed 42 home runs. McGwire was being compared (and not always favorably) to Fred McGriff, a steady but unspectacular long-ball hitting first baseman who was the same age.

But 1993 and 1994 were lost seasons for the tall redhead from Pomona, California. A heel injury the first year limited his appearances to just 27 games and 84 at-bats. He hit nine homers. The next season he injured his left arch and managed just nine long balls again. In their careers McGriff had now out-homered Mac by 27.

But McGwire came on strong in 1995, swatting 39 homers to land him just one behind the two men tied for second in the AL race. And he did it playing in only 104 games. His average of one homer for every 8.13 at-bats was the best for a full season ever, topping Ruth's 8.48 in 1920. McGwire was hurt again in 1996, but he still powered homers at exactly the same rate as in the record-setting previous year. In only 423 at-bats he hit 52 home runs. He also led the league in both on-base average and slugging percentage, with a breathtaking .730. People were starting to wonder, "If only McGwire could stay healthy…."

McGwire's home runs were huge in distance as well as quantity. On April 20, 1996, he knocked a pitch 514 feet over the left-field roof at Tiger Stadium. Then 10 days later he hit two home runs in the same game in Cleveland's Jacobs Field that went 459 and 485 feet. The second one put a dent in the top of the Budweiser scoreboard in left-center field. On June 24 he tore into a 97-mph fastball from Seattle's Randy Johnson and sent it 538 feet into the Kingdome's upper deck, just six rows from the back of the seating area—the longest homer in baseball since MCI had starting calculating them in 1992.

But the A's were going nowhere, McGwire's long blasts or not. With Mark on his way to free agency, the A's decided to trade him to the St. Louis Cardinals on July 31. He had already hit 34 homers. The A's got T. J. Mathews, Eric Ludwick, and Blake Stein.

The St. Louis fans took quickly to the big guy, and Mark fell in love with the city. Before long he signed a long-term contract to stay there. Then his bat got hot. He knocked 24 more out of the park to finish the season with 58, the most by any hitter since Roger Maris's record of 61 in 1961, and the fourth best home run season of all time. He also had a combined total of 123 RBI.

When asked about hitting home runs, McGwire explained: "I try not to swing too hard. I have a natural loft." And he put that "natural loft" to work on Opening Day, 1998, as he began the greatest home run season ever. He clubbed four in his team's first four games. By the end of April he had 11 homers.

By the end of May he had 27. Ten more flew off his bat in June, eight more in July. He hit his 50th and 51st homers in an August 8 doubleheader, passing Babe Ruth by becoming the only man to hit 50 three years in a row.

The whole nation was in love with Mark McGwire. And the exciting race that the Cubs' Sammy Sosa made with his record-breaking 20 homers in June gave everyone something to talk about every morning. "America is a baseball nation again," Tom Verducci wrote in the September 14 *Sports Illustrated*.

Even more amazing is how McGwire handled the absolutely unheard-of media pressure. The hounding from the press began in spring training. He was followed by as many as 600 media persons, yet he maintained incredible grace and decency throughout all the inane questions, endlessly repeated. When McGwire said he was happy just to be getting the chance, he was completely believable.

There were a few snappish moments, to be sure, but very few. In comparison to the torture the writers and broadcasters applied to Roger Maris when he chased the same record 37 years earlier, what McGwire was going through was a love-fest. Towns with bad teams going nowhere still sold out to see the Mark and Sammy shows. Opposing fans cheered Mac wildly, giving him standing ovations for his clouts—and booing their own pitchers for failing to give him a pitch to hit. When he hit No. 53 in Pittsburgh, the fans demanded a curtain call—the first time anyone could remember that happening for

Before he took down the most storied record in sports, McGwire set new marks in 1998 for homers in two and three consecutive seasons (128 and 180).

As he neared the record, Major League Baseball began instructing the umpires to use specially coded balls, so the "real" home run balls could be distinguished from phonies.

RESPECT FOR ROGER

Mark McGwire spent the 1998 season in a home run battle with three men: Sammy Sosa, who was hitting them almost as often for the Cubs as Mark was for the Cards; the incomparable Babe Ruth; and the much-maligned Roger Maris. McGwire's straightforward appreciation of what Maris had gone through during *his* home run chase (and who else could ever appreciate it so fully?) did much to revivify the memory of Roger's sensational feat. While America adored Mark and Sammy, Maris had seen his hair fall out in clumps from the pressure while fans and the press alike belittled what he was doing.

Immediately after McGwire circled the bases after slugging No. 62, and after he hugged his son and teammates, he rushed spontaneously into the stands and embraced the Maris family. It was a truly touching scene and showed America that Mark McGwire was a man of decency. "I told them," Mark said, "that their father was in my heart."

During the 1998 postseason, a commercial for Major League Baseball aired that showed McGwire, Sosa, Cal Ripken, and other heros of the 1998 season thanking the fans for a great year. In it McGwire says, "Together we celebrated a new record and gave honor to an old one." It was a class act all the way.

a visiting player. As he neared the record, Major League Baseball began instructing the umpires to use specially coded balls, so the "real" home run balls could be distinguished from phonies. Everyone loved what he was doing. Even opposing players.

When McGwire began to show signs of fatigue—both at the plate and in his press conferences—in early August, several players from other teams said to him, "Relax. Enjoy the ride. What you're doing is great for baseball." Ken Griffey Jr. (on his way to a 56-homer season himself) even hired an airplane to fly a sign of congratulations over Cincinnati's Cinergy Field when McGwire and the Cards were playing there.

Some of the press missed the point. When *The New York Times* in early September

McGwire's good times with the Oakland A's included shattering the league's home run record for rookies with 49 in his first full season.

thought they were uncovering a scandal by pointing out that McGwire was using an over-the-counter muscle enhancer, androstenedione (legal in baseball although banned in the Olympics), the whole world yawned. McGwire was a man all the world wanted to love; the attempt at muckraking, at diminishing his effort, was forgotten in days.

Before McGwire broke Ruth's legendary mark of 60 home runs, with a 430-foot poke off the Cubs' Mike Morgan on September 7, he had already pushed the Babe aside in some remarkable slugging categories. Not only had he become the first player to hit 50 three years in a row, but he also required the fewest at-bats to reach 400 homers in his career. Moreover, he shattered the records for homers in two and three consecutive seasons. McGwire's 61st homer came on his dad's 61st birthday.

Homer No. 62 came on September 8 in the Cards' 145th game. Surprisingly, it was his shortest of the year, a mere 341 feet. But the season was far from over. Sosa was still in the hunt. Going into the final Friday of the season, the two were

neck-and-neck with a remarkable 65 homers each. Sammy, with his team scrambling for a wild-card slot, would manage just one more homer. But McGwire finished with a flourish, knocking the ball out of the park five times in his final 19 swings of the season to end with the thoroughly sensational total of 70—10 more than Ruth's "unbeatable" record. In addition, McGwire moved past Ruth for the best career homer-per-at-bat ratio, with 8.91 to the Babe's 8.50.

Forty-eight of McGwire's long shots were calculated to have traveled more than 400 feet, including an amazing 13 in a row from June 18 through July 28. Five were listed at 500 feet or better, with the longest being a 545-shot to dead center field off Florida's Livan Hernandez, the longest home run ever hit at McGwire's home park, Busch Stadium.

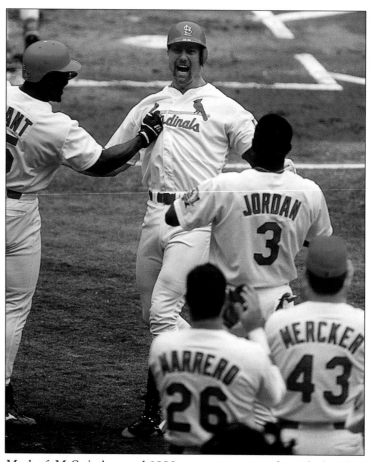

Much of McGwire's record 1998 season was spent downplaying the numbers and the 500-foot blasts. After catching Roger Maris, however, he talked freely about the accomplishment.

McGwire had 10 multiple-homer games in 1998—eight two-homer games, two three-homer performances. He hit 38 of his slams at home, 32 on the road. Fifty-five were sent downtown against right-handed pitching; just 15 against lefties. He also walked a National League-record 162 times, 28 of them intentional.

McGwire averaged a home run every 7.3 at-bats in 1998, much better than the Babe's 9.0 in 1927. A purist with a fondness for nitpicking might point out that Ruth drove in 17 more runs and batted 57 points higher, and of course his team won the pennant and swept the World Series while McGwire's Cards finished 19 games back. (Maris's 1961 Yanks were world champs, too.) The fact is, Ruth will always be Ruth, no matter how often McGwire hits more than 60 home runs. But now McGwire stands alone, at a level of home run power no one ever dreamed of before.

McGwire, like Ruth did, loves kids. His huge post-homer hugs of his 10-year-old son, Matthew (honorary batboy during Dad's long-ball chase), are some of the most indelible memories of the fairytale season. McGwire also has established a foundation to help sexually abused and battered children. He donates $1 million a year to it. On September 3, one of his few off days during the race, McGwire spent his day filming a public service announcement telling kids how they can get help in dealing with an abusive parent. Mac has become a hero in every sense of the word.

McGwire capped his magical season by swatting No. 70 against Montreal in the last game of the year. He homered once every 7.3 at-bats in 1998.

BY THE NUMBERS																
Year	Team	G	AB	R	H	2B	3B	HR	HR%	RBI	BB	K	BA	SA	SB
1986	Oak-A	18	53	10	10	1	0	3	5.7	9	4	18	.189	.377	0
1987	Oak-A	151	557	97	161	28	4	**49**	8.8	118	71	131	.289	**.618**	1
1988	Oak-A	155	550	87	143	22	1	32	5.8	99	76	117	.260	.478	0
1989	Oak-A	143	490	74	113	17	0	33	6.7	95	83	94	.231	.467	1
1990	Oak-A	156	523	87	123	16	0	39	7.5	108	**110**	116	.235	.489	2
1991	Oak-A	154	483	62	97	22	0	22	4.6	75	93	116	.201	.383	2
1992	Oak-A	139	467	87	125	22	0	42	9.0	104	90	105	.268	.585	0
1993	Oak-A	27	84	16	28	6	0	9	10.7	24	21	19	.333	.726	0
1994	Oak-A	47	135	26	34	3	0	9	6.7	25	37	40	.252	.474	0
1995	Oak-A	104	317	75	87	13	0	39	12.3	90	88	77	.274	.685	1
1996	Oak-A	130	423	104	132	21	0	**52**	12.3	113	116	112	.312	.730	0
1997	Oak-A	105	366	48	104	24	0	34	9.3	81	58	98	.284	.628	1
	StL-N	51	174	38	44	3	0	24	13.8	42	43	61	.253	.684	2
1998	StL-N	155	509	130	152	21	0	**70**	13.8	147	**162**	155	.299	**.752**	1
Total		13	1535	5131	941	1353	219	5	457	8.9	1130	1052	1259	.264	.576	11

EDDIE MURRAY

"Consistency" was Eddie Murray's middle name. By swatting about a homer a week for two decades, he landed among the top 15 home run hitters of all time.

EDDIE MURRAY NEVER hit 50 home runs in a season. In fact, he never hit 35. But as a dangerous switch-hitter with power to all fields, he hit around 25 to 30 many times over a long career. As opposed to the brilliant comet that flashes across the heavens and then is gone, Eddie Murray was there, for 21 seasons. Day-in, day-out, he performed as a consistently powerful clutch hitter. And he was almost never on the disabled list. He was a manager's dream, an opposing pitcher's nightmare.

Murray's Orioles were almost always in the thick of the pennant chase. Long after he left Baltimore, Eddie was in demand by teams who coveted his winner's attitude and clutch bat. In fact, at age 39, Murray was the first member of the Cleveland Indians to homer in their brand-new Jacobs Field. He also drove in the winning run in Game 3 of that year's World Series.

He did it all without drawing attention to himself. As longtime teammate Mike Flanagan put it in David Porter's *African-American Sports Greats*, "He doesn't feel comfortable in the spotlight. All he needs is the satisfaction that he did his job."

In Eddie's first season, 1977, he tallied 29 doubles, 27 homers, 88 RBI, and a .283 average, and was the easy choice for American League Rookie of the Year. In retrospect, it's remarkable that those numbers are almost exactly what Murray would average for the next 20 seasons. With the exception of strike years, 1986 (when injuries held him to 137 games), and the last season of his career, Murray played in more than 150 games every single season.

In 1978 Murray was named to the All-Star team, the first of seven times. That year he was second in the league in total bases. He started the 1979 season with a 17-game hitting streak. On August 29 of that year, he hit three homers. In the '79 American League Championship Series, he batted .417 and drove in five runs to propel the O's to the World Series. In 1980 he had a huge year, with two streaks of three consecutive games with at least one homer and 30 RBI in the month of

Above right: With the switch-hitting Murray on board, the Orioles had the winning edge. The Birds were almost always battling for the Eastern Division title, winning it in 1979 and 1983. Below: It was only fitting that Murray's 500th career home run came in 1996, the year he returned to Baltimore. Few sluggers have been better in clutch situations.

Year	Team	G	AB	R	H	2B	3B	HR	HR%	RBI	BB	K	BA	SA	SB
1977	Bal-A	160	611	81	173	29	2	27	4.4	88	48	104	.283	.470	0
1978	Bal-A	161	610	85	174	32	3	27	4.4	95	70	97	.285	.480	6
1979	Bal-A	159	606	90	179	30	2	25	4.1	99	72	78	.295	.475	10
1980	Bal-A	158	621	100	186	36	2	32	5.2	116	54	71	.300	.519	7
1981	Bal-A	99	378	57	111	21	2	**22**	5.8	**78**	40	43	.294	.534	2
1982	Bal-A	151	550	87	174	30	1	32	5.8	110	70	82	.316	.549	7
1983	Bal-A	156	582	115	178	30	3	33	5.7	111	86	90	.306	.538	5
1984	Bal-A	162	588	97	180	26	3	29	4.9	110	**107**	87	.306	.509	10
1985	Bal-A	156	583	111	173	37	1	31	5.3	124	84	68	.297	.523	5
1986	Bal-A	137	495	61	151	25	1	17	3.4	84	78	49	.305	.463	3
1987	Bal-A	160	618	89	171	28	3	30	4.9	91	73	80	.277	.477	1
1988	Bal-A	161	603	75	171	27	2	28	4.6	84	75	78	.284	.474	5
1989	LA-N	160	594	66	147	29	1	20	3.4	88	87	85	.247	.401	7
1990	LA-N	155	558	96	184	22	3	26	4.7	95	82	64	.330	.520	8
1991	LA-N	153	576	69	150	23	1	19	3.3	96	55	74	.260	.403	10
1992	NY-N	156	551	64	144	37	2	16	2.9	93	66	74	.261	.423	4
1993	NY-N	154	610	77	174	28	1	27	4.4	100	40	61	.285	.467	2
1994	Cle-A	108	433	57	110	21	1	17	3.9	76	31	53	.254	.425	8
1995	Cle-A	113	436	68	141	21	0	21	4.8	82	39	65	.323	.516	5
1996	Cle-A	88	336	33	88	9	1	12	3.6	45	34	45	.262	.402	3
	Bal-A	64	230	36	59	12	0	10	4.3	34	27	42	.257	.439	1
	Yr	152	566	69	147	21	1	22	3.9	79	61	87	.260	.417	4
1997	Ana-A	46	160	13	35	7	0	3	1.9	15	13	24	.219	.319	1
	LA-N	9	7	0	2	0	0	0	0.0	3	2	2	.286	.286	0
Total	21	3026	11336	1627	3255	560	35	504	4.4	1917	1333	1516	.287	.476	110

September. He finished fifth in the league in both homers (32) and RBI (116).

In 1981 Murray led the league in RBI and tied for the home run title. In 1982 he hit 32 homers, drove in 110, and batted .316. He finished second in the MVP voting to Robin Yount. In 1983 his 33-homer, 111-RBI season earned him a second-place league MVP finish to teammate Cal Ripken. In fact, Murray was in the Top 10 in MVP voting six consecutive years. And in the 1983 World Series, he belted two homers in the deciding Game 5 Baltimore victory.

There was no better proof of Eddie Murray's clutch performance than his grand slam total: 19. Only one man, Lou Gehrig, has hit more. In 1985 Murray hit three. In 1992 he was 10-for-15 with the sacks jammed. His lifetime batting average with three men on was .429.

In 1987 Murray became the first major-leaguer ever to homer from both sides of the plate in consecutive games. That year he batted .421 in late-inning pressure situations. And 1988 was the fifth time he led the Orioles in homers, batting average, and RBI in the same year.

Dealt to the Dodgers for the 1989 season, Eddie didn't stop. He led all Dodgers in homers, RBI, runs, total bases, walks, and games. In 1990 only Willie McGee's .335 average topped Murray's .330 among National Leaguers. In 1991 Murray's 19 homers were the 15th time he had hit 17 or more in a season. Only five players have exceeded that level of excellence. For his career he had 20 consecutive 75-plus RBI seasons. Hank Aaron had just 19. In 1994 Murray homered from both sides of the plate for the 11th time in his career, passing Mickey Mantle's 10.

But he was far from through. After two years (and 93- and 100-RBI seasons) as a Met, Murray returned to the American League with Cleveland. His .323 average in 1995 was the second highest of his career. That year he also swatted his 3,000th hit. In the first inning of Game 4 of that year's LCS, with a man on, Murray rapped a pitch 435 feet into the center-field stands to key a Tribe win.

Sent back to the Orioles during the 1996 season, Murray homered in his first game back. That year he hit .400 in the Division Series and swatted a homer in the LCS. On September 6 Murray hit his 500th homer, joining two men with 500 homers and 3,000 hits. Their names? Hank Aaron and Willie Mays.

Murray was never the game's most powerful player. However, with more than 500 homers and 3,000 hits over 21 seasons, he was among the most productive.

STAN MUSIAL

Most people don't mention Stan Musial when they list the game's greatest sluggers, which is a sad oversight, because until Willie Mays, "The Man" was probably the most complete offensive production machine ever.

Musial never led the league in home runs in 22 years in the bigs, but he hit 30 or more six times. His other specialties included the single, double, and triple.

BORN IN A STEEL TOWN in the Monongahela Valley, south of Pittsburgh, Stan Musial exemplified the town's work ethic. He applied that ethic to an impressive slate of physical skills: He could hit for average and for power and was very fast. "The Donora Greyhound" was one of his nicknames. He achieved his slugging with a style almost the direct opposite of many other bombers. Unlike Joe DiMaggio's or Jimmie Foxx's wide-open stances, Musial was compact, with feet close together and the bat tucked in behind his shoulder. He looked, some said, like he was peeking at the pitcher from around a corner.

Musial's completeness as a hitter is illustrated in this stat: He is the only man in the top 20 lifetime in singles, doubles, triples, and home runs. And he averaged just 33 strikeouts a season. He held most of the National League lifetime batting marks until Hank Aaron. From 1943 through 1954, he hit better than .330 every year but one. When he began to lose his famed foot speed, he moved to first base and became the first National Leaguer to play 1,000 games or more at two different positions.

Six times Musial led the league in hits, slugging percentage, and total bases. Eight times he led in doubles;

Few hitters could keep pace with Ted Williams (left), but Musial was close. He won seven batting titles and was one of the most complete players ever to don a cap.

in triples and runs five times. He was the top hitter for average in the NL seven times; only Honus Wagner and Tony Gwynn have done better. Musial won his last batting title with a .351 average when he was 36 years old. He hit .330 the year of his 42nd birthday. Musial was a model of consistency: He had exactly the same number of hits at home and on the road during his career—1,815 each. He scored 1,949 runs and drove in 1,951. He was the first National Leaguer to win the Most Valuable Player crown three times.

Musial began his pro career as a pitcher. In his first three minor-league seasons, he sported a 33–13 record. But with his batting skills, he began playing the outfield, too, and a fall on his pitching shoulder while making a catch turned him into a full-time batsman. In his first minor-league season as a regular outfielder, he slugged 29 home runs and knocked in 115, while batting over .350. He won his first major-league bat crown his second full season in the bigs. During his first four full major-league seasons, Musial's St. Louis Cardinals won four NL titles and three world championships.

In 1946 Musial cracked 50 doubles and 20 triples. It was the second time in his four-year career up to that point that he had hit 20 triples, and the third time he had hit at least 48 doubles. He also led the league in runs, hits, slugging, and batting average, and took the MVP Award.

In 1948 "Stan the Man" had one of the most spectacular offensive seasons in history. His .376 batting average was 43 points better than Richie Ashburn's, who finished second. He topped the league with 230 hits, which included 46 doubles and 18 triples, both league-leading numbers, too. His 131 RBI, .450 on-base average, and .702 slugging percentage were also

One of the more impressive feats in Musial's career was his record-tying mark of homering in four successive at-bats during the summer of 1962. Here, he's congratulated by Ken Boyer after rapping the third dinger.

the best among NLers. If he had hit just one more homer (he finished with 39), he would have tied Johnny Mize and Ralph Kiner for the home run title and taken the Triple Crown, something no National Leaguer had done since 1937 (or has done since). His 429 total bases that year are the sixth highest in any season by anybody. Only two men have come within 23 of the mark since then.

Musial won batting titles in 1950, '51, and '52, and he took the slugging title two of those years as well. On May 2, 1954, he belted five home runs in a doubleheader. After he batted just .255 in 1959, most people were willing to write him off as a hitter. But he came back, hitting .275, .288, and then .330. He finished his career with a .331 average.

When the All-Stars got together in mid-July each season to strut their stuff, Stan proved that he belonged. In 24 All-Star Games he averaged .317, with 20 hits. His six All-Star homers are the most ever, and he is tied with Willie Mays for most All-Star total bases with 40. In 1955 his 12th-inning homer won the game.

On the occasion of Musial's retirement, Ford Frick said of Stan the Man, "Here stands baseball's happy warrior. Here stands baseball's perfect knight." As Dodger broadcaster Vin Scully put it during a 1989 telecast, "How good was Stan Musial? He was good enough to take your breath away."

BY THE NUMBERS

Year	Team	G	AB	R	H	2B	3B	HR	HR%	RBI	BB	K	BA	SA	SB
1941	StL-N	12	47	8	20	4	0	1	2.1	7	2	1	.426	.574	1
1942	StL-N	140	467	87	147	32	10	10	2.1	72	62	25	.315	.490	6
1943	StL-N	157	617	108	**220**	48	**20**	13	2.1	81	72	18	**.357**	**.562**	9
1944	StL-N	146	568	112	197	51	14	12	2.1	94	90	28	.347	**.549**	7
1946	StL-N	156	624	**124**	**228**	50	**20**	16	2.6	103	73	31	**.365**	**.587**	7
1947	StL-N	149	587	113	183	30	13	19	3.2	95	80	24	.312	.504	4
1948	StL-N	155	611	**135**	**230**	46	18	39	6.4	**131**	79	34	**.376**	**.702**	7
1949	StL-N	157	612	128	**207**	41	**13**	36	5.9	123	107	38	.338	.624	3
1950	StL-N	146	555	105	192	41	7	28	5.0	109	87	36	**.346**	**.596**	5
1951	StL-N	152	578	**124**	205	30	**12**	32	5.5	108	98	40	**.355**	.614	4
1952	StL-N	154	578	105	**194**	42	6	21	3.6	91	96	29	**.336**	**.538**	7
1953	StL-N	157	593	127	200	**53**	9	30	5.1	113	**105**	32	.337	.609	3
1954	StL-N	153	591	**120**	195	41	9	35	5.9	126	103	39	.330	.607	1
1955	StL-N	154	562	97	179	30	5	33	5.9	108	80	39	.319	.566	5
1956	StL-N	156	594	87	184	33	6	27	4.5	**109**	75	39	.310	.522	2
1957	StL-N	134	502	82	176	38	3	29	5.8	102	66	34	**.351**	.612	1
1958	StL-N	135	472	64	159	35	2	17	3.6	62	72	26	.337	.528	0
1959	StL-N	115	341	37	87	13	2	14	4.1	44	60	25	.255	.428	0
1960	StL-N	116	331	49	91	17	1	17	5.1	63	41	34	.275	.486	1
1961	StL-N	123	372	46	107	22	4	15	4.0	70	52	35	.288	.489	0
1962	StL-N	135	433	57	143	18	1	19	4.4	82	64	46	.330	.508	3
1963	StL-N	124	337	34	86	10	2	12	3.6	58	35	43	.255	.404	2
Total	22	3026	10972	1949	3630	725	177	475	4.3	1951	1599	696	.331	.559	78

MEL OTT

At just 5'9" and 170 pounds, Mel Ott was the smallest of all the great sluggers in history. His success came because he knew how to get the most from what he had.

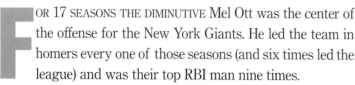

Above right: Ott (center), pictured with Bill Terry, joined the Giants right out of high school and quickly became the fan favorite. He played 22 seasons with the club. Below: Ott led the league in home runs six times and was the Giants' leader in that category a staggering 17 consecutive years. He finished his career with 511.

FOR 17 SEASONS THE DIMINUTIVE Mel Ott was the center of the offense for the New York Giants. He led the team in homers every one of those seasons (and six times led the league) and was their top RBI man nine times.

The first National Leaguer to swat 500 home runs, Ott's total of 511 was the all-time NL high until another Giant, Willie Mays, came along. Ott was a complete ballplayer. Longtime foe Pie Traynor said in *The Ballplayers,* "I can't name a player who has exerted as strong an influence on so many games."

There were two keys to Ott's continued brilliance. First was his unique left-handed batting stance. As the pitch came in, he raised his right leg high while he simultaneously lowered his bat until it was almost horizontal. With his body ready to propel into the pitch, his swing was exceptionally level. Despite all the movement in his body, his head remained still, as his manager, John McGraw, noted early on. In fact, Ott joined the Giants right out of high school and McGraw refused to send him to the minors, afraid some ambitious bush-league manager would mess with that stroke. McGraw sat the youngster next to him on the bench for what amounted to two years of training (1926 and 1927).

Ott's second advantage was his home park. The short right-field line in the Polo Grounds—just 257 feet away—was tailored for his pull hitting. And no player in baseball ever got more out of being at home. Ott's lifetime record of 323 home runs in one stadium (the Polo Grounds) is unmatched in history.

Given the right-field job at age 20 in 1928, Ott came through with a stellar season: a .328 average, 42 homers, 138 runs, 151 RBI, and a league-leading 113 walks. Like many bombers, Ott seldom saw a fat pitch. He was walked intentionally five times in one game in 1929.

Despite an off season for him (just 23 homers and 103 RBI) in 1933, Ott was a big star in the Giants' win over the Senators in that year's World Series. In Game 1 he went 4-for-4, with a two-run homer in the first inning. In Game 5 the score was tied at 3 in the top of the 10th when Ott powered a homer into the center-field bleachers, giving the Giants the victory—and the championship. He kept his hitting going throughout the 1934 season, when he led all NLers with 35 homers and 135 RBI while batting .326.

In 1936 Ott played a huge role in the Giants' miracle comeback to win the pennant. Eleven games back on July 15, in fifth place, the Giants swept a doubleheader. Ott won the next day's game with a two-run, eighth-inning homer. The Giants won 15 straight. After a loss, they swept two from the Cubs, with Ott winning the nightcap with a homer in the ninth inning. Ott led the National League in home runs, with 33, and slugging average, at .588. He was also in the top five in runs, walks, total bases, RBI, and on-base percentage.

With 1,860 lifetime RBI, Ott is eighth on the all-time list. His 1,859 runs rank ninth. Ott led the league in walks six times and in home run percentage 10 times. He hit two or more homers in a game 49 times. Twice he scored six runs in a single contest. He had a lifetime on-base percentage of .414.

Mel Ott was also the most popular Giant of his time and one of the most popular in the 116-year history of the club. Broadway stars often passed on their expensive box seats to sit in the right-field bleachers—"Ottville"—close to their hero. The story is told that famous New York restaurateur Toots Shor was conversing with Sir Alexander Fleming, the discoverer of penicillin, when Toots saw the Giants' slugger. "You'll have to excuse me," the restaurant manager said. "Someone important just came in."

Ott became the Giants' manager in 1942 and remained a full-time player through 1945. He was replaced midway through the 1948 season. Because he never played an inning of minor-league ball, and spent his entire career (22 years) with one team, he is one of the few men to "go from high school to the Hall of Fame wearing just one uniform," as historian Cappy Gagnon put it.

What Ott lacked in size he made up for with a marvelous swing that helped him become the first National Leaguer to swat 500 lifetime home runs.

BY THE NUMBERS

Year	Team	G	AB	R	H	2B	3B	HR	HR%	RBI	BB	K	BA	SA	SB
1926	NY-N	35	60	7	23	2	0	0	0.0	4	1	9	.383	.417	1
1927	NY-N	82	163	23	46	7	3	1	0.6	19	13	9	.282	.380	2
1928	NY-N	124	435	69	140	26	4	18	4.1	77	52	36	.322	.524	3
1929	NY-N	150	545	138	179	37	2	42	**7.7**	151	**113**	38	.328	.635	6
1930	NY-N	148	521	122	182	34	5	25	4.8	119	103	35	.349	.578	9
1931	NY-N	138	497	104	145	23	8	29	5.8	115	80	44	.292	.545	10
1932	NY-N	154	566	119	180	30	8	**38**	6.7	123	**100**	39	.318	.601	6
1933	NY-N	152	580	98	164	36	1	23	4.0	103	75	48	.283	.467	1
1934	NY-N	153	582	119	190	29	10	35	6.0	**135**	85	43	.326	.591	0
1935	NY-N	152	593	113	191	33	6	31	5.2	114	82	58	.322	.555	7
1936	NY-N	150	534	120	175	28	6	**33**	6.2	135	111	41	.328	**.588**	6
1937	NY-N	151	545	99	160	28	2	31	5.7	95	**102**	69	.294	.523	7
1938	NY-N	150	527	**116**	164	23	6	36	6.8	116	118	47	.311	.583	2
1939	NY-N	125	396	85	122	23	2	27	**6.8**	80	100	50	.308	.581	2
1940	NY-N	151	536	89	155	27	3	19	3.5	79	100	50	.289	.457	6
1941	NY-N	148	525	89	150	29	0	27	5.1	90	100	68	.286	.495	5
1942	NY-N	152	549	**118**	162	21	0	30	5.5	93	**109**	61	.295	.497	6
1943	NY-N	125	380	65	89	12	2	18	4.7	47	95	48	.234	.418	7
1944	NY-N	120	399	91	115	16	4	26	**6.5**	82	90	47	.288	.544	2
1945	NY-N	135	451	73	139	23	0	21	4.7	79	71	41	.308	.499	1
1946	NY-N	31	68	2	5	1	0	1	1.5	4	8	15	.074	.132	0
1947	NY-N	4	4	0	0	0	0	0	0.0	0	0	0	.000	.000	0
Total	22	2730	9456	1859	2876	488	72	511	5.4	1860	1708	896	.304	.533	89

FRANK ROBINSON

The ever-competitive Frank Robinson was inducted into the Hall of Fame the same day as Hank Aaron. Robinson, accepting his plaque before Aaron, nodded to Henry and said to the crowd, "I always knew I'd get here first."

Still intense as a skipper, Robinson resurrected the Orioles in 1989.

FRANK ROBINSON PLAYED with fire, with a controlled aggression that drove him to excellence. He didn't just want to beat you; he wanted to humiliate you. It's why only two men in baseball history were ever hit by pitches more often than Robinson. He stuck his head and upper body out over the plate, daring pitchers to pitch him inside, where he could snap his quick bat around to sting a line drive to left. His teammate, Gene Freese (and a pretty tough guy himself), was quoted in David Porter's *African-American Sports Heroes* as saying, "When it comes to guts, I've never seen anyone equal him."

Robinson is the only man ever to be selected as Most Valuable Player in both leagues. His 586 lifetime homers are fourth behind Hank Aaron, Babe Ruth, and Willie Mays. His 1,829 runs scored rank ninth all time; his 5,373 total bases are eighth. Although he hit more than 40 homers in a season only once (and that year he hit almost 50), Robinson cracked 30 or more homers 11 times. He hit two or more homers in a game 54 times.

Robby also swatted eight World Series, two LCS, and two All-Star home runs. And no one has ever hit homers in more parks than Robinson. His 32 parks homered in ties him with Aaron, Rusty Staub, Dave Winfield, and

19th-century sluggers Roger Connor and Harry Stovey. Robinson's lifetime slugging percentage of .537 places him in the Top 25. He was an All-Star 11 times.

Robinson began his professional career with a splash, hitting .348 with 17 homers and 83 RBI in just 72 games for Ogden of the Pioneer League. In his next season, with Columbia of the Sally League, he led the league with 112 runs scored while hitting .336 with 25 homers and 110 RBI. He seemed to be ready for the jump to Cincinnati, but a shoulder problem kept him in the minors for 1955, when he played in just 80 games.

As an intense, young African American playing in the southern minor leagues, and with that injury haunting him, he dealt with racial intolerance in a typically Robinson way. That year three drunks in the stands at a Sally League game crossed the line with their racist epithets, and Robinson took matters into his own hands. He charged into the stands after them, brandishing a bat. It took the strength of his manager and several teammates to stop him. After that incident, Robinson wanted to quit baseball, but the only other African American on the team talked him out of it. And baseball is glad.

Robinson arrived with Cincinnati, in more ways than one, in 1956. His 38 home runs tied the major leagues' then-rookie record, and he led the league by scoring 122 runs. He set another rookie record by being hit by a pitch 20 times. With the rookie Robinson leading the way, and Ted Kluszewski, Wally Post, Gus Bell, and Ed Bailey pitching in, the Reds tied the then-record for home runs by a team in one season, with 221.

In 1957, the first year of fan voting for the All-Star Game, Robinson was one of eight Reds to be voted a starter. Commissioner Ford Frick overturned the obvious ballot-box stuffing. Only Robinson was felt deserving and allowed to keep his starting role. He followed his sensational first season with 29 homers in '57. Then he hit 31 or more the next five in a row. Robinson was acknowledged as one of the game's young stars (and there were two guys named Aaron and Clemente also playing right field in the National League at the time), but his team was going nowhere. In 1959 he hit for the cycle in one game and hit three homers in another.

Robinson (right), pictured with Vada Pinson, learned that the best way to overcome adversity on a baseball diamond was to keep hitting home runs. He did it 586 times.

Visibly upset after sitting on the bench for the entire first All-Star Game that year, Robinson responded in typical fashion when he replaced Stan Musial at first early in the year's second All-Star Game. He cracked three hits, including a homer. A few days later, his hard slide into Milwaukee Brave Eddie Mathews provoked a huge fight, one of the first ever between black and white stars. Robinson was booed unmercifully by the Milwaukee fans, but once again he responded as he knew best. He hit a grand slam later in the game. It kicked off a hot streak for him that was capped by his three-homer game against the Phils on August 22.

For the decade of the '60s, Robinson was third behind only Aaron and Mays in runs and total bases. He was also third in doubles, RBI, and walks and fourth in home runs. Robinson led the National League in slugging in 1960 (he was also second in on-base percentage and fifth in homers), then repeated the feat in 1961, when he was second in on-base percentage and third in homers with 37. He also scored 117 runs and stole 22 bases in 25 tries. His Reds took the National League title, although they were dumped in the World Series in five games by the Maris-Mantle-Ford Yankees. Robinson was named the NL's Most Valuable Player.

Robinson hit two home runs in the 1971 World Series before his Orioles lost to the Pirates in seven games. The O's also lost the '69 Series, but they won in 1970.

In 1962 the National League slugging crown was his again, and he added 39 homers and 136 RBI, plus 51 doubles and a .342 average for a truly monumental season. He could have won the batting and total-base titles that year, but the Dodgers-Giants three-game playoff gave Tommy Davis a chance to creep past Robinson in batting average—and Willie Mays to edge him in total bases.

Injuries dampened Robinson's effectiveness in 1963, but his pride wouldn't let him give up. He came back with a .306 average, 29 homers, and 96 RBI, and in 1965 he did almost the same—.296, 33, 113. But the Reds were looking to make a change, and before the 1966 season Robinson was dealt to the Orioles for Milt Pappas and two others. Asked why he would trade the 30-year-old Robinson, Reds general manager Bill DeWitt spoke words that have gone down in baseball infamy: "He's an old 30." Reds fans still groan when they remember the deal. In *Baseball Digest* in August 1996, historian Eddie Gold ranked it as one of the 10 worst trades of all time.

Robinson seemed to revel in a challenge. "Pitchers did me a favor when they knocked me down," he said. "It made me more determined." In 1966 he showed DeWitt how old he really was. Hit by a pitch in his first American League plate appearance (no surprise there), he followed with a homer that game and another one the next, and the Orioles won 12 of their first 13 games.

In May of that year, Frank became the first man to hit the ball completely out of Baltimore's Memorial Stadium. It supposedly reached 451 feet on the fly and landed 540 feet from home. For the season all Robinson did was win the Triple Crown, with a .316 average, 49 homers, and 122 RBI plus 122 runs scored. He also slugged .637, even more remarkable when

Robinson, the only man ever to earn MVP honors in both leagues, took home several awards for a 1966 season in which he hit 49 homers and won the Triple Crown.

you consider that only one other man in the league hit better than .300 that year. Naturally, Robinson was chosen AL MVP.

The Orioles took the flag, then demolished the highly vaunted Dodgers in the World Series. The men from Los Angeles didn't score a run after the first game. Robinson hit two homers in the Series, both off Don Drysdale. The second was the only run scored in the fourth and final game. Robinson was chosen Series MVP, too. Writer Bob Broeg, in his *Superstars of Baseball,* called Robinson's season "one of the most inspirational examples of 'I'll-show-those-guys' ever."

With the "old" Robinson as their head slugger, the Orioles won four pennants and two World Series in the next six years. Robinson also played a key role in the clubhouse as the organizer and administrator of their "kangaroo court." Wearing a mop as a judicial wig, Robinson fined players, coaches, and even the manager for lapses in play, thinking, or demeanor. It was the perfect good-natured antidote to skipper Earl Weaver's boiling temper. And it worked.

Robinson might have been on his way to a second consecutive Triple Crown in 1967. Late in June, with his batting average at .337, he suffered a serious head injury in a violent collision at second base. He had to sit out for a month, and he suffered from double vision for a year and a half. Then, in 1968, as he was beginning to come around, he got the mumps and tore a muscle in his right shoulder.

PIONEERING SKIPPER

Frank Robinson learned a lot from Earl Weaver about managing. And it wasn't long thereafter that Frank began to pay his managerial dues. He worked as a manager in the Caribbean winter leagues for six seasons to learn the ropes. His big chance came in 1975.

After being traded to Cleveland late in the 1974 season, he was named the Indians manager for the next year, making him the first African American to win that job. He responded in typical Robinson fashion, knocking a home run to help the Indians to victory. Although officially a playing manager, Robinson wrote his name into the lineup only 85 times in 1975–76. Others might have been tempted to give themselves a shot at 600 homers or 3,000 hits (he finished 14 homers and 57 hits shy), but Robinson was more interested in winning than in personal stats.

Frank's Indians sported a 79–80 record in 1975 and finished fourth. They went 81–78 in 1976 under Robby. But after a slow start in 1977, Robinson was fired.

Robinson joined the Giants as their manager in 1981. To go along with his other claims to two-league greatness, he became the first African American manager in the National League as well. After three years with the Giants, he was replaced. He returned to manage his old team, the Orioles, early in 1988, and stayed there for three-plus seasons. In 1989 he was the American League Manager of the Year.

But, of course, Robinson had made a living rising above adversity. He came back in 1969 to finish second in runs scored and second in on-base percentage, while knocking 32 homers, driving in 100, and batting .308. In 1970 he swatted grand slams in back-to-back innings and batted .306 for the season. In 1971 he stroked 28 homers and knocked in 99 runs. With Frank and Boog Powell providing the power and Brooks Robinson, Paul Blair, and Mark Belanger handling the leather—and under the leadership of the feisty Weaver—the Orioles were a juggernaut. Winning more than 100 games every year, the Orioles went to the World Series three seasons in a row.

Although they were topped by the Mets in the 1969 World Series and the Pirates in '71, the O's beat Cincinnati in the 1970 fall classic. In true sweet-revenge style, Robinson hit two homers in the '70 Series. He repeated the effort in the '71 classic, and it was his hustle to score on a short fly ball in the ninth inning of the sixth game that forced a Game 7.

Sent to the Dodgers before the 1972 season in a six-man trade, Robinson had his lowest batting average ever, .251, and hit only 19 homers. Shopped to the Angels in a seven-man deal before the 1973 season, Frank hit 30 homers and drove in 97 runs. Still up for another challenge, Robinson became the first African American manager in major-league history, taking over the reins of the Cleveland Indians in 1975.

> "Pitchers did me a favor when they knocked me down. It made me more determined."
> —Robinson

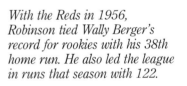

With the Reds in 1956, Robinson tied Wally Berger's record for rookies with his 38th home run. He also led the league in runs that season with 122.

BY THE NUMBERS

Year	Team	G	AB	R	H	2B	3B	HR	HR%	RBI	BB	K	BA	SA	SB
1956	Cin-N	152	572	122	166	27	6	38	6.6	83	64	95	.290	.558	8
1957	Cin-N	150	611	97	197	29	5	29	4.7	75	44	92	.322	.529	10
1958	Cin-N	148	554	90	149	25	6	31	5.6	83	62	80	.269	.504	10
1959	Cin-N	146	540	106	168	31	4	36	6.7	125	69	93	.311	.583	18
1960	Cin-N	139	464	86	138	33	6	31	6.7	83	82	67	.297	.595	13
1961	Cin-N	153	545	117	176	32	7	37	6.8	124	71	64	.323	.611	22
1962	Cin-N	162	609	134	208	51	2	39	6.4	136	76	62	.342	.624	18
1963	Cin-N	140	482	79	125	19	3	21	4.4	91	81	69	.259	.442	26
1964	Cin-N	156	568	103	174	38	6	29	5.1	96	79	67	.306	.548	23
1965	Cin-N	156	582	109	172	33	5	33	5.7	113	70	100	.296	.540	13
1966	Bal-A	155	576	122	182	34	2	49	8.5	122	87	90	.316	.637	8
1967	Bal-A	129	479	83	149	23	7	30	6.3	94	71	84	.311	.576	2
1968	Bal-A	130	421	69	113	27	1	15	3.6	52	73	84	.268	.444	11
1969	Bal-A	148	539	111	166	19	5	32	5.9	100	88	62	.308	.540	9
1970	Bal-A	132	471	88	144	24	1	25	5.3	78	69	70	.306	.520	2
1971	Bal-A	133	455	82	128	16	2	28	6.2	99	72	62	.281	.510	3
1972	LA-N	103	342	41	86	6	1	19	5.6	59	55	76	.251	.442	2
1973	Cal-A	147	534	85	142	29	0	30	5.6	97	82	93	.266	.489	1
1974	Cal-A	129	427	75	107	26	2	20	4.7	63	75	85	.251	.461	5
	Cle-A	15	50	6	10	1	1	2	4.0	5	10	10	.200	.380	0
	Yr	144	477	81	117	27	3	22	4.6	68	85	95	.245	.453	5
1975	Cle-A	49	118	19	28	5	0	9	7.6	24	29	15	.237	.508	0
1976	Cle-A	36	67	5	15	0	0	3	4.5	10	11	12	.224	.358	0
Total	21	2808	10006	1829	2943	528	72	586	5.9	1812	1420	1532	.294	.537	204

BABE RUTH

When Babe Ruth hit his 700th homer, only two other people had hit 300. When he retired with 714, he had twice as many as the next guy. If you make the claim that Ruth invented the home run, you wouldn't be far from the truth.

How times have changed. Ruth's 700th home run ball was worth $20 and an autograph in 1934. Retriever Leonard Beals was undoubtedly thrilled.

BABE RUTH WAS NOT only the greatest hitter ever to play professional baseball. He was a unique personality, a huge man with huge appetites who was so in love with life and fame and success that he lit up any room he ever walked near. As writer Roger Kahn put it, in *Let's Play Ball* by William Humber, "As he moved, center stage moved with him." Ruth himself said, as quoted by William Safire in *Words of Wisdom,* "I swing big, with everything I've got. I hit big or I miss big. I like to live as big as I can."

In 1918 a Boston sportswriter said, "The more I see of Babe, the more he seems a figure out of mythology." Ruth was 24 years old at the time. In the 1920s Ruth's name appeared in print more often than anyone's except those of the presidents of the United States.

Paul Gallico, in the New York *Daily News,* described Ruth's prowess at the bat. "I have seen hundreds of ballplayers at the plate, and none of them managed to convey the message of impending doom to a pitcher that Babe Ruth did with the cock of his head, the position of his legs and the little gentle waving of the bat, feathered in his two big paws."

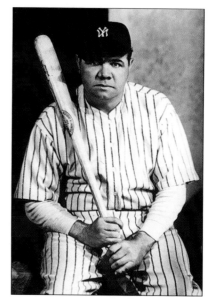

Ruth's career highs include a .393 batting average, 60 homers, 171 RBI, and 177 runs.

Yes, Ruth was an athlete of imposing skills, but we have had plenty of those. He was a grand performer in the arena of professional sports, but there seems to be a new one of those every weekend. What made him so unique and endearing was the way all those things were wrapped up in one boyish, fun-loving package.

And isn't it wonderful that the best player ever had one of the greatest nicknames of all time? The story goes that when George Herman Ruth first signed with Jack Dunn's International League Baltimore Orioles at the age of 19, a fan in the bleachers noted the pink-cheeked youth taking the pitching mound and bellowed, "There goes another one of Dunn's babes." And a Babe is what he always was: a kid in an immensely talented man's body.

When Ruth was seven, he was legally labeled "incorrigible" and committed to St Mary's Industrial School for Boys. In 1914 he signed with Baltimore for $600 a month. That pay was tripled by the end of July. Sold to the Red Sox, Ruth signed for $3,500 a year—nearly six times what he had begun the season making. By the time his career ended, he had reached the stratospheric salary level of $80,000, plus millions more in endorsements.

Bob Broeg, in *The Ballplayers,* said, "Trying to capture Babe Ruth with cold statistics would be like trying to keep up with him on a night out." That's probably true. But here's an overview of his slugging feats. Hold onto your seat:

Ruth's 714 career homers remained the most ever by a hitter for 38 years (and it took Hank Aaron 3,000 more at-bats to pass him). Ruth is still second, 54 ahead of the next guy. He had a lifetime batting average of .342. His lifetime slugging percentage is an almost unbelievable .690. Ted Williams is second, with a remarkable, though distant, .634. When Ruth died, he was the major-league record holder in 56 different categories, and the American League's top man in 10 more.

He led the AL in home runs 12 times, six of those consecutively. He led in on-base percentage 11 times and in slugging percentage 13 times—including a breathtaking total of nine

Ruth cast an imposing shadow at the plate, where he was capable of striking fear in the hearts of opposing pitchers with nothing more than a twitch of his bat.

years with SPs above .700, plus one of .697. In the history of the game, that level of power has been reached only 30 times by everybody put together (14,000-plus players in 160 years).

Babe led the AL in walks 11 times (including the still-record 170 in 1923), in runs scored eight times, and in RBI six times. He also won one batting title. When the new baseball statisticians compile their "total player rating," Ruth tops everyone, with 107.7. The No. 2 finisher is 94.2, and only two other men rate higher than 90. And by the way, Ruth had only four fewer triples than Willie Mays.

Ruth started as a pitcher in the Red Sox system until leaving the mound in 1919. At one time he was considered the best left-handed hurler in the league.

Let's put these stats into an historical context. To fully understand Ruth's impact on the game, it's important to realize that the feat of hitting 20 home runs in a season had been accomplished only a handful of times before Ruth. From 1900 until Ruth, the home run titlist had hit 10 or fewer 18 times.

Home runs were considered freak events; no one was supposed to try for them. This isn't to say that there weren't great sluggers before Ruth. It's just that the parks were often huge, one ball was used for the entire game, and the big bombers were the guys who led their leagues in doubles and triples. So when Ruth bombed 29 homers in 1919, that was *10 more* than all but two men had hit in the 20th century. And when he hit 54 the very next year, well, he had definitely changed what baseball was all about.

Let's take a look at some of Ruth's greatest years and see how they stack up:

1919: During the previous season Red Sox teammate Harry Hooper suggested to his manager that Babe's power might be more useful if he didn't have to pitch (despite the fact that Ruth was probably the best left-hander in baseball at the time). As a part-time outfielder and part-time pitcher, Babe had hit 11 home runs in 1918 to lead the American League while appearing in just 95 games. When he left the mound for good in 1919, Ruth's 29 long balls that season were 19 more than the second-place finisher—and more than the number hit by half of the teams in the American League and all but two in the National. Ruth also led the league in RBI, total bases, on-base percentage, and slugging average. That December the Yankees' money came beckoning, and Ruth became a New Yorker.

1920: Fifty-four home runs! The total was beyond belief, since no one had ever hit 30 before. It was more than any team in baseball except one. Ruth batted .376 that year, fourth best in the league. No one came close to his league-leading numbers in runs, RBI, walks, on-base percentage, slugging, and total bases. His slugging average that year, .847, was the highest by any player ever, before or since. Only four men in history (besides the Babe himself, of course) have ever had a slugging average within 100 points of that number.

1921: If any hitter in history was ever a more sensationally dominant offensive machine than Ruth in 1921, he has managed to keep it a secret. The 1921 season was a year after Ray Chapman's death from a pitched ball, and baseball ruled that only clean, white balls be used, with dirty and scuffed ones removed from play. Babe took to the notion.

WOULD-BE MANAGER

Babe Ruth's awesome inborn physical skills were evident to everyone. Teammate Joe Dugan, quoted in Noel Hynd's *The Giants of the Polo Grounds,* said, "Babe Ruth wasn't born; he dropped from a tree." However, only a few people, such as teammate Waite Hoyt, realized that the Babe was a true student of the game.

Babe always felt that he deserved a chance to be a big-league manager, hopefully with his beloved Yankees. When the Yanks replaced Bob Shawkey as their manager after the 1930 season, Babe lobbied for the job, but it was given to Joe McCarthy. Ruth couldn't live down his by-now ancient reputation as the baddest of bad boys. "If you can't manage yourself, how can you manage the Yankees?" he was told.

After the 1933 season Ruth was asked to manage Newark (one of the strongest Triple-A teams of all time), but he refused, confident he already knew enough to be a big-league manager. Allegedly the Detroit Tigers were interested in making Ruth their field boss, but, typically, he failed to show up for the meeting.

When the Braves signed him in 1935, it was supposed to be as player, assistant manager, and vice-president. Babe could only feel the managerial job would be his soon. The Braves were kidding. The Dodgers signed Ruth as a coach for the 1938 season, and once again Babe figured he was the logical choice to step in as manager. But they hired Leo Durocher instead, and Babe was left out in the cold.

Ruth's wife, Claire, had sad memories of those times. As she said in Bill Guttman's *Giants of Baseball,* "Babe would often sit by the phone, waiting for the call that never came. Sometimes, when he couldn't take it any longer, he'd break down, put his head in his hands, and weep."

Ruth led all American League batsmen that year in runs, home runs, total bases, RBI, walks, on-base percentage, and slugging average. In the stat categories created in recent years, he was tops in runs produced, runs created, and total average. He was second in doubles and only two behind the league leaders in triples. Oh, and he batted .378, too.

But what's truly outstanding about Ruth's 1921 season is how far he was ahead of everybody else in everything, even though the other batsmen had that bright, white ball to hit, too. The 177 runs he scored were 45 more than the man who finished second. Ruth's 59 homers were 35 more than Ken Williams's 24—and more than nine other *teams* managed to hit. He had 92 total bases more than the second-place finisher, and 32 more runs batted in.

Ruth walked 41 times more than the No. 2 guy. His on-base percentage was 60 points higher than second-place finisher Ty Cobb. And his slugging average was a merely Ruthian .846, an absolutely outstanding 240 points better than No. 2 guy Harry Heilmann. It's no wonder the Yankees figured they needed a

new stadium. And don't forget, this was *nine years* before the introduction of the "lively ball." In 1921 Ruth broke the lifetime record for home runs (136), held by 19th-century great Roger Connor. He'd hold that top spot for 52 years.

A scuffle between Ruth and Commissioner Kenesaw Mountain Landis over Babe's postseason barnstorming adventures went to Landis. Ruth was suspended for the first six weeks of the 1922 season and spent the rest of the year in a crabby mood. Battles with umps got him suspended three more times before the year was out. His manager, Miller Huggins, fined him $5,000—10 percent of his salary. But in barely over 400 at-bats, Ruth still cracked 35 homers and drove in 99. It was the first time he had not led the American League in homers since 1917. He would fail to top the league just once more in the next nine years.

1923: Ruth makes a "comeback." It was the year that the Yankees opened their new stadium, which was quickly dubbed the "House That Ruth Built." Babe belted a three-run homer to win the Yanks' first game there. He finished the season with

Babe led the league in runs scored eight times in a 10-year span. His incredibly high on-base average got him to first, while Lou Gehrig often moved him around.

41 homers, and added 45 doubles and 13 triples, too. He also had a batting average of .393, second only to Heilmann. Once again, Babe led the American League in homers, runs, RBI, walks, on-base percentage, and slugging average—at .764, 132 points ahead of Heilmann. His "total player rating" that year was the best ever.

1924: This year the Babe was the top AL player in home runs, runs, walks, on-base percentage, and slugging average. He also won the batting title, with a .378 average. But he finished behind Goose Goslin, whose Washington Senators won the pennant, in runs batted in, with 121 to Goose's 129. Otherwise, Babe would have had a Triple Crown title to go with his many other achievements. The only men who had clear-cut Triple Crown seasons before '24 were Nap Lajoie, Ty Cobb, and Rogers Hornsby.

1926: A spring training illness kept Babe hospitalized for seven weeks in 1925, and he didn't play until June 1. In 1926 he returned to form, hitting 47 homers and driving in 146 runs. He also had some help in the power department with the addition

Right: Ruth and Lou Gehrig (right) were the giants of their day, giving the mighty Yankees star power long before television took sports heroes into the living rooms of America. Below: Youngsters gravitated toward the Babe, who lived life to its fullest off the field while, on it, established legendary home run standards that still inspire awe.

of Lou Gehrig. Once again Ruth sat firmly atop the American League in the familiar six categories: runs, homers, RBI, walks, on-base percentage, and slugging average. And his .372 batting average was second in the league.

Ruth carved himself a small corner of infamy in the 1926 World Series. He tried to steal second base with two outs in the last of the ninth of Game 7, with his team down by a run and Bob Meusel at the plate. When Rogers Hornsby applied the tag, the Series was over and the Yanks had lost.

1927: While much has been made of Ruth's 60-homer season in 1927, it actually didn't fit in the top tier of his work. It was just spectacular; not truly, well, Ruthian. He did not lead the league in RBI, trailing Gehrig 175 to 164. Babe didn't lead the league in total bases (only the second time that had happened in six seasons), either. Of course, with Larrupin' Lou establishing himself as one of the all-time greats, Babe didn't have to carry the show all by himself. In their seven seasons together, the two *averaged* 84 homers and 303 RBI a year.

1928: With 54 home runs, Ruth was again tops in the American League, but it was to be his last great year. Only a second-place finish to Gehrig in on-base percentage kept the Babe from leading in the familiar six categories. Although he would still ring up three more home run titles, three slugging-average and on-base average crowns, and four walk titles, Ruth would never again top the American League in either runs scored or RBI.

The Yankees won the American League flag six of the first nine seasons that Babe was with them. But from 1929 through 1931, their spot at the top of the league was usurped by the incredible, but unsung, Philadelphia A's. Babe was still a potent force at the plate, hitting 46 homers twice and 49 once during those years, but the Yankee pitching couldn't match what the A's were throwing. The Yanks returned to the Series for the last time with the Babe on board to sweep the Chicago Cubs in 1932, in a series noted for Ruth's "called shot."

Only four men in history (besides the Babe himself, of course) have ever had a slugging average within 100 points of his .847 mark in 1920.

In an era when 20 home runs in a year was considered a great achievement, Ruth swatted 40 or more 11 times. He also eclipsed 50 in four different seasons.

Ruth played in 10 World Series in his career, three as a member of the Red Sox. His team won seven times. In consecutive Series appearances in 1927, 1928, and 1932, Ruth's Yanks won 12 straight games—three four-game sweeps. In those Series, Babe batted .400, .625, and .333 and compiled slugging averages of .800, 1.375, and .733.

In 1933 Ruth belted 34 homers but finished a distant second to Jimmie Foxx's 48. Ruth led the league in walks again, and was in the top five in slugging and on-base average, but his career was nearing its end. A kid named DiMaggio was on his way to New York. After only 22 long balls in 1934, Ruth was dealt to the Boston Braves, where he hoped he would earn the chance to manage—his lifelong dream. But despite a host of promises, the poor Braves were only looking for Babe to juice their box-office receipts.

Braves teammate Elbie Fletcher remembered the Babe's final season in *Total Baseball:* "We were all awed by his presence. He still had that marvelous swing—and what a beautiful follow-through! But he was 40 years old. He couldn't run, couldn't bend down for a ground ball, and, of course, couldn't hit the way he used to. It was sad seeing those great skills fade away. To see it happening to Babe Ruth, to see Babe Ruth struggling on a ballfield . . . well, that's when you realize we're all mortal and nothing lasts forever."

On May 25, 1935, the Babe homered twice in his first two at-bats against the Pirates. The third time he singled. In his final plate appearance, he knocked a ball completely over the high right-field roof of Forbes Field, the first time that had ever been done. "Boy, that last one felt good," he said. Although that was not his last game, as the movies would have you believe, he ended his career after just a few more games.

BY THE NUMBERS

Year	Team	G	AB	R	H	2B	3B	HR	HR%	RBI	BB	K	BA	SA	SB
1914	Bos-A	5	10	1	2	1	0	0	0.0	2	0	4	.200	.300	0
1915	Bos-A	42	92	16	29	10	1	4	4.3	21	9	23	.315	.576	0
1916	Bos-A	67	136	18	37	5	3	3	2.2	15	10	23	.272	.419	0
1917	Bos-A	52	123	14	40	6	3	2	1.6	12	12	18	.325	.472	0
1918	Bos-A	95	317	50	95	26	11	11	3.5	66	57	58	.300	.555	6
1919	Bos-A	130	432	103	139	34	12	29	6.7	114	101	58	.322	.657	7
1920	NY-A	142	458	158	172	36	9	54	11.8	137	148	80	.376	.847	14
1921	NY-A	152	540	177	204	44	16	59	10.9	171	144	81	.378	.846	17
1922	NY-A	110	406	94	128	24	8	35	8.6	99	84	80	.315	.672	2
1923	NY-A	152	522	151	205	45	13	41	7.9	131	170	93	.393	.764	17
1924	NY-A	153	529	143	200	39	7	46	8.7	121	142	81	.378	.739	9
1925	NY-A	98	359	61	104	12	2	25	7.0	66	59	68	.290	.543	2
1926	NY-A	152	495	139	184	30	5	47	9.5	146	144	76	.372	.737	11
1927	NY-A	151	540	158	192	29	8	60	11.1	164	138	89	.356	.772	7
1928	NY-A	154	536	163	173	29	8	54	10.1	142	135	87	.323	.709	4
1929	NY-A	135	499	121	172	26	6	46	9.2	154	72	60	.345	.697	5
1930	NY-A	145	518	150	186	28	9	49	9.5	153	136	61	.359	.732	10
1931	NY-A	145	534	149	199	31	3	46	8.6	163	128	51	.373	.700	5
1932	NY-A	133	457	120	156	13	5	41	9.0	137	130	62	.341	.661	2
1933	NY-A	137	459	97	138	21	3	34	7.4	103	114	90	.301	.582	4
1934	NY-A	125	365	78	105	17	4	22	6.0	84	103	63	.288	.537	1
1935	Bos-N	28	72	13	13	0	0	6	8.3	12	20	24	.181	.431	0
Total	22	2503	8399	2174	2873	506	136	714	8.5	2213	2056	1330	.342	.690	123

MIKE SCHMIDT

If Mike Schmidt had begun his career with a good team, it might have been over in a hurry. But Schmidt's hard work helped him grow with his team and become the heaviest hitting third baseman of all time.

Greg Luzinski (left) and Schmidt gave the Phillies plenty of power. Schmidt once hit four home runs in a 1976 game against the Cubs.

AFTER A HORRIBLE FIRST season in the major leagues in 1973—a .196 batting average and 136 strikeouts in just 367 at-bats—Mike Schmidt went to play winter ball. While there, he experienced a batting epiphany. In the flash of just one instant, he realized the value of being relaxed at the plate. When the new season started, Schmidt was ready. And how!

He led the National League in homers in 1974 with 36. His slugging average of .546 was also the best in the league. He finished second in total bases and in RBI. He struck out two more times than the year before but batted a quite respectable .282. And the Phillies finished third in their division, their highest finish in 10 years.

Strikeouts would haunt Schmidt his entire career. His lifetime total was exceeded by only three men. In 1975 his 180 whiffs were the third most ever. But he also led the league in homers once again, this time with 38. His Phils finished in second place.

With Mike as their slugging centerpiece and Greg "Bull" Luzinski as the Gehrig to Mike's Ruth, the Phils were suddenly a National League powerhouse. They won consecutive National League East flags in 1976, 1977, and 1978, although they were dumped each year before they could reach the World Series.

On April 17, 1976, Schmidt did something Babe Ruth never did—knock four homers in a single game. His Phils had been trailing the Cubs 13–2 at one point in the game, but Mike powered them back with a two-run dinger in the fifth, a solo shot in the seventh, and a three-run blast in the eighth. His two-run belt in the 10th provided the winning runs in an 18–16 victory. He finished the game with eight RBI and 13 total bases—just

The 1986 MVP trophy was just one of several honors Schmidt attained in his career. Mike is widely hailed as the best third baseman the game has ever known.

BY THE NUMBERS															
Year	Team	G	AB	R	H	2B	3B	HR	HR%	RBI	BB	K	BA	SA	SB
1972	Phi-N	13	34	2	7	0	0	1	2.9	3	5	15	.206	.294	0
1973	Phi-N	132	367	43	72	11	0	18	4.9	52	62	136	.196	.373	8
1974	Phi-N	162	568	108	160	28	7	36	6.3	116	106	138	.282	.546	23
1975	Phi-N	158	562	93	140	34	3	38	6.8	95	101	180	.249	.523	29
1976	Phi-N	160	584	112	153	31	4	38	6.5	107	100	149	.262	.524	14
1977	Phi-N	154	544	114	149	27	11	38	7.0	101	104	122	.274	.574	15
1978	Phi-N	145	513	93	129	27	2	21	4.1	78	91	103	.251	.435	19
1979	Phi-N	160	541	109	137	25	4	45	8.3	114	120	115	.253	.564	9
1980	Phi-N	150	548	104	157	25	8	48	8.8	121	89	119	.286	.624	12
1981	Phi-N	102	354	78	112	19	2	31	8.8	91	73	71	.316	.644	12
1982	Phi-N	148	514	108	144	26	3	35	6.8	87	107	131	.280	.547	14
1983	Phi-N	154	534	104	136	16	4	40	7.5	109	128	148	.255	.524	7
1984	Phi-N	151	528	93	146	23	3	36	6.8	106	92	116	.277	.536	5
1985	Phi-N	158	549	89	152	31	5	33	6.0	93	87	117	.277	.532	1
1986	Phi-N	160	552	97	160	29	1	37	6.7	119	89	84	.290	.547	1
1987	Phi-N	147	522	88	153	28	0	35	6.7	113	83	80	.293	.548	2
1988	Phi-N	108	390	52	97	21	2	12	3.1	62	49	42	.249	.405	3
1989	Phi-N	42	148	19	30	7	0	6	4.1	28	21	17	.203	.372	0
Total	18	2404	8352	1506	2234	408	59	548	6.6	1595	1507	1883	.267	.527	174

one off the all-time record. That four-homer day helped Schmidt to a total of 11 homers for the month, tying two others for the most ever in April.

In the Astrodome Schmidt once hit a ball 117 feet high that landed 329 feet from home plate. It was on pace to travel 500 feet. But the ball hit a speaker in the ceiling, and Schmidt was awarded only one long single.

In 1978 Schmidt did something few successful sluggers would have tried: He changed his batting style. Instead of trying to pull everything, he began to look for pitches he could drive anywhere. The new technique worked: In 1979 Schmidt hit 45 homers, setting a personal high. That year he found himself right in the middle of the biggest slugfest of all time, the incredible battle between the Phillies and (who else?) the Cubs at (where else?) Wrigley Field on May 17. The final score was 23–22; the teams combined for 11 homers. Mike Schmidt hit the first homer of that game as well as the last—the one that won the game for the Phils in 10 innings.

Schmidt's 48 home runs in 1980 set the major-league season record for third basemen. He also led the league in RBI for the first time, with 121, and slugged an impressive .624. For these feats he won the NL Most Valuable Player Award. And his Phils won the World Series for the first time ever. After Schmidt batted at a .381 clip in the Series and was the batting star in three games, he was named Series MVP.

In 1981, despite the strike-abbreviated season, Schmidt won the home run and RBI crowns and batted .316, fourth best in the league—not too far from the Triple Crown. Yet another highlight for Schmidt's ever-expanding résumé was the two-run homer he smashed to give the National League a 5–4 win in that year's All-Star Game. At the end of the season, Schmidt came away with League MVP honors once again.

In 1982, when a broken rib forced him to miss two weeks of the season, he finished just two homers behind the league leader. Schmidt then won three more homer titles and two more RBI crowns before retiring early in the 1989 season. In an overwhelming show of support, the fans elected him to the All-Star Game anyway that year, although he declined the honor.

All told, this baseball legend slugged 548 home runs, seventh on the all-time list. He led the National League in homers eight times, an NL record. Only Ruth did it more often. Schmidt's 13 seasons of 30 or more long balls was surpassed

only by Hank Aaron. His 11 years of 35 or more was bested only by the Babe. Schmidt and Ralph Kiner remain the only two men to hit homers in four consecutive at-bats twice in their careers. Schmidt reached the 100-RBI plateau nine times and led his league in slugging percentage five times. He walked 100 times or more in a season seven times.

Also a winner of 10 Gold Gloves, Schmidt is universally considered the greatest third baseman of all time.

Schmidt's 548 career home runs included eight seasons as the National League leader. Only Babe Ruth, who dominated the American League, won more long-ball titles in his career.

SAMMY SOSA

Until Sammy Sosa started to break loose in 1993, he had never hit more than 15 homers in a season. But even in the mid-1990s, nobody expected that Sosa would realize the feats he accomplished in the magical 1998 season.

Above right: During his memorable 1998 home run race with Mark McGwire, Sosa's clutch hitting and relaxed demeanor helped the Cubs to their first postseason trip since 1989. Below: Sosa is the most beloved player in the Dominican Republic—and perhaps in the United States. Of course, 66-home run seasons tend to endear you to fans.

SAMMY SOSA ISN'T JUST a great slugger; he is a beloved crowd-pleaser. During Sosa's jaw-dropping 66-homer season in 1998, he went through a stretch of 15 consecutive series in which he belted at least one out of the park. If you went to a game looking to see Sammy go yard, there was a very good chance you'd get your wish. And he'd kiss his fingers and tap his chest to let you know he loved you, too.

Sosa grew up in a poor neighborhood in San Pedro de Macoris, Dominican Republic. As a kid, he lived through the worst of poverty. He sold oranges and shined shoes to raise enough money to keep his family going. But every second he could manage to break free from work, he could be found playing ball.

Signed as a skinny 17-year-old by the Texas Rangers in 1987, Sammy's minor-league stats were far from compelling. Although he led his leagues in doubles once and triples once, he never reached the .300 batting mark and only once hit as many as 11 homers. Texas gave him a brief chance in the bigs in 1989, and then he was traded with Wilson Alvarez to the White Sox. In Chicago in 1990, his first full season in the majors, he did manage 15 homers and 26 doubles, but he batted only .233. In March 1992 Sosa joined the crosstown Cubs in a trade when they tired of moody slugger George Bell.

By June 10 that year Sammy had five homers. He slugged two more that day, then in the next game an inside fastball broke his right hand. After a stint on the disabled list, he went 15-for-39 with three homers, eight runs scored, and nine RBI in his first nine games back. The next game he fouled a pitch off his ankle, breaking it. His season was over.

At long last, a healthy Sammy moved into the top ranks of big-league sluggers in 1993. That year showcased a streak of nine consecutive hits, including six in one game, which firmly established him as a super streak hitter. Sosa finished the season with 33 homers, and he also stole 36 bases to make him the first Cub ever to reach the 30–30 level. The next year he hit .300 and added 25 homers.

From 1995 through 1998 Sammy was spectacular. In 1995 his 36 homers and 119 RBI were second best in the league. He further solidified his place in Cubs history when his 13th-inning homer on May 21 gave the Chicagoans a win—the 9,000th Cubs victory. His August 14th long ball that year was the 10,000th home run hit by a Cub. During a seven-game span in August, Sosa slugged seven homers, drove in 14 runs, and homered in four straight games.

Sammy continued to improve: In 1996 he had 40 homers and 100 RBI by August 20, and people were starting to mention his name in the same breath as the names Ruth and Maris. Unfortunately, at the plate with the bases loaded, he was hit by a pitch, again breaking his hand and ending his season. He still finished fifth in the league in long balls. He returned in 1997 to belt 36 homers and knock in 119.

And then came 1998. While Mark McGwire started the season hot, Sammy did not. By May 24 Mark had 24 homers, Sammy only nine. Then Sosa embarked upon one of his amazing hot streaks. He homered twice on May 25 and again on May 27.

This was just a prelude to what was to come in June, the greatest slugging month ever.

Sammy homered in his first and his last at-bat in June. In between he knocked 18 more balls out of the park, breaking the previous record for homers in a month by two and shattering the previous June record of 15. He racked up 40 RBI that month, too.

Sammy had reached 246 career home runs without a grand slam (breaking a record previously held by Bob Horner), but on July 27 he cleared the bases with his first grand slam. And then, the next day, he hit another. He added a third in September for good measure.

Even though McGwire broke Roger Maris's home run record first, Sosa was right behind him. Both men had 65 homers when the final weekend of the season began, but

Sammy could manage only one the rest of the way, while Mark added five. Actually, from May 25 through the end of the season, Sosa outhomered McGwire 57–46.

Sammy's 66 homers were 10 more than the old National League record. His 158 RBI were the most anyone had driven in in 49 years. He also led the league in runs scored. His 11 multiple-homer games tied Hank Greenberg for the all-time season record. And the truly amazing stat: Sosa's 416 total bases were the most in baseball since 1948. He was named NL MVP.

Sosa actually outhomered McGwire over the last four months of 1998, thanks to a big-league record 20 clouts in June. Sosa won NL MVP honors in a landslide.

						BY THE NUMBERS									
Year	Team	G	AB	R	H	2B	3B	HR	HR%	RBI	BB	K	BA	SA	SB
1989	Tex-A	25	84	8	20	3	0	1	1.2	3	0	20	.238	.310	0
	Chi-A	33	99	19	27	5	0	3	3.0	10	11	27	.273	.414	7
	Yr	58	183	27	47	8	0	4	2.2	13	11	47	.257	.366	7
1990	Chi-A	153	532	72	124	26	10	15	2.8	70	33	150	.233	.404	32
1991	Chi-A	116	316	39	64	10	1	10	3.2	33	14	98	.203	.335	13
1992	Chi-N	67	262	41	68	7	2	8	3.1	25	19	63	.260	.393	15
1993	Chi-N	159	598	92	156	25	5	33	5.5	93	38	135	.261	.485	36
1994	Chi-N	105	426	59	128	17	6	25	5.9	70	25	92	.300	.545	22
1995	Chi-N	144	564	89	151	17	3	36	6.4	119	58	134	.268	.500	34
1996	Chi-N	124	498	84	136	21	2	40	8.0	100	34	134	.273	.564	18
1997	Chi-N	162	642	90	161	31	4	36	5.6	119	45	174	.251	.480	22
1998	Chi-N	159	643	134	198	20	0	66	10.3	158	73	171	.308	.647	18
Total	10	1247	4664	727	1233	182	33	273	5.9	800	350	1198	.264	.493	217

WILLIE STARGELL

He was the greatest slugger in Pittsburgh Pirates history, but Willie Stargell's biggest impact may have been less the power in his bat than the power of his personality.

THE GAME'S SUPPOSED to be fun," Willie Stargell often said. "The umpire says 'play ball,' not 'work ball.'" And fun is what Willie Stargell had a lot of in his 21-year big-league career. Of course, the opposing pitchers he belted his 475 homers off of might have disagreed. As Don Sutton put it in *Total Baseball,* "He doesn't just hit pitchers; he takes away their dignity."

Stargell was just a big, rawboned kid when he joined the Pirates organization in 1959. But he grew into a man in front of the eyes of baseball fans everywhere. He learned the art of leadership from Roberto Clemente, and when Clemente tragically died while on a mission of charity in 1972, Stargell stepped in to fill the role of team leader. The Pirates of his era were a raucous, rowdy bunch, and no one had more fun than Willie. But when the game was on the line, or when a youngster needed a jolt of confidence (or ribbing), Stargell took charge. *New Yorker* writer Roger Angell called him "the most admired and admirable player of his time."

Above right: A batting tip from Stargell was worth putting into practice. The popular Pirate twice led the National League in homers, smashing 48 in 1971 and 44 in 1973. Below: A young Stargell (center, to the right of Roberto Clemente) saw his home run production limited by the pitcher-friendly Forbes Field, but he accounted for seven of the 18 balls that cleared the stadium's right-field roof.

Willie's power numbers his first few years in the big leagues weren't the stuff of legend. He hit 21 homers his second full year (1964), 27 the third, and 33 the fourth, but wouldn't top 30 again until his eighth season with the Pirates. Part of the reason, of course, was that Stargell played his home games in Forbes Field, where a 28-foot-high screen on top of the 9½-foot right-field wall eliminated the possibility of a cheap homer. Nearly every year he hit more homers on the road than at home. But when Stargell hit them, he hit them well. During the 61 seasons in which major-league baseball was played in Forbes Field, the right-field roof was cleared by a homer just 18 times. Babe Ruth did it. Mickey Mantle did it. Willie Stargell did it, too—seven times.

When the Bucs moved to Three Rivers Stadium in 1970, Stargell found the dimensions much more to his liking. He belted the first Pirate homer in the new park, and he hit the first four shots to make it into the right-field upper deck. On the road he swatted some tape-measure jobs, too. He is the only man to twice hit a ball completely out of Dodger Stadium. He also hit a ball an estimated 535 feet into the upper level of Montreal's Olympic Stadium.

In 1971 Stargell started out hot, with two three-homer games in April and a total of 11 for the month, a major-league record. He finished the season with 48 homers, leading the NL, and finished second in RBI and slugging percentage. Joe Torre beat him out for the NL Most Valuable Player Award.

In 1973 Stargell had another colossal year. His 44 homers, 43 doubles, 119 RBI, and .646 slugging percentage all led the league. He missed a .300 average by a single point. But he fin-

In his first World Series, in 1971, Stargell struggled mightily, batting just .208 with one RBI in seven games. His Pirates, however, prevailed over the Orioles.

ished second in the MVP voting again, this time to a guy named Pete Rose from Cincinnati.

Injuries and aging slowed down the Stargell swing for the next several years. He slugged 25 homers in 1974, but hit fewer and fewer each of the next three years, falling to a mere 13 in 1977. His season was shortened that year when he tried to break up a fight on the field and suffered a pinched nerve in his elbow. In 1978, however, Stargell was named Comeback Player of the Year as he swatted 28 homers and drove in 97 runs, and his Pirates battled the Phillies to the final weekend of the season before finishing second.

In 1979, at the age of 39, Stargell had his greatest year ever. He batted only 424 times, but he slugged 32 homers and drove in 82 runs. He was the ultimate team leader, handing out "Stargell Stars" to those who excelled. The Pirates took the National League East crown, and Stargell finished in a tie with Keith Hernandez for Most Valuable Player. But Willie still had more to do. In the National League Championship Series he batted .455. His three-run homer in the 11th inning won Game 1 for the Bucs; he delivered a double and a single in their 3–2 Game 2 victory; and he homered, doubled, and knocked in three runs in Game 3 as the Pirates swept the Reds, avenging previous

LCS defeats in 1970, '72, and '75. Stargell was named Most Valuable Player of the NLCS.

In that year's World Series, Stargell was even more amazing. He batted .400, hit three homers (including the two-run shot that put the Pirates ahead for good in Game 7), and had four doubles and seven RBI. His 25 World Series total bases are the most anyone has ever had in a Series. Not surprisingly, he was named Series MVP, completing a highly rare trifecta.

Stargell remained with the Pirates for three more seasons, by then contributing mainly with his clubhouse presence. Although his bat had slowed, his contributions were not—and never will be —forgotten. His 296 homers in the 1970s were the most by anybody, while his 475 lifetime clouts tie him with Stan Musial for 17th all time.

BY THE NUMBERS															
Year	Team	G	AB	R	H	2B	3B	HR	HR%	RBI	BB	K	BA	SA	SB
1962	Pit-N	10	31	1	9	3	1	0	0.0	4	3	10	.290	.452	0
1963	Pit-N	108	304	34	74	11	6	11	3.6	47	19	85	.243	.428	0
1964	Pit-N	117	421	53	115	19	7	21	5.0	78	17	92	.273	.501	1
1965	Pit-N	144	533	68	145	25	8	27	5.1	107	39	127	.272	.501	1
1966	Pit-N	140	485	84	153	30	0	33	6.8	102	48	109	.315	.581	2
1967	Pit-N	134	462	54	125	18	6	20	4.3	73	67	103	.271	.465	1
1968	Pit-N	128	435	57	103	15	1	24	5.5	67	47	105	.237	.441	5
1969	Pit-N	145	522	89	160	31	6	29	5.6	92	61	120	.307	.556	1
1970	Pit-N	136	474	70	125	18	3	31	6.5	85	44	119	.264	.511	0
1971	Pit-N	141	511	104	151	26	0	**48**	9.4	125	83	154	.295	.628	0
1972	Pit-N	138	495	75	145	28	2	33	6.7	112	65	129	.293	.558	1
1973	Pit-N	148	522	106	156	**43**	3	**44**	8.4	**119**	80	129	.299	**.646**	0
1974	Pit-N	140	508	90	153	37	4	25	4.9	96	87	106	.301	.537	0
1975	Pit-N	124	461	71	136	32	2	22	4.8	90	58	109	.295	.516	0
1976	Pit-N	117	428	54	110	20	3	20	4.7	65	50	101	.257	.458	2
1977	Pit-N	63	186	29	51	12	0	13	7.0	35	31	55	.274	.548	0
1978	Pit-N	122	390	60	115	18	2	28	7.2	97	50	93	.295	.567	3
1979	Pit-N	126	424	60	119	19	0	32	7.5	82	47	105	.281	.552	0
1980	Pit-N	67	202	28	53	10	1	11	5.4	38	26	52	.262	.485	0
1981	Pit-N	38	60	2	17	4	0	0	0.0	9	5	9	.283	.350	0
1982	Pit-N	74	73	6	17	4	0	3	4.1	17	10	24	.233	.411	0
Total	21	2360	7927	1195	2232	423	55	475	6.0	1540	937	1936	.282	.529	17

TED WILLIAMS

When fans debate about who was baseball's greatest hitter, two names are bandied about the most: Babe Ruth and Ted Williams. In the career rankings for slugging average, they rank first and second.

WHILE OTHER LEGENDARY figures in the game are identified by nicknames (the Babe, the Mick, the Ole Perfesser), Ted Williams alone is defined by his own words. His frequently stated goal was simple: "When I walk down the street, I want people to say, 'There goes the greatest hitter who ever lived.'" Williams's lifetime stats are equaled only by Babe Ruth's, and it must be remembered that Williams lost roughly 4½ seasons during his prime because he served his country.

Like the Babe, Williams was a larger-than-life hero. But while Ruth was the man who partied harder than anyone, Ted was the man who devoted his life to excellence as a batsman. Williams had exceptional vision, and he combined this awesome physical gift with hours in the batting cage. His batting eye was legendary. He struck out 64 times his first season, 54 the next, and never again more than 51. Meanwhile, he finished second only to Ruth in lifetime walks received. Here's what he accomplished:

Williams was voted Most Valuable Player in the American League twice. He did not win MVP Awards the year he batted .406 (1941) *or* the year he won the Triple Crown (1942). No one has come within 15 points of that .406 average in the 57 years since. Williams won six batting titles, and if today's standards had been applied, he would have won two more. (Because he walked so often, he failed to get enough at-bats. Nowadays the standard is plate appearances, not at-bats.) From 1940 through 1960, he finished in the top three in the batting race every year he was eligible.

With his superlative batting eye, Williams led the league in walks eight times, including six years in a row. He led in home runs and RBI four times each, in doubles twice. He was tops in slugging percentage eight times, in on-base average a dozen times. He scored *and* drove in 100 runs nine times in the same season, eight consecutively. His lifetime on-base percentage is a totally remarkable .480. Today, a .480 OBP will lead the league almost every year.

The "Splendid Splinter" won his sixth batting title when he was 41 years old. And in his final big-league at-bat, he hit a homer that has been immortalized in literature. It was his 29th long ball that season. In only one full season in his career did he hit fewer than 24.

In one of those wonderful "what if?" scenarios that are so much a part of baseball history, Ted Williams almost signed with the Yankees. But his mother refused, demanding that he complete high school. In the year he turned 19, 1937, he homered in every Pacific Coast League park and finished with 23 homers and 98 RBI. The next year he won the Triple Crown for Minneapolis of the American Association, putting together a .366 average, 43 homers, and 142 RBI.

Ted arrived in the bigs with a huge chip on his shoulder. He was destined to be the best, and he let everyone know it. When his manager gave an ultimatum—the kid or me—ownership wisely sided with the youngster, and the manager backed down. In 1939 Williams drove in 145 runs, the most ever by a rookie, and had the sixth highest batting average in the

Above right: It took Williams just three seasons to crack the .400 mark, as he led the league in 1941 with a .406 average at age 23. His 37 homers were also tops among AL sluggers. Below: Williams led the league in runs six times during his career, but never after returning in 1953 from his tour of duty as a fighter pilot over Korea. He was a standout there as well.

American League. He also slugged 31 homers, including seven into the right-field bleachers at Fenway Park, where only five other men had ever sent a ball. The next year he hit .344, third best in the AL, and led all others in runs scored and on-base percentage.

But in some ways 1941 was his crowning glory. When the season started he was only 22 years old, but on May 15 he began the longest hitting streak of his career. Over 23 games of hitting successfully, he batted a sensational .488. It raised his average for the season to .430. In that year's All-Star Game, Williams hit a two-out, three-run homer in the ninth inning to turn a likely AL defeat into a 7–5 victory. He said it was the most memorable moment of his career.

Williams went into the final day's doubleheader against the Philadelphia A's batting .39955, technically a .400 season.

When offered the chance to sit down and protect his average, Ted refused. He went out and rapped six hits in the two games to finish at .406. Nevertheless, he wasn't overwhelmed by his feat. "I was being paid $30,000 a year. The least I could do was hit .400," he supposedly said. Williams also led the AL in runs, homers, walks, and on-base and slugging averages. With five more RBI, he would have tied DiMaggio and earned the Triple Crown. But Joe DiMaggio's 56-game hitting streak won him the Most Valuable Player Award.

In 1942 Ted did win the Triple Crown, with 36 homers, 137 RBI, and a .356 average. He scored more runs and got more walks than anyone else in the league, and he also topped all others in on-base and slugging. However, Williams finished second in the MVP voting once again, this time to Yankees second baseman Joe Gordon, who batted .322.

Williams rarely missed a pitch he liked. He struck out fewer than 50 times in 17 of his 19 seasons—remarkable numbers for a power hitter.

In 1943 Williams became a member of the U.S. fighting forces, and he didn't return until the 1946 season. That year he finished with a .342 average, 38 homers, and 123 RBI (all of which placed second in the league). In the 1946 All-Star Game, he swatted two homers, one off Rip Sewell's famous 25-foot-high "eephus" pitch. The film shows the glee on Williams's face as he rounded the bases, enough to light up the whole place.

The 1946 season was also the year that Cleveland manager Lou Boudreau invented the "Williams Shift." He placed all but one infielder on the right side of the diamond to counteract Ted's incredible pull-hitting capability. For the most part Williams refused to change his stroke, believing he was still good enough to overcome the shift. He did, however, hit an inside-the-park homer to left to help clinch the pennant for the Red Sox. Late in the season he was hit on the elbow by a pitch and performed poorly in Boston's World Series defeat. It was his only Series appearance.

Williams had his second Triple Crown season in 1947, topping all AL batters with a .343 average, 32 homers, and 114 RBI. He led in runs scored again, for the fifth consecutive season. DiMaggio beat him out for the Most Valuable Player title by a single vote. In 1949 Ted failed to win the Triple Crown when George Kell outbatted him by .0002 points. But the writers gave Ted his second MVP Award anyway.

Although never a superstar defensively, "Teddy Ballgame" took pride in playing his position well. Long gone were the times when he would practice his batting stroke while he stood in the outfield. During the 1950 All-Star Game, Williams made a spectacular catch, crashing into the Comiskey Park fence to corral a screaming liner by Ralph Kiner. Although he stayed to play nine innings, Ted discovered his elbow was broken. He played in only 89 games that year.

After a 30-homer, 126-RBI season in 1951 (both second in the league), Williams left early in 1952 to rejoin the military for

Mickey Mantle (right) *hit 15 more homers than Williams—536 to 521. Ted missed about 700 games due to military service.*

pilot duty in Korea. The club held a Ted Williams Day at Fenway Park, and he homered in his final at-bat.

Many people felt Williams, not yet 34 years of age, would not be returning to baseball. Ted was as big a star in the air over Korea as he had been on the fields of the American League. He flew 39 missions as a fighter pilot, and he even crash-landed once after being hit by small-arms fire. John Wayne, who reminded many people of Ted (and vice versa) but was only a war hero in the movies, would have been proud.

When Williams came back, on August 6, 1953, he hadn't swung a bat in 16 months. Of course, he slugged a homer in his first Fenway plate appearance. He finished the season with a .407 average and 13 homers in only 91 at-bats. His slugging average for that short season was an extraordinary .901.

Aches and pains and a fractured collarbone dogged Williams for the next three seasons. He never reached 30 homers or 90 RBI in any of them. Nevertheless, he would have won the batting titles in 1954 (.345) and 1955 (.356) if he had enough at-bats. He posted a .703 slugging average in 1955.

MR. SENATOR

Although Ted Williams loved to talk about hitting (and could do it for hours on end), he never worked for any team as a full-time hitting instructor. He was often with the Red Sox during spring training, offering advice to any and all who would listen, and he has had well-documented confabs with batters as famous as Carl Yastrzemski and Tony Gwynn.

But Williams surprised everyone when he took the job of managing the lowly Washington Senators in 1969. An expansion team in 1961, they had kept up the tradition of their namesake predecessors as perennial doormats. In the eight years before Ted arrived, they had finished higher than eighth (in a 10-team league) only once.

Williams began his lectures on how to hit from day one of spring training. The No. 1 rule, of course, was "get a good pitch to hit." And it worked. At least for one year.

In their first year with Ted at the helm (and with no major personnel changes), the Senators scored 170 more runs than they had the year before and batted 27 points higher as a team. The result was an improvement of 21 wins. They finished fourth, 10 games *over* .500, and Williams received Manager of the Year honors. Unfortunately, the tutoring didn't hold. The next year they scored 68 fewer runs and fell back to sixth. Williams left in 1972, one year after the club moved to Texas.

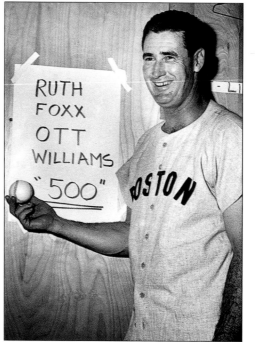

Williams joined exclusive company in 1960 when he hit his 500th career home run at Cleveland.

In the 1946 World Series, the Cardinals employed the "Williams Shift," a move Cleveland manager Lou Boudreau had concocted earlier that season. Williams refused to alter his swing.

In 1957, on his way to turning 40, Williams belted 38 homers, hit .388 to win his fifth batting title, and had sensational on-base (.528) and slugging averages (.731). He was only five hits shy of another .400 season (five hits that a younger, speedier Ted would have probably beaten out). In the second half of the year, he batted .453. Ted finished second in the MVP voting again, this time to Mickey Mantle.

In 1958, turning 41, Williams won another batting title, this time with a .328 average. He led the AL in on-base percentage that year, too, for the 12th time. After a poor season in 1959, in which he batted only .254 (his lowest average ever—by 62 points), many thought he should retire. But Teddy Ballgame had no desire to leave with numbers that puny. He returned in 1960 and batted .316 (even though Ted didn't qualify for the batting title, only one man hit higher that year). In just 310 at-bats he swatted 29 homers. And his final at-bat was another Fenway homer, the 248th time he had gone deep in his home park. John Updike's article "Hub Fans Bid Kid Adieu," about that day, is an all-time classic in baseball writing.

Much has been made of Williams's vitriolic battles with the members of the press. He didn't like or respect the "knights of the keyboard" (as he called them), and that may have had something to do with his failure to win Most Valuable Player crowns when he had all the stats. But no matter what was said about him in the papers, Williams was a decent, committed man. He worked tirelessly for the Jimmy Fund, an organization to combat children's cancer. And in his Hall of Fame induction speech, he scolded baseball for failing to bring into the Hall the great players of the Negro Leagues who had been denied playing in the majors because of the color of their skin.

BY THE NUMBERS																
Year	Team	G	AB	R	H	2B	3B	HR	HR%	RBI	BB	K	BA	SA	SB
1939	Bos-A	149	565	131	185	44	11	31	5.5	**145**	107	64	.327	.609	2
1940	Bos-A	144	561	**134**	193	43	14	23	4.1	113	96	54	.344	.594	4
1941	Bos-A	143	456	**135**	185	33	3	**37**	**8.1**	120	**145**	27	**.406**	**.735**	2
1942	Bos-A	150	522	**141**	186	34	5	**36**	6.9	137	145	51	**.356**	**.648**	3
1946	Bos-A	150	514	**142**	176	37	8	38	7.4	123	**156**	44	.342	**.667**	0
1947	Bos-A	156	528	**125**	181	40	9	**32**	6.1	114	**162**	47	**.343**	**.634**	0
1948	Bos-A	137	509	124	188	**44**	3	25	4.9	127	**126**	41	**.369**	.615	4
1949	Bos-A	155	566	**150**	194	**39**	3	**43**	7.6	159	**162**	48	.343	**.650**	1
1950	Bos-A	89	334	82	106	24	1	28	8.4	97	82	21	.317	.647	3
1951	Bos-A	148	531	109	169	28	4	30	5.6	126	**144**	45	.318	**.556**	1
1952	Bos-A	6	10	2	4	0	1	1	10.0	3	2	2	.400	.900	0
1953	Bos-A	37	91	17	37	6	0	13	14.3	34	19	10	.407	.901	0
1954	Bos-A	117	386	93	133	23	1	29	7.5	89	**136**	32	.345	.635	0
1955	Bos-A	98	320	77	114	21	3	28	8.8	83	91	24	.356	.703	0
1956	Bos-A	136	400	71	138	28	2	24	6.0	82	102	39	.345	.605	0
1957	Bos-A	132	420	96	163	28	1	38	**9.0**	87	119	43	**.388**	**.731**	0
1958	Bos-A	129	411	81	135	23	2	26	6.3	85	98	49	**.328**	.584	1
1959	Bos-A	103	272	32	69	15	0	10	3.7	43	52	27	.254	.419	0
1960	Bos-A	113	310	56	98	15	0	29	9.4	72	75	41	.316	.645	1
Total	19	2292	7706	1798	2654	525	71	521	6.8	1839	2019	709	.344	.634	24

CARL YASTRZEMSKI

Perhaps no player in history can match Carl Yastrzemski's unique combination of abilities. Not only was he a consistent star for many years, but when the pressure was on, he was absolutely sensational.

IN JOHN HOLWAY's *The Sluggers,* legendary hitting coach Charlie Lau said this of Carl Yastrzemski: "He was possibly the hardest working hitter I've ever seen." Yaz knew he had to work; the man he was replacing in the Boston outfield was none other than Ted Williams.

Shortly into his first big-league year, 1961, Yaz found himself pressing—and slumping. The Red Sox located Williams, off on a fishing trip, and brought him to talk to the rookie. One of the things Williams said was "don't ever let anyone monkey with your swing." In his Hall of Fame induction speech, Yaz publicly thanked Ted for the advice.

In his second year in the bigs, Yaz hit .296, knocked in 94 runs, rapped 43 doubles, and clubbed 19 homers. He had found his place. The next year, 1963, he won the batting title for the first of three times. He also led the league in walks, doubles, hits, and on-base percentage, although he homered just 14 times.

Over the next three seasons, Yaz hit 20 homers only once, but he batted .312 one year, led the American League in doubles twice, and was the top batsman in on-base percentage and slugging in one season.

While Carl was performing well, his team was not. They barely avoided the cellar with ninth-place finishes in 1965 and 1966. But 1967 would be different. It was a season they still call the

"Impossible Dream" in New England. No one expected much from the Red Sox that year. Yaz, despite a new off-season weight-lifting regimen, was hitting just .260 with two homers on May 14. But during a series between Boston and Chicago, White Sox manager Eddie Stanky, known during his playing career as "The Brat," said something he shouldn't have. He called Yastrzemski "an All-Star from the neck down." The next day Yaz went 6-for-9 in a doubleheader and homered in his last at-bat. (Some say he tipped his cap to Stanky as he rounded the bases.) Carl then went on a tear that brought the Red Sox to the World Series for the first time in 21 long years.

The pennant race that year was furious. Four teams were in the hunt with less than a week to go. Yaz didn't just perform; he tore the cover off the ball. On the next to last day of the season, when a Sox defeat would have eliminated them, Yaz swatted three hits and knocked in four runs. On the final day, with the outcome still very much in doubt, Carl erased a 2–0 deficit with a two-RBI single—and had three more hits. In his final dozen games of that season—with the pressure to win seemingly unbearable—Yaz batted an earth-shattering .523 (23-for-44), clubbed five homers, scored 14 runs, and drove in 16. He also contributed some dazzling clutch defense.

Yaz didn't let up in the World Series, either. He batted .400, with three homers and five RBI, although his Sox lost to St. Louis. For the season Yaz's .326 average, 44 homers, and 121 RBI landed him the Triple Crown. (No player in either league has won it since.) He also led the AL in runs, hits, and on-base and slugging averages. He missed being the unanimous Most Valuable Player by one vote.

The 1968 season was called the "Year of the Pitcher." Yaz's .301 batting average was the lowest ever to win a bat crown. While some may scoff, statisticians who study such things claim that, taken in context, Yaz's average was on a par with Bill Terry's .401 in 1930. Yaz was the only man in the major leagues to have an on-base percentage over .400 in '68.

In 1969 Yaz slugged 40 homers and drove in 111. The next year he swatted another 40, compiled a .329 batting average, and topped the AL in runs, on-base average, and slugging per-

Right: Only three players preceded Yaz in compiling 3,000 hits and 400 home runs—Stan Musial, Willie Mays, and Hank Aaron. Not bad company for a man who prided himself on hard work. Below: Yastrzemski, pictured with fellow All-Star outfielder Al Kaline of the Tigers, won his first of three batting titles in 1963. He finished his career with 452 home runs.

centage. Several off years followed, but when the Sox recaptured the AL East flag in 1975, Yaz proved he was up to the pressure once again. He batted .455 against the Oakland A's in the ALCS, then hit .310 in that season's memorable World Series against Cincinnati.

Yastrzemski's power numbers were dropping steadily by that point in his career, although he managed a three-homer game in May 1976. In the sensational '78 season, Yaz homered to put his Sox ahead in the one-game playoff for the AL East against the Yankees, but he popped out with the winning run on base to end the game in defeat.

When Yastrzemski retired in 1983, he was only the fourth player to have 3,000 hits and 400 homers, joining Stan Musial, Willie Mays, and Hank Aaron. On the career lists, Yaz ranks second in games, third in at-bats, sixth in hits, seventh in doubles, 11th in RBI, and 13th in runs scored. He ripped 452 home runs.

	BY THE NUMBERS														
Year	Team	G	AB	R	H	2B	3B	HR	HR%	RBI	BB	K	BA	SA	SB
1961	Bos-A	148	583	71	155	31	6	11	1.9	80	50	96	.266	.396	6
1962	Bos-A	160	646	99	191	43	6	19	2.9	94	66	82	.296	.469	7
1963	Bos-A	151	570	91	183	40	3	14	2.5	68	95	72	.321	.475	8
1964	Bos-A	151	567	77	164	29	9	15	2.6	67	75	90	.289	.451	6
1965	Bos-A	133	494	78	154	45	3	20	4.0	72	70	58	.312	.536	7
1966	Bos-A	160	594	81	165	39	2	16	2.7	80	84	60	.278	.431	8
1967	Bos-A	161	579	112	189	31	4	44	7.6	121	91	69	.326	.622	10
1968	Bos-A	157	539	90	162	32	2	23	4.3	74	119	90	.301	.495	13
1969	Bos-A	162	603	96	154	28	2	40	6.6	111	101	91	.255	.507	15
1970	Bos-A	161	566	125	186	29	0	40	7.1	102	128	66	.329	.592	23
1971	Bos-A	148	508	75	129	21	2	15	3.0	70	106	60	.254	.392	8
1972	Bos-A	125	455	70	120	18	2	12	2.6	68	67	44	.264	.391	5
1973	Bos-A	152	540	82	160	25	4	19	3.5	95	105	58	.296	.463	9
1974	Bos-A	148	515	93	155	25	2	15	2.9	79	104	48	.301	.445	12
1975	Bos-A	149	543	91	146	30	1	14	2.6	60	87	67	.269	.405	8
1976	Bos-A	155	546	71	146	23	2	21	3.8	102	80	67	.267	.432	5
1977	Bos-A	150	558	99	165	27	3	28	5.0	102	73	40	.296	.505	11
1978	Bos-A	144	523	70	145	21	2	17	3.3	81	76	44	.277	.423	4
1979	Bos-A	147	518	69	140	28	1	21	4.1	87	62	46	.270	.450	3
1980	Bos-A	105	364	49	100	21	1	15	4.1	50	44	38	.275	.462	0
1981	Bos-A	91	338	36	83	14	1	7	2.1	53	49	28	.246	.355	0
1982	Bos-A	131	459	53	126	22	1	16	3.5	72	59	50	.275	.431	0
1983	Bos-A	119	380	38	101	24	0	10	2.6	56	54	29	.266	.408	0
Total		23	3308	11988	1816	3419	646	59	452	3.8	1844	1845	1393	.285	.462	168

Yaz helped power the Red Sox in their magical 1967 season. He came up big down the stretch of a tight pennant race and stayed hot in the World Series, though Boston lost to St. Louis.

RUTH CLOUTS 60 HOMERS

AS HAD BECOME HIS custom, Babe Ruth spent ample time over the winter of 1927 haggling with Yankees owner Jacob Ruppert over his latest contract—eventually settling on $70,000 a season for three years. No other member of the defending American League champs would even earn $20,000, and the average big-league pay was just $7,000. Ruth, however, deemed himself worth every penny. The Babe was quick to tell reporters upon signing the pact that he was still in great shape at age 32, and he expected to be wearing out AL pitchers for years to come.

Most writers picked the Yankees to contend for the AL pennant again, but nobody thought their title defense would be so easy. The 1927 New York club has been called the best in baseball history, posting a record of 110–44 and sweeping Pittsburgh in the World Series.

At the center of it all was Ruth. The Babe had been trying to outdo his own major-league record of 59 homers since setting the mark in 1921, but he had never gotten closer than the 47 he hit in '26. Now, with cleanup hitter Lou Gehrig reaching

his own full potential as a slugger, the Yankees had the type of dangerous batter following Ruth in the lineup who could force pitchers to throw to the Babe rather than around him. Ruth would still walk a league-high 138 times in 1927, but thanks to Lou's presence he also got many more strikes to hit.

Each of these two players seemed to thrive on the presence of the other. Ruth hit his first home run in the club's fourth game on April 15 against Philadelphia, and Gehrig responded with a pair of blasts two days later versus the Red Sox. Overall, Babe had just four homers in April, but he added 12 in May and another nine in June. Gehrig kept the pace, and at the beginning of July he actually led Ruth 28 to 25. Nobody else was close, either to this duo or to the Yankees in the standings. New York was running away with the pennant, leaving fans to focus on the battle being waged by "Babe and the Buster."

Ruth slugged nine more home runs in July (including an inside-the-parker), but he still trailed his teammate 38 to 35 on August 10. Then, in the final 50 games of the season, the Babe put his prodigious power into overdrive. He caught and passed Gehrig and entered September with 43 homers. This meant he would still have to hit 17 more during the final month to reach 60, and skeptics figured this was too tall an order even for the great Bambino.

It was not. Gehrig drew even the next week, and on September 6 he actually passed Babe a final time with his 45th homer during the first game of a doubleheader at Boston. Lou's lead was brief. Just one inning after Lou's blast, Babe answered with a shot most agreed was the longest ever hit in Fenway Park. Ruth went on to add another homer in the same game, then yet another in the back end of the twinbill. By the time Babe added Nos. 47 and 48 against the Red Sox the following day, Gehrig was in the taillights and fading fast. Lou would finish with 47 homers, more than anyone but the Babe had ever hit before, but good for only a footnote this season.

Above right: Ruth accounted for a staggering 14 percent of all the home runs hit in the AL in 1927. After his 60 and Gehrig's 47, no other player hit more than 18 that year. Below: The 1927 Yankees scored 975 runs, a new American League record and 134 more than any other big-league team. Earle Combs (left) tallied a .356 average, 231 hits, 23 triples, and 137 runs. Bob Meusel (right) rapped .337 with 103 RBI.

Now Ruth's only opponent in the race for 60 was time, which was running out. Even after his five-homer spree vs. Boston and another blast on September 11, he still needed 10 round-trippers in his last 17 games to reach the magic figure. It was a fantastic rush to the finish. Babe slugged two on September 13, then four more over the next six days. The crowds at Yankee Stadium (where Ruth hit each of his last 10 homers) were not particularly large during the final weeks, but those who did come were quite demonstrative in their feelings. After home run No. 54 landed in the Yankee Stadium right-field seats on September 17, a 10-year-old boy grabbed the ball, leaped onto the field with a pen, and got Ruth to sign it. When the Bambino slugged No. 56 on the 22nd, he carried his bat with him around the bases and was chased from third to home by another youngster, who pounded on his back while grabbing at the seemingly magic club.

No. 57 came off Philadelphia A's legend Lefty Grove on September 27, leaving Ruth with three to go entering a season-ending three-game series against Washington. He got his 58th and 59th in the first contest, then faced lefty screwballer Tom Zachary before a Yankee Stadium crowd of approximately 10,000 in the middle game on September 30. After a walk and two hits in his first three at-bats, Babe connected on a low, inside fastball from Zachary in the eighth inning and sent a shot to right. The ball curved dramatically toward the corner, then landed just fair halfway up the right-field bleachers. Ruth had done it.

How incredible was the feat? Consider these numbers: Other than Gehrig's runner-up total of 47, no other AL player hit more than 18 home runs in 1927. Ruth by himself outhomered 12 of the 15 major-league teams (not including the Yankees), and his 60 smashes represented 14 percent of the 439 round-trippers hit in the AL that season. In contrast, Mark McGwire's 70 homers for the St. Louis Cardinals in 1998 were just 2.7 percent of the National League's 2,565 long balls.

"Sixty! Count 'em, sixty!" Babe exalted after slugging his record breaker. "Let's see some other SOB match that!"

For 34 years, nobody would.

Ruth admires his 60th home run of the 1927 season. It came in front of just 10,000 fans at Yankee Stadium on an inside-fastball offering from Tom Zachary.

MARIS ONE-UPS THE BABE

WHEN ROGER MARIS broke Babe Ruth's 34-year-old standard with 61 homers in '61, he achieved the feat amidst a sea of controversy. Major-league expansion had led to an extension of the regular-season schedule for 1961, from 154 to 162 games. Once Roger started belting the ball at a record clip that summer, baseball Commissioner Ford Frick—an old friend of the Babe—took steps to assure Ruth's legacy would remain untarnished.

In a decision opposed by the majority of fans, media representatives, and players, Frick ruled in July 1961 that the name of any player who broke Babe's revered 1927 mark of 60 homers that season could only appear in record books if accompanied by an asterisk (*) or further clarification that the feat had been accomplished with the "help" of a longer schedule. Never in Maris's lifetime would the injustice be reversed.

Even before Frick's decision became final, Maris was not able to fully enjoy his exploits. The media horde that surrounded him as he approached No. 60 was tough for Roger to bear. An intensely private man, he preferred to let his actions on the field speak for themselves. His inability to warm up to the task of describing them continuously for newspaper reporters earned him a label as a moody, sullen malcontent. In his opinion,

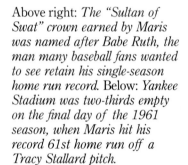

the Yankees didn't take the proper steps to help him cope with the frenzy. "They had publicity people working with that ballclub, and they just let me hang out to dry by myself," Maris recalled in a 1981 TV interview. "Being a young kid, it was very difficult."

Contrary to what some historians now suggest, the quiet, 27-year-old slugger did not emerge as a bolt out of the blue in 1961. During his first season with the Yankees the previous year, Maris had edged out teammate Mickey Mantle in voting for the American League MVP Award—leading the league with 112 RBI and a .581 slugging percentage while winning a Gold Glove and finishing one behind Mantle with 39 homers. Even better numbers were expected of Roger in '61, but at first he couldn't seem to get untracked. In mid-May his average was a shaky .218, and he

Above right: The "Sultan of Swat" crown earned by Maris was named after Babe Ruth, the man many baseball fans wanted to see retain his single-season home run record. Below: Yankee Stadium was two-thirds empty on the final day of the 1961 season, when Maris hit his record 61st home run off a Tracy Stallard pitch.

had hit just three home runs in 29 games—a pace that made reaching even the 20-homer mark look like a long shot. Sixty round-trippers? That was something for Mantle to think about. Off to one of the best starts of his career, Mickey was pacing the league in the category.

The fans got on Maris horribly for his lack of production, but Yankees President Dan Topping told Roger not to worry about his average or the boos and concentrate solely on hitting homers. This simple request seemed to immediately lift Maris out of his slump, and by the end of May he was up to 12 home runs. Things got even better from there. Maris slugged eight more long balls before June was 12 days old, and by the end of the month had accumulated 27 in 66 games. Reporters rushing to their record books discovered Roger was 12 games ahead of Ruth's famous 60-homer pace of 1927. Mantle, the Yankees' golden boy and fan

favorite, was right behind with more than 20 round-trippers of his own.

Through all of the booing that Maris endured as the villain in this shootout, he kept right on hitting. He slugged 13 homers in July, slammed 11 more in August, and entered the final month with 51. Two more on September 2 gave Roger 53; Mantle was still right behind with 50. Only when fate intervened did the race let up: Mickey went down with a hip injury after reaching 54 homers, and Maris was left to chase Ruth's ghost alone.

Suffering from both insomnia and nightmares, and seeing his hair fall out in clumps, Roger still managed to reach 58 four-baggers going into the 154th game of the season at Baltimore on September 20. To tie Ruth's mark and avoid an asterisk, he needed to hit two homers in that game. He got No. 59 off Orioles starter Milt Pappas in the third inning, but despite a couple long foul balls in ensuing at-bats couldn't add another. Frick's ruling would stand.

Roger, however, wasn't through. Baltimore's Jack Fischer was the victim when he bashed No. 60 at Yankee Stadium in New York's 159th game. With the days dwindling down to a handful, Maris's next move shocked everyone: He decided to sit out the following game. The pressure had finally worn Roger completely down, and with Topping's approval he spent the day shopping in Manhattan with his wife, Pat, while the Yankees and Orioles squared off in the Bronx. Maris later said the respite was the most relaxing day he had felt all season.

On October 1, still stuck at 60, Maris suited up for New York's final regular-season game at Yankee Stadium. The contest with the Red Sox drew just 23,154 fans (one-third of capacity), many of whom clustered in the right-field grandstand to get a better shot at catching the record breaker. Roger flew out in his first at-bat, then sent a 2-and-0 fastball from rookie Tracy Stallard deep to right in the fourth. Watching as it cleared the wall for No. 61, Maris showed no more emotion than on any of the previous homers he had slugged during that year. He rounded the bases, went straight to the dugout, and had to literally be pushed by his teammates back up the steps for a quick wave of his cap to the fans.

Baseball had a new home run king—asterisk and all.

Maris deposited No. 61 into the right-field seats. Watching as it cleared the fence, Maris showed no more emotion than usual, but he was sure glad that the chase was finally over.

AARON HAMMERS NO. 715

T WOULD HAVE BEEN a lot easier on his sanity, Hank Aaron admitted later, if he could have just hit one more home run during the 1973 season.

At the age of 39, coming to bat only 392 times, the Atlanta Braves superstar had managed to slug 40 out of the park in '73—an incredible feat, but one that still left him a single homer short of Babe Ruth's career record of 714 round-trippers. The long standing ovation Aaron received from the home crowd at Atlanta Fulton County Stadium after popping out in his final at-bat of the year gave him a good feeling to take into the winter. Still, he knew it would be six long months of waiting before he could take his rightful place as the new Home Run King.

Making the delay all the more trying were the daily reminders that not everybody was crazy about the idea of a black man breaking the most revered record in sports. Often addressed "Dear Nigger" or "Dear Jungle Bunny," the hate letters to Aaron had begun coming in droves during the '73 season—and didn't let up even after the World Series. Hank, in fact, received more pieces of mail (930,000) than any American besides President Richard Nixon during 1973. The vast majority of letters were supportive of his efforts to surpass Ruth, but a frightening amount were racist in tone.

Many bigots warned that they would shoot Aaron to death if he played in a particular game, and Hank often took the field not knowing if and when a crackpot might go through with the threat. At one point his daughter, Gaile, began receiving harassing phone calls while away at Fisk University in Nashville, and rumors she would be kidnapped led Aaron to seek FBI intervention. Then there were the folks who, racist or not, felt the need to let Hank know he couldn't carry Babe Ruth's shoes. Time and again he was reminded that he had come to bat over 2,800 times more than the Babe during his career, and "Aaron is Ruth-less" bumper stickers began popping up on cars throughout the South.

Then, as spring training drew near in 1974, things got even more tense. Despite knowing Hank's anxiousness to get the record over with quickly, Braves owner Bill Bartholomay told Aaron that the organization wanted him to sit out the first three games of the '74 season at Cincin-nati, thereby increasing the likelihood of his setting the new home run mark in Atlanta. Aaron accepted the proposal, recalling later in his autobiography, *I Had a Hammer*, that "I kind of liked the idea of being able to show my grandchildren the spots where 714 and 715 landed."

Some folks, however, weren't so enamored with Bartholomay's plan to intentionally hold up history. New York sportswriters were particularly harsh. Dave Anderson of *The New York Times* called the move "a brazen defiance of baseball's integrity." Dick Young of the *Daily News* claimed that "baseball has gone crooked." To quiet the critics, baseball Commissioner Bowie Kuhn ruled that Aaron would have to start at least two of the three games in Cincy. Hank wasn't happy with the decision, but he accepted it.

Spring training itself was no less aggravating. Reporters and cameramen from around the world seemed to be everywhere Aaron went. The fans were just as obtrusive, chasing him for autographs and even leaping onto the field during exhibition games to get their pictures taken with him. By the time the Braves broke camp and headed to Cincinnati for the Thursday, April 4 opener, Aaron had endured enough. As

Opposite page: Aaron had to wait out a trying winter with 713 home runs before tying Babe Ruth with his first homer in 1974. He then hit his record 715th on April 8. Above right: Aaron was more relieved that it was over than thrilled with the feat of becoming baseball's all-time home run king. He finished his career with 755 homers. Below: The Dodgers' Al Downing served up the pitch that Aaron swatted for No. 714 in front of 53,775 fans on "Hank Aaron Night."

teammate Paul Casanova later revealed in *I Had a Hammer,* Hank told him en route to Ohio that he was going to tie Ruth's record in the first game against the Reds, rest a little, then break it in the home opener back in Atlanta.

Aaron stepped to the plate in the first inning on Opening Day. With his first swing of the year, he drilled a 3–1 pitch to left for a three-run homer off veteran Jack Billingham. Hank had tied Ruth with one at-bat, and as he rounded the bases his eyes grew moist. "For the first time in several long years," Aaron later recalled of the moment, "I wasn't chasing anybody."

After a day of rain, Aaron sat out Saturday and was in Sunday's lineup. Hank went 0-for-3 with two strikeouts before being removed once Atlanta built a large lead. Some reporters later claimed that Aaron went hitless on purpose so his family and the Atlanta fans could witness his record breaker in person. Hank, of course, denied all such charges.

Several hundred reporters and the biggest crowd in team history—53,775—showed up at Fulton County Stadium for Monday's home opener and "Hank Aaron Night." Keeping his promise to Casanova, the guest of honor did not disappoint. After Aaron's father, Herbert, threw out the first ball, Hank walked on five pitches in his initial at-bat against Los Angeles Dodgers lefty Al Downing. In the fourth Aaron came up with Darrell Evans on first. At 9:07 P.M. he hit a 1–0 slider from Downing on a line toward left-center. Dodger left fielder Bill Buckner gave chase and leaped at the fence, but the ball went over his glove and into the Braves' bullpen—where it was caught by Atlanta relief pitcher Tom House. At long last, No. 715 was in the record books.

As Aaron reached home plate, he was met with back slaps from his teammates and a powerful hug from his mother. The flashing scoreboard said it all: "Move Over Babe, Here Comes Henry." Or maybe Hank himself summed it up best when he told the crowd, "Thank God it's over."

MAC, SAMMY BLAST PAST MARIS

BEFORE THE MAGICAL summer of 1998, Mark McGwire and Sammy Sosa appeared to be at opposite ends of the baseball spectrum. McGwire was the prototypical slugger, a massive, slow-footed giant in the Paul Bunyan mold. By age 34, he had become the most prolific fence-buster (in terms of home runs per at-bat) since the mighty Babe Ruth. If anybody had a shot at breaking Roger Maris's single-season record of 61 homers in 1998, it was "Big Mac."

Sosa, on the other hand, had to be considered a huge long shot for such a feat. The Chicago Cubs outfielder was a streak hitter with a mediocre .257 career average and little discipline at the plate. Sammy had never hit more than 40 round-trippers in one season, and the 36 he collected in 1997 were accompanied by 174 strikeouts and a .251 average. A much less imposing physical presence than Big Mac at 6'0", 185 pounds, he was blessed with far more speed and athleticism than his bulky counterpart. Unfortunately, he was also known as a "hot-doggish" performer, obsessed with statistics and unable to perform up to his talent level.

The differences didn't end there. Unlike McGwire, who had grown up in a nice neighborhood in southern California, Sosa spent his poverty-stricken childhood shining shoes and selling oranges to support his widowed mother in the Dominican Republic. He didn't become an overnight success in the majors like Mac, but once he did develop into a quality player he was bursting with pride—and wanted everyone to know about it. Whether by wearing expensive "30–30" jewelry to symbolize

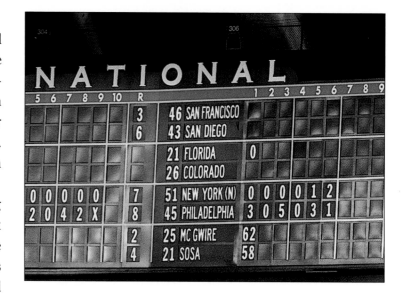

Above right: The old scoreboard at Wrigley Field added a new feature late in 1998. Throughout the United States, most fans were more interested in the home race than the nightly scores. Below: *Wrigley Field curtain calls were commonplace as Sosa powered his way through the 1998 season. As he neared Roger Maris's mark, even road fans wanted a salute.*

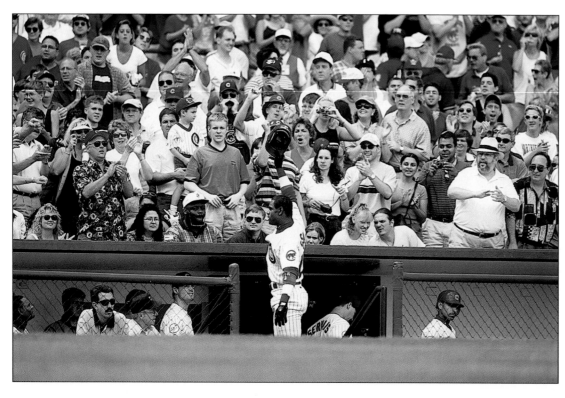

his achievements as the first 30-homer, 30-steal performer in Cubs history, or by engaging in friendly banter with the fans seated behind him at Wrigley Field, Sosa was as flashy and emotional as McGwire was low-key.

Suggesting at the start of the '98 campaign that this unlikely duo would by year's end be forever linked in friendship, the Hall of Fame, and the hearts of countless fans would have been sheer lunacy. An assault on the Maris home run record by McGwire and Seattle Mariners slugger Ken Griffey Jr. (who had hit 56 homers in '97) was expected to be *the* baseball story of the year, but most people simply penciled in Sosa for his usual numbers and then promptly forgot about him. Mac's face adorned the covers of countless preseason publications. And when he tied Willie Mays's 1971 record by homering in his first four games of the season, the media frenzy only increased. One ESPN broadcaster even joked that McGwire was "now on pace for a 162-homer season."

For a while the script ran according to plan. McGwire continued crushing the ball with authority, routinely hammering drives that traveled 450 feet or more while drawing huge crowds at home and on the road—even during batting practice. He talked the Cardinals organization into letting his 10-year-old son, Matthew, become a team batboy, then promptly slugged three home runs against Arizona the night Matt made his debut. After his National League-leading 27th homer of the year at San Diego on May 30, McGwire was 13 games ahead of the famous pace established by Maris en route to his 61 in '61.

Griffey was playing his part as well. Leading the American League with 19 homers through May, he, too, was on pace to crack the 61 barrier. Several other sluggers were also smashing balls out at an impressive clip—Andres Galarraga of the Braves and Greg Vaughn of the Padres among them—but Sosa was far back of the pack. In fact, when McGwire stroked his

24th home run on May 24 (in just his 47th game), Sammy had only nine big flys to his credit.

The only hint that Sosa was going to have his own season to remember was his unaccustomed place among the NL batting leaders, with a .340 average through May. Off-season work with Cubs hitting coach Jeff Pentland had improved Sammy's selectivity at the plate, and his concentration in the field showed a marked maturity as well. He was succeeding in areas in which he had struggled in the past: hitting in the clutch, going to the opposite field, and taking more walks. In short, Sosa was, at age 29, finally performing like a team player—and the Cubs were off to a surprisingly strong start as a result.

Still, even the most optimistic Cubs fans were not ready for what came next. Once the temperatures started to rise, Sosa grew red-hot. The line drives that had sprayed off his bat during the spring were suddenly drifting over the vine-covered walls of Wrigley, and often onto Waveland Avenue beyond the last row of bleacher seats. In one phenomenal stretch Sammy hit 21 homers in 22 games, and his 20 clouts in June broke Rudy York's 1937 record for the most in a single calendar month. Included in the outburst were five two-homer games and one three-bomb effort versus Milwaukee, a team against which Sosa would eventually slug 12 round-trippers during the season—another record. For the first time all season, Mac was being upstaged.

People across the country, many of them getting their first close look at Sammy, were delighted by his open displays of enthusiasm for the game. Each inning he sprinted from the dugout to his position in right field, often waving to fans in the bleachers upon his arrival. Whenever he sent a ball over the fence, he completed his home run trot by looking into the TV cameras, tapping his heart with two fingers, and then blowing a kiss to his mother back home in San Pedro de Macoris. Even the broken English Sosa delivered with a toothy grin was infectious: Asked how he felt about his hot streak, he simply smiled and said he was happy to be helping his team win. The explanation sounded refreshingly sincere.

His wild month enabled Sosa to quickly close the 15-homer gap between him and McGwire. By the All-Star break in early July, "Slammin' Sammy" stood just four behind Mac—whose 37 jacks tied Reggie Jackson's 1969 record for most home runs by the midsummer classic. Griffey was wedged between them with an AL-leading 35 homers, and Greg Vaughn was the only other slugger near the trio with 30. It looked like a three-horse race.

Looks, however, can be deceiving. A long dry spell in July and August, during which he hit just three home runs in

Sosa insisted throughout the 1998 home run chase that McGwire was "The Man," but Cubs fans and voters for the National League MVP Award felt otherwise.

33 games, dropped Griffey out of the record hunt—and out of the spotlight. Junior would eventually finish with 56 homers for the second straight year, a fantastic feat in itself. For now, however, all eyes turned to Mac and Sammy. Newspapers throughout the country began carrying "Maris Watch" boxes. Many sports departments began sending writers to cover Cardinals and Cubs games.

What reporters found were two clubs heading in opposite directions. Thanks in large part to Sosa, the Cubs were in the thick of an NL playoff race for the first time since 1989. But the Cardinals, despite similar heroics from McGwire, were instead struggling along with a sub-.500 record. Redbird rooters focused their full attention toward the red-headed slugger with the Ruthian power.

Sammy loved the attention, but he shed his selfish image by deflecting all praise toward McGwire. "Mark's the man," Sosa continuously told reporters inquiring about his chances of passing Maris first. "Mac is my hero. He is going to break the record."

This respect for his rival further endeared fans to Sammy, and it had its impact on McGwire as well. Mac was noticeably uncomfortable with the attention thrust upon him from the first day of spring training onward, and he smiled little during the early months of the season. At one point in June, saying he "felt like a caged animal," he asked the Cardinals to set up strict pre- and post-game interview guidelines. Now, taking a cue from Sosa's happy-go-lucky approach to the questions coming his way, McGwire suddenly began having more fun in front of reporters and cameras.

What resulted was a love-fest between these two players and baseball fans across the country that grew as the season

St. Louis fans were understandably more enamored with McGwire than Sosa, although both received loud ovations during the series in which Mac hit his 62nd.

Seemingly every kid in St. Louis wanted to be like Mac. Kids and adults flocked to Busch Stadium early just to watch McGwire take batting practice.

moved toward its climax. The more people found out about Sammy and Mac, the more folks liked them. Both sluggers were extremely charitable: McGwire donated $1 million of his salary each year to help abused children. Sosa built shopping malls in his hometown, and he responded to news that Dominican schools needed more computer equipment by personally shipping brand-new PCs to the president's palace. Both had warm, loving relationships with their families, adored the city they played in, and were praised as great teammates. Both respected each other.

And—most importantly—both kept hitting balls out of the park. In mid-August Sosa finally caught McGwire with his 47th homer, and on August 19 he actually went ahead for the first time with No. 48 when the Cubs and Cardinals met in Chicago. He didn't stay in front long—Mac came back with two in the same game—but for the final five weeks of the regular season the duel was on. Fans couldn't get enough of the battle. *Newsweek* and *Time* dedicated cover stories to the race, and word of the latest blasts led off nightly national newscasts. Both players entered September at 55 and counting, and everyone knew it was only a matter of time before someone toppled Maris from his 37-year-old throne.

McGwire got there first, completing an incredible stretch of 15 homers in 66 at-bats with No. 62 at home on September 8 against (who else?) the Cubs. The incredible feat was made all the more memorable by the celebration surrounding it. After hitting Steve Trachsel's pitch 341 feet to left field (his shortest homer all year) for

While Sosa was known for blowing kisses to fans, McGwire returns the favor to his new pal. Some credit McGwire and Sosa with revitalizing baseball with their uplifting and dramatic race. Each packed the house in August and September.

the record breaker, Mac rounded the bases as Sosa applauded from the outfield, then went through a series of emotional embraces: one for his son waiting at home plate, six more for Maris's children seated in the front row, and a final bear hug for Sammy. Then he accepted gifts, including a Cardinal-red '62 Corvette from the Cardinals organization.

If Sosa was disappointed at being second fiddle, he didn't show it. Six days later he got to 62 himself, clubbing two homers vs. Milwaukee and stunningly tying McGwire. The question turned again to which player would finish on top and thereby establish the new record. McGwire, of course, could swing for the fences since his team was long out of the race, while Sosa's Cubs were battling the Giants and Mets for the final NL playoff berth. Mac went ahead 65 to 63, but Sammy

snapped an 0-for-17 slump with three homers in three days to go ahead 66–65. Then, just when it seemed that nothing more incredible could happen, McGwire slugged five round-trippers during the final three games of the season—one on Friday, two on Saturday, and two on Sunday—ending the year with an astronomical total of 70.

Sosa was anything but a loser. Although his 66 homers were good for only runner-up status, Chicago defeated the Giants in a one-game playoff to earn a wild-card spot in the postseason. The Cubs lost in the Division Series to Atlanta, but for batting .308 and leading the major leagues with 158 RBI (the most in 50 seasons) and 134 runs scored, Sammy was named NL MVP. As far as McGwire was concerned, it couldn't have happened to a nicer guy.

Few players in history have hit home runs with anything approaching the force of Big Mac, whose rocket shots of 1998 will be talked about for years to come.

MAGICAL BLASTS

RUTH'S CALLED SHOT

FEATURING FIVE FUTURE Hall of Famers on their roster—including Babe Ruth and Lou Gehrig—the 1932 Yankees cruised to the American League pennant with a 107–47 record. Their opponent in the World Series was the Chicago Cubs, a club with a lineup nowhere near as daunting as New York's "Murderer's Row" and just 90 victories to its credit. Most oddsmakers anticipated a Yankee cakewalk, and the Bronx Bombers didn't disappoint. They swept their National League foes in four straight games.

On the surface it was a rather dull Series, yet buried within the boxscores was an interesting sideshow. Former Yankees shortstop Mark Koenig had been brought up by the Cubs late in the '32 season and hit .353 during the pennant drive, yet he had been voted only a half share of Chicago's World Series pot. The decision by Koenig's new teammates to slight him upset his old pals. Led by the always boisterous Ruth, the Yankees began hurling insults at their "cheapskate" opponents from the dugout and batter's box. The Cubs retaliated, and pretty soon

Above right: Ruth and Lou Gehrig seemed to draw a chuckle from their long-ball torture of the Cubs in 1932, though the Babe's "called shot" was nothing more than a great story in the making. Below: Artistic license allows painters and movie-makers to portray a scene that has no documented truth. Ruth pointed to the Cubs' dugout but probably not to the outfield seats.

an all-out war of words was being waged along with the games.

By the third contest in Chicago, the 50,000 fans at Wrigley Field were in on it, too, hurling lemons at Ruth during batting practice. He and Gehrig responded to the taunts with early home runs off righty Charlie Root, but the Cubs had pulled even at 4–4 when Ruth stepped in against Root during the fifth. Babe was in a playful mood. He grinned, took a called strike from Root, then looked over to the Cubs dugout and raised one finger on his left hand. The following two pitches were balls, then the next another strike. Ruth had still not swung, and the jeers grew louder.

At this point, Cubs catcher Gabby Hartnett claimed to hear Ruth say, "It only takes one to hit it." Then, as if on cue, he crushed the following pitch for a 435-foot home run far into the center-field bleachers. Ruth jabbered with Chicago infielders as he rounded the bases, and in a photo of him crossing the plate and shaking hands with Gehrig, the two seem almost to be laughing. Gehrig belted Root's very next pitch for *his* second homer of the day, and the Yanks won 7–5. They wrapped up the Series the next day with a 13–6 victory.

Those are the facts as best remembered by those involved. What has emerged over time is something far different. Ruth didn't just lift a finger to the Cubs dugout, the tale now goes, but he pointed to center field as if to call his shot. The image has been chronicled countless times in artwork and film, yet there seems no substantial proof that it occurred. Ruth supposedly even denied it himself when questioned by Root years later, but added with a laugh, "It makes a hell of a story, doesn't it?"

That it does.

THE HOMER IN THE GLOAMIN'

NIGHT GAMES ARE NOW an accepted part of baseball, more the norm than the exception. There was a time, however, when sunshine was the only source of illumination at ballparks, and umpires often called games on account of darkness. Teams in the lead as evening approached were known to stall in an attempt to preserve victories, and the lack of visibility as dusk crept in made all facets of play—especially hitting—a monumental struggle.

This was the situation the Chicago Cubs faced on September 28, 1938. After trailing the Pittsburgh Pirates in the National League pennant race by 8½ games at the beginning of the month, they had rallied to within 1½ games of the top when the two clubs met for three late-season contests at Chicago's lightless Wrigley Field. The Cubs took the first game 2–1 behind sore-armed Dizzy Dean, but they went into the bottom of the sixth the next day trailing 3–2.

Then Chicago player-manager Gabby Hartnett went to work. The NL's premier catcher for much of the decade, Gabby was now 37 years old and nearing the end of the line. He caught just 88 games in '38—ending a record string of eight straight 100-game seasons behind the plate—and his average had fallen from .354 the year before to just .274. Still, he had a few more big moments left in him. Leading off the Chicago sixth with a double, he scored moments later on a two-bagger by Rip Collins. When Collins came home on a groundout, it was 3–3. The Pirates went up 5–3 in the eighth, but Chicago rallied to tie it again in the bottom of the inning.

Darkness was now descending, and if the game was called it would end a tie—and Pittsburgh would remain in first. In the top of the ninth, the Pirates got a man on first, but Hartnett gunned him down at second attempting to steal. Umpires debated before letting the game continue, and when Gabby came up with two outs in the bottom of the ninth and the score still 5–5, it was clear he would be the final batter. After falling behind 0–2, he swung at a curve from Mace Brown and sent it deep to left field. Most of the nearly 35,000 people on hand couldn't see the ball, but it reached the bleachers for a game-winning homer.

Wrigley erupted, and a crowd of fans rushing the field put Hartnett on their shoulders as he rounded second base. Eventually Gabby broke free and made it to home plate before being mobbed again. "He would have soon been lost in the throng," columnist Red Smith wrote of the moment, "except for that tomato face glistening with sweat and the grin that glowed like a street lamp in the dark." Boosted into first place, the Cubs went on to win their third pennant in seven seasons—thanks to Gabby's "Homer in the Gloamin'."

Night baseball actually arrived at Wrigley long before the lights, as Hartnett put an end to a crucial 1938 win over the Pirates with a ninth-inning, twilight smash.

GREENBERG'S PENNANT-WINNING SLAM

JUST AS THE REST of America slowly returned to normalcy in the days following the end of World War II, major-league baseball worked its way back into shape during the late summer of 1945. Players who had spent the previous one to four years serving their country traded in their guns for bats, often finding that their abilities with the latter were a bit rusty. One soldier-turned-slugger who didn't have this problem, however, was Detroit Tigers outfielder Hank Greenberg.

The first major-leaguer to be enlisted in the Armed Forces, in May 1941, Greenberg had originally served eight months in the Army before being released on December 5 of the same year. Two days later the Japanese attacked Pearl Harbor, and

Hank immediately reenlisted for the duration of World War II. Rising to the rank of captain, he was discharged again in June '45. He immediately reported to the first-place Tigers. Any concerns over his rustiness were erased when the 34-year-old slugger belted a home run before 55,000 home fans in his first game back on July 1. Somehow, this seemed fitting: In his last contest before entering the service in '41, Hank had stroked two homers.

Detroit led the second-place New York Yankees by 3½ games upon Greenberg's return. Hank played nearly full-time down the stretch, and overall he hit .311 with 13 homers and 60 RBI in just 270 at-bats spread over 78 games. The Yankees faded, but the Tigers held just a one-game lead over the Washington Senators heading into a season-ending double-header against the St. Louis Browns on September 30. A win in either game of the twin bill at St. Louis would earn Detroit a World Series berth, but two losses would mean a pennant playoff with Washington— which had already completed its schedule.

Bad weather threatened to cancel both contests, and just over 5,000 shivering souls turned out at the Browns' Sportsman's Park. Playing on a muddy field through constant rain, the Tigers trailed screwballer Nelson Potter 3–2 heading into the ninth inning of the opening game. Detroit got men to second and third with one out, and Browns manager Luke Sewell walked Doc Cramer to load the bases and set up a double play. This was a risk with Greenberg being the next batter, but—perhaps considering the weather and Hank's lack of foot speed—Sewell was willing to take the gamble.

Greenberg made him pay, dispatching a Potter screwball into the left-field bleachers (and just inside the foul pole) for a pennant-clinching grand slam. "It was a strange thing," he recalled thinking as he rounded the bases and leaped into the arms of his teammates at home plate. "I wasn't sure if I was awake or dreaming." For a guy who had gone more than four years between major-league at-bats, Hank had made quite a comeback. And in the World Series that followed, he punctuated his return with two more homers as Detroit beat the Chicago Cubs in seven games.

Nothing beats a grand slam— especially one that clinches a pennant like Greenberg's did for the Tigers in 1945. He homered twice more in a seven-game World Series win over the Cubs, one of which is pictured.

THE SHOT HEARD 'ROUND THE WORLD

ON AUGUST 12, 1950, the Brooklyn Dodgers held a commanding 13½ game lead in the National League pennant race. Their lineup included the likes of Jackie Robinson, Duke Snider, Roy Campanella, and Pee Wee Reese, and their pitching staff was paced by ace Don Newcombe. With a sparkling record of 75–30, this group seemed all but assured of making its third World Series trip in five seasons.

The only problem with Brooklyn's plan was that the second-place New York Giants refused to play along. Managed by former Dodgers skipper Leo Durocher and ignited by a young rookie named Willie Mays, the Giants made a late-season rush of incredible proportions. They went 39–8 down the stretch to catch their hated rivals on the final weekend of the season. A three-game playoff was scheduled to determine the league champion, and the clubs split the first two contests—a 3–1 Giants win followed by a 10–0 Brooklyn triumph.

The season now came down to a third and final match at the Polo Grounds, home of the Giants. Brooklyn took a 1–0 lead in the first inning on two walks and a Robinson single, and it

stayed that way into the seventh as hurlers Sal Maglie and Newcombe locked up in a tense pitcher's duel. A sacrifice fly by Giants third baseman Bobby Thomson in the seventh tied the game, but the Dodgers then rocked Maglie for four hits in the eighth and went into the final inning with a 4–1 edge.

It looked like the Brooklynites would get the last laugh after all, but the Giants still had one more comeback in them. In the bottom of the ninth they finally got to Newcombe. Alvin Dark and Don Mueller singled, and with one out Whitey Lockman doubled into the gap in left-center to make it 4–2. Dodger swingman Ralph Branca was called in to put out the fire. Thomson stepped to the plate, and rather than intentionally walk the slugger who had homered off him two days earlier, Branca was told to pitch to him. Mays, slumping but ever dangerous, was on deck.

Branca delivered a fastball taken for a called strike. The next pitch came in high and inside, and Thomson swung— sending a shot to left that at first kept rising and then quickly started to sink. Left fielder Andy Pafko ran to the wall in pursuit, but it was gone into the seats just beyond the 315-foot marker. Thomson rounded first base, then began clapping his hands as pandemonium broke loose at the Polo Grounds. Radio broadcaster Russ Hodges shouted out the words that would be replayed more than any in baseball history: "The Giants win the pennant! The Giants win the pennant! The Giants win the pennant!"

Nearly a half-century later, fans still remember where they were at that moment. Thomson's blast remains the home run against which all others are measured for sheer drama.

Above: *The Dodgers could have walked Thomson in 1951, but with Willie Mays on deck they decided to pitch to him. A high, inside fastball wound up in the left-field seats.* Left: *No home run in baseball history carried the drama of Thomson's "Shot Heard 'Round the World," a 1951 home run that sent Giants fans into a frenzy.*

MAZ'S SERIES-WINNING SMASH

I T IS PERHAPS THE MOST common of all childhood athletic fantasies, a scenario played out in countless backyards and daydreams by young baseball fans. A home run in the bottom of the ninth inning to win the World Series is a concept as American as John Wayne and apple pie. Yet it took nearly six decades of fall classics before this script ever presented itself in real life.

No one told the gritty Pirates that they were not supposed to beat the Yankees in the 1960 World Series, which they did on Mazeroski's dramatic homer at Forbes Field.

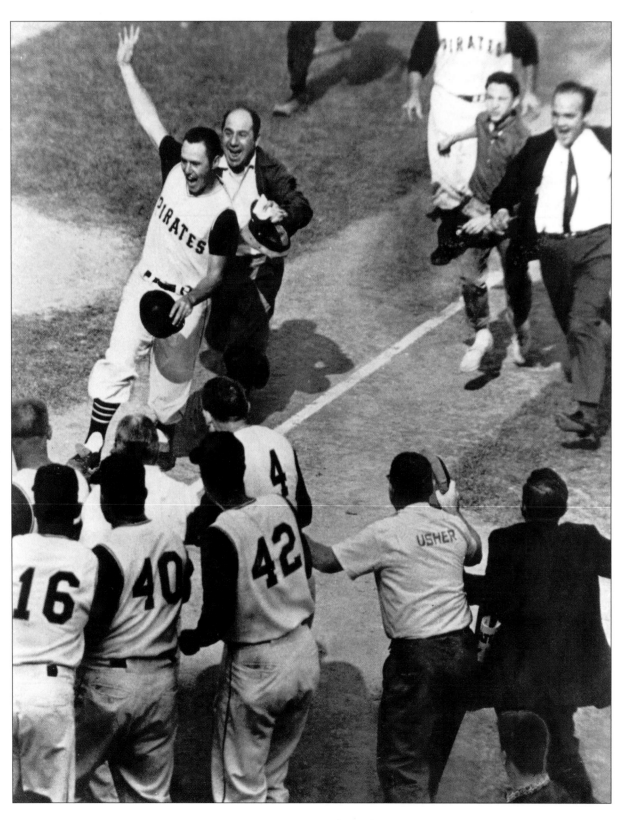

The 1960 Series matched up the powerful New York Yankees of Mickey Mantle, Roger Maris, and Yogi Berra against the scrappy, never-say-die Pittsburgh Pirates of Roberto Clemente, Dick Groat, and Bill Mazeroski. Many experts thought the Pirates didn't even belong on the same field as Casey Stengel's team, and the lopsided triumphs of 16–3, 10–0, and 12–0 rung up by the Yanks in Games 2, 3, and 6 seemed to justify these opinions. What happened during the rest of the Series, however, was a different story. Although they did so in far less convincing fashion— by scores of 6–4, 3–2, and 5–2—the Pirates claimed three victories themselves to set up a winner-take-all finale at Pittsburgh's Forbes Field.

This seventh contest would prove a seesaw affair. The Pirates took a 4–0 lead through four innings, only to fall behind 7–4 when their usually dependable relief pitching failed in the middle frames. Then came a wild Pittsburgh eighth. Gino Cimoli led off with a walk, and Bill Virdon's ensuing double-play grounder took a strange hop at the last instant and hit Yankees shortstop Tony Kubek in the throat. Both runners were safe, and Groat followed with a single to drive in Cimoli and make it 7–5. Two outs later, with men on second and third, Clemente hit what looked like an inning-ending chopper to first baseman Bill Skowron—but wound up an infield hit when pitcher Jim Coates failed to cover first on the play. Another run scored, Hal Smith stepped up, and before the crowd had a chance to relax Smith sent it to new heights of delirium with a three-run homer.

Down 9–7, the Yankees rallied in the ninth for three hits and two runs to tie things up 9–9. Leading off the bottom of the inning was Mazeroski, a Gold Glove second baseman not known for his power. New Yankees hurler Ralph Terry delivered a heater high and inside for a ball, then got his second pitch down a bit—just where Maz wanted it. Taking the season's final swing, he sent a shot over Berra's head and into the left-field stands.

Dancing wildly around the bases, Mazeroski whirled his arm with glee as fans rushed onto the field to shake his hand. The first diehards reached him before he even stepped on home plate, and when he finally did touch it the Pirates had claimed their first World Series title since 1925.

Kids watching could take note: Sometimes dreams *do* come true.

FISK'S LATE-NIGHT HEROICS

IT HAS BEEN CALLED the greatest World Series game ever played, which is quite a statement considering the number of dramatic battles waged through the decades. Yet for those who saw Game 6 of the 1975 fall classic between the Cincinnati Reds and Boston Red Sox, there is little argument against the claim—especially considering the emotional high on which the contest ended.

On paper the '75 Series looked to be a mismatch. The Reds had romped to the National League pennant with a 108–54 record and a star-studded veteran lineup that included Pete Rose, Joe Morgan, Johnny Bench, and Tony Perez. The Red Sox had fought off Baltimore and the Yankees to reach the playoffs with 95 victories, thanks largely to the sparkling play of two rookies—outfielders Fred Lynn and Jim Rice. And with Rice lost for the World Series with a broken hand, the Red Sox were considered even bigger underdogs.

As is often the case, things played out much differently than predicted. Three of the first five Series contests were decided by a single run, including one in the ninth and one in extra innings. Cincinnati was up three games to two going into Game 6 at Boston, but Red Sox fans were still confident: Three days of rainouts allowed the Sox to start ageless ace Luis Tiant when play resumed at Fenway Park, and "Looie" had already beaten the Reds twice in the Series.

Lynn gave Boston a quick 3–0 lead on a first-inning homer. After chipping away at Tiant to tie the score, the Reds took a 6–3 lead in the eighth. Boston's Bernie Carbo then knotted things again in the bottom of the eighth with his second pinch-hit homer of the Series, a three-run shot. The Sox loaded the bases with none out in the ninth, but George Foster caught a fly ball and nailed Denny Doyle at the plate for a double play.

Morgan hit a smash in the 11th that seemed like a sure homer, but Boston's Dwight Evans chased it down and made a twisting, running catch in front of the short wall in right field to start a double play. When Rose stepped to the plate that same inning, he said to Red Sox catcher Carlton Fisk, "This is some game, isn't it?"

Fisk led off the bottom of the 12th. At 12:34 A.M., he pulled Pat Darcy's first pitch (a sinker) toward the left-field corner. It

was not clear if the ball would stay fair, and as Fisk ran to first he did all he could to "will" it so by leaping, yelling, and waving his arms. Fans watching the path of the ball missed his theatrics, but the TV audience saw the whole act.

Eventually the ball struck the mesh netting attached to the foul pole for a home run, and Fisk thrust his arms over his head in celebration. The hit didn't win the Series (the Reds did the following night), but it is still remembered as the greatest moment in Red Sox history.

Carlton Fisk's memorable and oft-replayed Game 6 blast capped what some consider the greatest game in World Series history, though the Red Sox lost Game 7 to the Reds.

REGGIE! REGGIE! REGGIE!

A FLASHY SLUGGER who talked a big game and had the ability to back up his boasts when it counted, Reggie Jackson was a winner. Over the course of his long career, he reached the postseason 11 times, played on five World Series champions, and was usually in the thick of things when titles were on the line. He earned the nickname "Mr. October" for his autumn exploits, and never was his ability to perform best on center stage more evident than in Game 6 of the 1977 fall classic.

Only a few months earlier, Jackson had been at the center of controversy. Signed as a free agent by the defending American League champion New York Yankees before the season, Reggie quickly declared himself "the straw that stirs the drink" on his new club—words that irked the team's acknowledged leader and captain, hard-nosed catcher Thurman Munson. In addition, Jackson's lackluster outfield play and frequent strike-outs overshadowed his mammoth home runs and drove fiery Yankee manager Billy Martin nuts. In June, with a packed crowd at Boston's Fenway Park and a nationwide TV audience

watching, skipper and player nearly came to blows in the dugout when Martin pulled Reggie off the field in mid-inning for not hustling after a fly ball.

At the time Jackson and the team were both struggling, but Reggie wound up with 32 homers and the Yankees won their second straight AL pennant. In the World Series they met the Los Angeles Dodgers. After winning three of the first five games, New York headed back to Yankee Stadium one victory away from the title. Reggie already had two home runs in the Series, including one in his final at-bat of the fifth contest.

The best was to come. After walking on four pitches his first time up in Game 6, Jackson came to the plate in the fourth inning with the Dodgers leading 3–2. Taking his trademark from-the-heels swing, he turned on Burt Hooton's first offering and blasted it into the right-field stands for a two-run homer. The Yanks had a 5–3 advantage when he batted again in the fifth. This time reliever Elias Sosa was the victim, as Reggie struck *his* first pitch to right for another two-run blast.

By Jackson's next at-bat in the eighth against Charlie Hough, the entire park seemed to be chanting, "Reggie! Reggie! Reggie!" He gave them just what they needed: a 450-foot smash to center for his third first-pitch homer of the game and fourth in his last four swings. The chants continued when Reggie took his place in right field to start the ninth, and it was almost an afterthought when New York wrapped up the title with an 8–4 victory. Jackson had tied a record with five home runs in one fall classic, and the Yankees were once again world champions after a 15-year layoff.

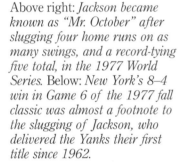

Above right: Jackson became known as "Mr. October" after slugging four home runs on as many swings, and a record-tying five total, in the 1977 World Series. Below: New York's 8–4 win in Game 6 of the 1977 fall classic was almost a footnote to the slugging of Jackson, who delivered the Yanks their first title since 1962.

BUCKY DENT AND THE "CURSE"

THE HISTORY OF THE Boston Red Sox is one filled with hard-luck defeats and blown opportunities. The run of near misses that has kept the Sox from capturing a World Series championship since 1918 is known in New England as the "Curse of the Bambino," since Babe Ruth's sale to the New York Yankees occurred just one season after that title year—and because in the decades since those very Yankees have often been the ones to deflate the hopes of Boston's fandom.

Never was the Curse—or the Yankees—deemed more responsible for the woes of Red Sox followers than in 1978. The Red Sox held a commanding lead in the American League East that July, while the defending world-champion Yankees sat in fourth place, 14 games behind. Boston possessed great sluggers in Jim Rice, Carlton Fisk, and Carl Yastrzemski as well as top-notch pitchers in Dennis Eckersley, Luis Tiant, and former Yankees ace Mike Torrez. New York's club was decimated by injuries to key performers, and manager Billy Martin had been fired in midseason and was replaced by Bob Lemon. It looked like Boston's year.

Then, quickly, the tide turned. The Yankees got healthy, the Red Sox went cold, and in two months New York made up the entire 14-game deficit. They took over first shortly after a four-game sweep at Fenway Park that was quickly dubbed the "Boston Massacre." The Sox eventually fell 3½ games back, then rebounded to win 12 of their last 14 and tie the Yanks at the top. Each team had 99 victories, but just one game would decide the division title.

The playoff was held at Fenway on a cool afternoon, and the Sox took an early 2–0 lead against 24-game winner Ron Guidry on a homer by Yastrzemski and an RBI single by Rice. Torrez held his old teammates score-less through six innings, but in the seventh Chris Chambliss and Roy White singled for New York with one out. Torrez got the next man, bringing up light-hitting shortstop Bucky Dent. A .240 hitter with just four home runs, Dent had been especially unproductive during September.

After taking the first pitch for a ball, Dent fouled the second off his foot and fell to the ground in pain. Breaking his bat on the play, he went to get a new club and shake off the injury. When he hit Torrez's next offering to left field, Yastrzemski drifted back for what at first seemed a routine fly—only to watch in horror as the ball kept carrying and settled in the net above Fenway's famed 37-foot "Green Monster" wall. It was barely 310 feet from home plate, but a three-run homer nonetheless.

There would be plenty more action in this game, but Dent's blast had shifted the momentum. The Yanks eventually led 5–2, held on for a 5–4 victory, and wrapped up their second straight world championship a few weeks later. The Curse of the Bambino had struck again.

Dent's playoff home run at Fenway Park remains a sore subject among Red Sox fans, whose team cannot seem to escape the "Curse of the Bambino."

GIBSON'S PINCH-HIT HEROICS

BASEBALL HAS LONG BEEN a favorite subject for filmmakers. But if a director in 1988 had come up with the story of hobbling Kirk Gibson and his World Series heroics, it would have been dismissed as a plot too corny for consideration. That said, it seems appropriate that this real-life tale took place in Hollywood's backyard.

A long-time standout on the Detroit Tigers, Gibson signed with the Los Angeles Dodgers as a free agent before the '88 season. The former college football star turned outfielder played the game with reckless abandon. Four years before, he had led the Tigers to a World Series title with his intense, gung-ho approach and dramatic homer in the clinching game. Dodgers management believed he could do the same for them in 1988, and Kirk rewarded their confidence with an MVP season. Besides giving Los Angeles veteran leadership, he batted .290 with 25 homers and 31 steals.

The gimpy Gibson's pinch-hit home run in the 1988 Series was a moment of drama that Hollywood could not have gotten away with. A's fans know all too well that it was for real.

Then came trouble. During a victorious NLCS against the Mets, Gibson hit two crucial home runs but also suffered a severely pulled left hamstring and strained ligaments in his right knee—injuries that threatened to sideline him for the World Series. He could barely walk, and he didn't suit up for Game 1 against the heavily favored Oakland Athletics at Dodger Stadium. He even sat in the clubhouse as his teammates took the field for opening introductions.

Gibson's only chance at seeing action was to take an anti-inflammatory shot that would temporarily ease the pain in his right knee and—coupled with ice treatments—possibly numb the swelled joint enough for him to bat. He took the long-needle shot in the clubhouse, then iced the knee and watched on TV as the Dodgers fell behind 4–3. When he heard broadcaster Vin Scully say "Gibson will not be available tonight," Kirk decided that, pain or no pain, he would try and ready himself to pinch-hit. Eliciting help from clubhouse batboy Mitch Poole, he limped to a batting cage beneath the stands and began hitting balls off a stationary tee.

In the bottom of the ninth, Gibson got his chance. Los Angeles still trailed 4–3 and faced Oakland's dominant closer, Dennis Eckersley. With two outs Mike Davis coaxed a walk, and the call came for Kirk. After 55,983 fans on hand and millions watching on TV had been told he wouldn't play, here he was hobbling to the plate.

Two fastballs later Gibson was down 0–2 and stumbling in agony, but somehow he worked the count full before Eckersley came in with a slider. Gibson took a one-legged swing, lunged at the ball, and sent it toward right field. As it settled into the stands for a game-winning homer, Kirk limped around the bases and pumped his fist in triumph. "It didn't hurt at all, believe me," Gibson told writer Dan Valenti later. "I don't know why, but fate was on my side."

And on the side of the Dodgers. Gibson never batted again in the Series, but his heroics launched Los Angeles to a five-game triumph.

CARTER'S CLIMACTIC CLOUT

H E WAS ONLY SEVEN months old when Bill Mazeroski of Pittsburgh hit his bottom-of-the-ninth homer to win the 1960 World Series, so it's safe to say that Joe Carter's only recollections of the blast were culled from old TV footage. Still, Carter admits that like millions of other kids—and hundreds of fellow big-leaguers—he imagined himself in Mazeroski's place, winning it all for his team on just such a blow.

Since the clubs he played on never finished higher than fourth place during his first eight seasons in the majors, Joe must have wondered if his chance would ever come. Then a trade prior to the 1991 season brought him to the Toronto Blue Jays, and suddenly Carter was with a contender. The Jays won the American League East that year, and in '92 they went all the way to a World Series championship. Carter contributed more than 30 homers and 100 RBI each year, and he even made the final putout of the '92 fall classic at first base. It wasn't a Mazeroski moment, but it was fun.

Joe had another standout season in '93, slugging 33 homers and driving in 121 runs as Toronto made a return trip to the World Series. The opponent this time was the Philadelphia Phillies, and the Blue Jays took two of the first three games heading into a wild fourth contest at Philadelphia. Toronto went up 3–0 in the first, fell behind 6–3 in the second, moved back in front 7–4 in the third, went back behind 12–7 in the fifth, and entered the eighth still down 14–9. Then came the rally to end all rallies: six runs, including five off Phillies closer Mitch "Wild Thing" Williams. When the dust settled, the Jays were 15–14 victors.

Philadelphia regrouped to win the next day 2–0, and the Series headed back to Toronto for Game 6. Once more the Blue Jays went up 3–0 in the first inning, and they still led 5–1 before the Phillies erupted for five runs in the seventh. Down 6–5 heading into the bottom of the ninth, Toronto was three outs away from facing a seventh-game showdown. Rickey Henderson walked against Williams to lead things off, and Paul Molitor slapped a one-out single. Now Carter came to the plate, a man with nearly 300 career homers looking to achieve the ultimate smash. Working the count to 2–2, he crushed the next pitch over the left-field fence and joyously danced around the bases. The Jays were 8–6 winners and champions again.

"It was a low pitch into my power," Carter told reporters after the game. "We had been talking about wouldn't it be great for something good to happen, something you dream about: bottom of the ninth, two strikes, and you hit a home run to win the World Series. It was a storybook finish."

Indeed it was.

Sports offers few spectacles like a game-winning home run to clinch the World Series, and Joe Carter produced just that to lift the Blue Jays over the Phillies in 1993.

HOME RUN HAVENS

AMONG BASEBALL'S GREATEST assets is the unique design of each ballpark. Unlike other fields of play, a baseball diamond is not bound by uniform measurements. The outfield wall in some parks is closer to home plate than it is in others, therefore posing a new challenge for hitters and pitchers in each city.

The dimensions of some parks favor the pitcher while others benefit the batter. And then there are those seemingly designed with the home run hitter in mind. It is within the walls of such places that baseball's big men do much of their damage. They are among baseball's home run palaces, where cleanup hitters begin to salivate during the cab ride to the park.

The first home run hit at **Tiger Stadium** in Detroit came off the bat of St. Louis Browns rookie Del Pratt on May 5, 1912. Pratt would enjoy a steady 13-year career in the major leagues, but no one could have predicted the legacy he started with that fateful swing in 1912.

Tiger Stadium has played host to 10,879 home runs, the most of any park in baseball history. While the majority of them have been as innocent as Pratt's inaugural blast, others have left a lasting impression on the game of baseball.

Above right: More home runs have been hit in Tiger Stadium than in any other big-league ballpark. If you keep your fly ball away from dead center, it's got a chance. Below: The "friendly confines" of Wrigley Field are no treat for the men on the mound. Players such as Andre Dawson and Sammy Sosa enjoyed career power years as Cubs and became favorites of the Bleacher Bums.

The primary reason that Tiger Stadium is such a homer-friendly park is that the outfield fences extend to center field in straight lines from each foul pole. The entire field, like most old ballparks, resembles a true diamond. The shape of the outfield at Tiger Stadium means the power alleys in left- and right-center measure a cozy 365 feet and 375 feet, respectively. Making things more appetizing for lefties is the fact that the upper-deck overhang in right field is 10 feet closer to the field than the ground-level right-field fence. The only challenge in Detroit is center field, which is 440 feet away from home plate and the deepest center field in the majors.

The Tigers have built their teams around sluggers, employing such power hitters as Hank Greenberg, Norm Cash, Al Kaline, Frank Howard, Kirk Gibson, and Cecil Fielder. "Tiger Stadium is a good hitting park," said the 6'7" Howard. "The background there is just great to hit off. It's a marvelous place for a power hitter to have the privilege to play in. There is great tradition inside that park, some great memories of our game."

Greenberg is the most prolific slugger in franchise history, having topped the AL in homers four times. In 1938 he connected for 58 home runs, 39 of them at home. Kaline is the career leader with 226 of his 399 career long balls occurring in Detroit. The Yankees' Babe Ruth hit his 700th home run in Detroit and leads opponents with 60 four-baggers at Tiger Stadium. Another Yankee, Mickey Mantle, hit his 535th homer in Detroit, which, at the time, moved him into third place on the all-time home run list.

Since 1938, when the park was renovated, 33 home runs have been hit out of Tiger Stadium. Of the 33, 29 traveled over the right-field roof while just four have exited over the more distant left-field roof. The four who have rocketed blasts out of

left are Harmon Killebrew, Howard, Fielder, and Mark McGwire.

On July 13, 1971, Detroit played host to the All-Star Game. On that night future Hall of Famers Johnny Bench, Hank Aaron, Roberto Clemente, Reggie Jackson, Frank Robinson, and Harmon Killebrew all left the yard. Jackson's colossal shot hit the light tower on the right-field roof.

Ranking second to Tiger Stadium in career home runs is **Wrigley Field** in Chicago. Those "Friendly Confines" have indeed been friendly to the long-ball hitter. Wrigley was erected in 1914, and the park has witnessed 9,801 home runs in its history.

Again, it's the shallow power alleys—368 feet in both left-center and right-center—that accommodate a high rate of home runs. The dimensions have helped some Cubs post extraordinary power numbers. In 1930 Chicago's Hack Wilson hit what was then a National League-record 56 home runs (33 of them at Wrigley) and drove in a major league-record 190 RBI. Hall of Fame shortstop Ernie Banks hit more than 40 homers in a season five times and launched his 500th career four-bagger at Wrigley Field in 1970.

In 1987 the Cubs led the NL with 209 home runs, while MVP Andre Dawson contributed 49 (27 at Wrigley). Three seasons later Ryne Sandberg swatted an NL-high 40 homers, the third best single-season total ever for a second baseman.

Wrigley took center stage during the home run chase of '98 waged by McGwire and Cubs slugger Sammy Sosa. McGwire hit four of his record 70 blasts in Chicago, while Sosa hit 39 of his 66 at home, including Nos. 60, 61, and 62.

Fenway Park in Boston and Tiger Stadium have two things in common. They opened on April 20, 1912, and both are known as a hitter's park. From Jimmie Foxx to Ted Williams to Carl Yazstremski to Mo Vaughn, some magnificent power hitters have worn the Red Sox uniform. On nine occasions a member of the Red Sox has led the AL in home runs. Foxx hit 50 in 1938 but finished second to Greenberg's 58. Of Foxx's 50 homers that season, 35 came at Fenway.

The Green Monster, a looming, 37-foot-high wall in left field, is among the most imposing sights in baseball. But because it's only 315 feet away from home plate, it's been an inviting target for such right-handed Boston sluggers as Foxx, Jim Rice, and Tony Armas.

Red Sox batters, with a little help from hitter-friendly Fenway Park, have led the AL in home runs nine times since the classic yard opened in 1912.

The remainder of Fenway is a hitter's dream and an outfielder's nightmare. Center field measures 390 feet from home plate, but the outfield inexplicably juts out farther to 420 feet in what is known as "Deep Center Field." The measurement of "Deep Right Field" is 380 feet, but the fence declines rapidly to the foul pole, which stands 302 feet away. In 1940, in an effort to help Williams, bullpens were built in right-center, reducing the distance by 23 feet. That area became known as Williamsburg.

The park with the shortest outfield dimensions in history was Chicago's **Lake Front Park,** home of the Chicago White Stockings in 1883 and '84. Starting from the left-field foul pole, the fences measured 186, 280, 300 (center field), 252, and 196 feet. In 1883 a ball hit over the left-field fence was counted only as a ground-rule double. The following season it counted as a homer, and Chicago totaled 142 home runs that season, including a NL-leading 27 by Ned Williamson. Three of Williamson's teammates also cracked the 20-homer barrier that year.

While many parks have been conducive to the home run, only one was built because of the home run and designed to accommodate the game's greatest home run hitter: **Yankee Stadium**.

The New York Giants were the rage of the Big Apple in the post-World War I era. So confident of their stature among the city's fans, the Giants allowed the Yankees to rent their park, the Polo Grounds, while they traveled. Then in 1920, the Yanks acquired Ruth from the Red Sox, and he responded with 54 home runs. The allure of the long ball quickly began to generate more interest than John McGraw's Giants, and the Yanks began to outdraw their landlords. Suddenly, the cozy relationship between baseball's roommates was over. "The Yankees will have to build a park in Queens or some other out-of-the-way place," said McGraw. "Let them go away and wither on the vine."

On April 18, 1923, Yankee Stadium opened in the Bronx, a long fly ball across the Harlem River from the Polo Grounds. Ruth hit the first homer in the stadium, and it would forever be known as the "House That Ruth Built." It could just have easily been called the "House Built for Ruth." With management aware of their marquee player's prodigious power, the stadium was designed with the right-field foul pole a cozy 295 feet away from home plate. It stayed that way until 1939, when the fence was moved back one foot. When Yankee Stadium was renovated after the '73 season, the right-field line was pushed back to 314 feet.

The friendly porch in right allowed left-handed sluggers to thrive throughout the team's glorious history. Among the stars who took advantage of the stadium's design were Ruth, Lou Gehrig, Mickey Mantle (a switch-hitter), Roger Maris, Reggie Jackson, Don Mattingly, and Tino Martinez.

In the course of the stadium's 75-year history, the team has lived up to its nickname as the Bronx Bombers. In 1961 six Yanks—Maris, Mantle, Yogi Berra, Johnny Blanchard, Elston Howard, and Moose Skowron—had at least 21 homers, and the team slugged a record 240 circuit clouts. The stadium was also home to Ruth's 60th home run in 1927, Maris's 61st in 1961, and Jackson's three homers in Game 6 of the 1977 World Series.

The noticeably deeper left field at Yankee Stadium hurt right-handed hitter Joe DiMaggio, but lefties such as Babe Ruth and Reggie Jackson feasted.

Of today's modern ballparks, Minnesota's **Metrodome** (a.k.a. the "Homer Dome") and Seattle's **Kingdome** are considered homer-friendly stadiums. While the dimensions at the Metrodome appear normal, the ball simply carries better inside the dome. According to the book *Green Cathedrals,* there are more home runs hit at the Metrodome when the air conditioner is turned on, which leads to the speculation that air flow generated by the air conditioning blows out like a subtle wind.

Seattle's Kingdome has a smaller version of the Green Monster in right field. The wall is 23 feet high, is painted blue, and is called the Walla Walla (after the city in Washington). Unlike the Metrodome, the air conditioning vents blow air toward the field, which would seem to prevent home runs. Therefore, the high rate of home runs at the Kingdome in recent years can be attributed to its moderate right-field fences and a lineup that has boasted the likes of Ken Griffey Jr., Jay Buhner, Edgar Martinez, and Alex Rodriguez.

The one modern ballpark that can turn a hitter with warning-track power into a bona fide long-ball threat is **Coors Field,** the home of the Colorado Rockies. The park appears to be large. The dimensions are 347 to left field, 414 in center, and 350 to right. But those distances are hardly enough to contain a baseball moving through the high altitude of Denver. In such rarified air, baseballs travel further and curveballs tend to flatten out. When compensating for the altitude, the equivalent sea-level dimensions of Coors Field shrink to 315 in left, 377 in center, and 318 in right.

Prior to the existence of the Rockies, Atlanta's **Fulton County Stadium** was the highest ballpark in the majors, standing more than 1,000 feet above sea level. It was known as the "Launching Pad" and was home to Hank Aaron's 715th career home run. In 1973 the Braves' Aaron, Darrell Evans, and Davey Johnson (who never eclipsed more than 18 homers before or after) became the first trio of teammates in major-league history to hit 40 or more homers.

Coors Field, though, sits 5,200 feet above sea level. In 1996 the Rockies' Andres Galarraga, Ellis Burks, Dante Bichette, and Vinny Castilla combined to hit 158 home runs. Of that number, 104 of them were hit at Coors Field. Galarraga, Castilla, and Burks also became the second trio of teammates to hit 40 or more homers in a season.

The following year the Rockies hit an NL-record 239 home runs. The notable exception in Colorado's power surge was Larry Walker. During his MVP season in '97, Walker hit 49 dingers, with only 20 coming at Coors Field.

Where there is bliss for batters typically means misery for pitchers. The Rockies' pitching staff posted a bloated 5.00 ERA in 1998, second worst in the league. Consider the case of Darryl Kile. As a member of the Houston Astros, Kile posted a 2.57 ERA in 1997, third best in the NL. In 1998, his first season with the Rockies, Kile's ERA ballooned to 5.20.

Above left: *Home run hitters love a hot day in Minneapolis, because an air-conditioned game in the Metrodome is the perfect setting for the deep fly.* Below: *Pitchers have nightmares about Coors Field, where 12–10 is not an unusual score. Curveballs lose their hook in Denver's altitude, and balls seem to carry forever.*

ONE-YEAR WONDERS

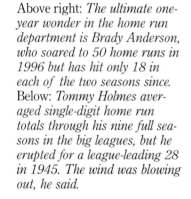

EVERY FEW YEARS, there emerges in baseball a home run Cinderella. For one year, the sudden slugger finds a power zone that sends his line drives to the bleachers and his pop flies to the upper deck. Then, all too quickly, the groove is gone, and the player in question is back to his old self—never to find the mysterious slugging source again.

There is no better example of this phenomenon than the 1996 season experienced by **Brady Anderson** of the Baltimore Orioles. An outstanding defensive outfielder and leadoff man, Anderson had never hit more than 21 homers in a season prior to '96—and over the previous four years had averaged 15.5 per annum. That fateful spring, however, Brady started bashing them in bunches, and by the All-Star break he was among the American League leaders with 30 round-trippers. A well-chiseled 6'1", 190 pounds, Anderson had been lifting weights religiously for a decade. Still, nobody—including Brady himself—could explain his sudden surge of power.

Despite an acute attack of appendicitis that briefly sidelined him in mid-July, Anderson fell just a bit off this frenetic pace following the break and slugged his 50th homer on the final day of the season. The 13th major-leaguer in history to reach this mark, he was the first to have also stolen 50 bases in one year (1992) during his career. But whatever magic-mashing potion he had found was gone by the following spring. Brady fell back down to 18 homers in 1997, then hit another 18 in '98. His prodigious power disappeared as fast as it came.

This tale is not unique. One of the greatest power seasons turned in by any player during the 1980s was the MVP year **Andre Dawson** had with the Chicago Cubs during 1987. As an All-Star outfielder with the Montreal Expos, Dawson had averaged a solid 23 home runs over nine years before joining the Cubs as a free agent prior to '87. Rejuvenated after years of pounding his injury-riddled knees on Astroturf, Andre thrived when given the chance to play on real grass. He slugged an NL-best 49 homers for the Cubs that year, a career high that he never came close to approaching again. He dropped off to 24 homers in 1988 and 21 in '89.

Speaking of 1989, **Kevin Mitchell** of San Francisco blasted 47 home runs that year, 28 more than ever before. He'd enjoy a couple more slugging seasons (35, 30) before dropping out of sight.

Go back a decade and you come across another surprising 50-homer man in **George Foster.** A vital cog in the Cincinnati "Big Red Machine" that won back-to-back World Series titles in 1975–76, Foster leaped from a career-high 29 homers in '76 to 52 big flys the following season—then the third highest total ever by an NL batter. The 28-year-old slugger was named MVP for his efforts, but over the next

Above right: The ultimate one-year wonder in the home run department is Brady Anderson, who soared to 50 home runs in 1996 but has hit only 18 in each of the two seasons since. Below: Tommy Holmes averaged single-digit home run totals through his nine full seasons in the big leagues, but he erupted for a league-leading 28 in 1945. The wind was blowing out, he said.

two years slid to 40 and then 30 home runs. Word got around among pitchers that Foster couldn't lay off low curveballs. In seven more seasons after '79, he never hit more than 28 out of the park.

The Brady Anderson of the 1970s was **Davey Johnson**, a slick-fielding second baseman who averaged nine homers a year during seven full seasons with Baltimore before being traded to the Atlanta Braves in 1973. Taking a tip from new teammate Hank Aaron, Davey switched to a lighter bat. By the end of '73, Johnson had skyrocketed from five to 43 homers in a single year, finishing just one behind NL leader Willie Stargell in the category and three ahead of Hammerin' Hank. Alas, by the next spring Davey's power days were going, going, gone. Johnson fell off to 15 circuit clouts in 1974 and never reached double figures again.

Maybe it's something in the Maryland water, but a few years earlier yet another Oriole had unexpectedly joined—and left—the power ranks. While most of the country focused on the slugging exploits of Roger Maris and Mickey Mantle during 1961, Baltimore first baseman **Jim Gentile** quietly leaped from 21 to 46 homers that year. By the time anybody noticed "Diamond Jim," he was back down to 33 home runs in '62, and he never managed to crack the 30 mark again in his remaining four big-league campaigns.

Of course, **Maris** was a bit of a one-year wonder himself. Although he was named MVP in 1960, his jump from 39 to a record 61 homers in 1961 was astonishing nonetheless—as was his drop down to 33 the following season. When you consider Roger averaged just 25 homers over his 12-year career, what he accomplished in '61 seems all the more remarkable.

A couple of other home run champions are also members of the one-year wonder club. Boston Braves outfielder **Tommy Holmes** led the NL in long balls with 28 during 1945, a year in which he also paced the league in hits, doubles, and slugging percentage while finishing second in batting. A great contact hitter throughout his career, Tommy was never a home run threat before or after that splendid summer. He was back down to six homers in '46 and averaged less than 10 during nine full big-league seasons. His explanation for his sudden—and short-lived—power? "The wind was blowing out that year."

Rounding out this list is Cubs outfielder **Hack Wilson.** Maybe it's a bit of a stretch to call a Hall of Famer and four-time home run champion a one-year wonder, but a closer look at the numbers supports the claim. Wilson averaged 30 homers per year from 1926 to '29, but then leaped from 39 to 56 in 1930—the same season he set a major-league record that still stands with 190 RBI. A severe drinking problem was the main reason this 5'6" ball of fire plummeted to 13 homers in '31.

The lesson to be learned? Enjoy the homers while you can—you never know when they'll stop coming.

The Giants' Kevin Mitchell led the NL with 47 homers in 1989, one year after a 19-home run season. He never topped 35 again.

TAPE-MEASURE SHOTS

THERE ARE HOME RUNS that sneak over the fence and then there are home runs that are launched into orbit. While the boxscore does not discriminate between the two, baseball history does. The moon shots are the ones that live forever.

At the end of the home run chase of 1998, just four homers separated **Mark McGwire** and Sammy Sosa. But it was McGwire's mammoth drives that truly separated baseball's dynamic duo. Of his record-breaking 70 home runs, 21 traveled more than 450 feet and five of them eclipsed 500. In contrast, Sosa hit six of his 66 better than 450 feet and only one surpassed 500.

It was truly a "shattering" season for Big Mac. He hit a 545-foot blast that dented a *St. Louis Post-Dispatch* billboard in center field. A short time later, a huge bandage appeared over the spot where McGwire's drive landed. He also caused $2,000 worth of damage to a scoreboard at Bank One Ballpark in Phoenix. In 1997 McGwire made headlines against Seattle fireballer Randy Johnson, a showdown one sportswriter called Ali vs. Frazier at 60 feet, six inches. Johnson struck out 19 but lost the game due in part to McGwire's 538-foot upper-deck home run, the Kingdome's longest recorded homer.

McGwire was not baseball's first interior redecorator. In 1967 Harmon Killebrew smacked a home run that landed six rows into the upper deck at Metropolitan Stadium in Minnesota. The blast traveled 530 feet and shattered two seats upon landing. The broken seats were painted orange and were never sold again.

Mickey Mantle's 1963 bomb off the facade rimming the right-center-field roof is among the most revered homers at Yankee Stadium. Mantle, a switch-hitter batting left-handed, came within six inches of going over the 108-foot-high stadium roof. The ball was still rising when it crashed into the facade, and it is believed that it would have traveled 620 feet.

Mantle exhibited tremendous power from either side of the plate. Batting right-handed at Griffith Stadium, he became one of only two men to hit a ball over the left-field bleachers. The drive came to rest in a neighborhood backyard some 565 feet away. The other man to go over those bleachers was Negro League legend **Josh Gibson**, who did it twice.

Legend also has it that Gibson hit a ball clear out of Yankee Stadium, a feat no player has matched. Although there is no documentation to substantiate it, eyewitnesses said Gibson hit a fair ball down the left-field line and out of the stadium during a 1934 Negro League doubleheader. The June 3, 1967, issue of *The Sporting News* also credits Gibson with hitting a shot two feet from the top of the wall behind the center-field bleachers at Yankee Stadium, about 580 feet away from home. Had the ball cleared that wall, it may have reached 700 feet.

Numerous players have hit balls onto Waveland Avenue behind Wrigley Field. But in 1976 the Mets' **Dave "King Kong" Kingman** blasted a pitch *over* Waveland Avenue. When the drive finally came to earth, it hit a house on Kenmore Avenue some 550 feet away, nearly crashing through a window.

Babe Ruth and **Lou Gehrig** contributed some long-distance clouts. It's believed that Gehrig hit a ball over the 40-foot-high center-field wall at Clark Field in Austin, Texas. The blast came during a 1929 exhibition game between the Yankees and Texas Longhorns and is said to have traveled 611 feet.

Ironically, Ruth's longest blasts did not come while wearing Yankee pinstripes. According to Robert Creamer's book *Babe,*

Above right: Mark McGwire stretched the phrase "tape measure" to its limits in 1998, hitting five of his home runs 500 feet or more. His 545-footer gave Busch Stadium a bandage. Below: Waving goodbye to Waveland, Dave Kingman once hit a ball over the famed avenue behind Wrigley Field and against a house on Kenmore, some 550 feet from the plate.

the longest shot of Ruth's career came in 1919 as a member of the Red Sox. During an exhibition game against the New York Giants at a Tampa, Florida, racetrack, Ruth hit a monstrous drive to right-center that cleared a small fence and rolled across the track. After the game several reporters asked the Giants outfielder to point out the precise spot where it landed. Some reports said the ball traveled 500 feet, while others claimed it went 600 feet. The unofficial measurement Creamer stands by is 579 feet.

The last blast of Ruth's career was among his mightiest. On May 25, 1935, Ruth, 40 years old and a Boston Brave, was facing the Pittsburgh Pirates at Forbes Field. He had already homered twice and singled when he stepped to the plate in the seventh inning. With the bases empty, Ruth launched the ball over the 186-foot-high right-field roof for his third round-tripper of the day. At the time, no one had hit a ball over the Forbes Field roof.

Reggie Jackson, another southpaw slugger, saved his longest homers for baseball's biggest showcases. In the 1971 All-Star Game at Tiger Stadium, Jackson hit a ball into the lights that sit on top of the right-field roof. In Game 6 of the 1977 World Series, at Yankee Stadium, Jackson hit three consecutive homers, the last one landing all the way in the black seats of the center-field bleachers.

Willie Stargell is another modern-day rocket launcher. Among Stargell's many clouts are four upper-deck blasts at Cincinnati's Riverfront Stadium and seven over the right-field roof at Forbes Field. He also hit the first two homers out of Dodger Stadium (Mike Piazza in the only other man to do it), and he once deposited a 535-foot four-bagger into the 500 level of Olympic Stadium in Montreal.

There is one home run, though, that would make Stargell, McGwire, and Ruth envious. At Crosley Field in the 1930s, Cincinnati Reds catcher **Ernie Lombardi** hit a home run over the center-field fence that landed in a truck behind the stadium. The truck drove 30 miles away before the ball was discovered, easily making Lombardi's drive the most well-traveled home run in history.

Mickey Mantle, one of the most powerful hitters ever, joined Josh Gibson as the only men to hit a ball over the left-field bleachers at Griffith Stadium.

UNSUNG SLUGGERS

Buzz Arlett played only one major-league season, hitting 18 home runs in 418 at-bats for Philadelphia in 1931. In the minors, though, he clubbed 432 homers, including two four-homer games.

YOU WON'T FIND THEIR deeds recorded in major-league record books, and their likenesses are not emblazoned on plaques at the Hall of Fame. Mule Suttles, Bunny Brief, and Hector Espino are anything but household names, but just like the legends enshrined at Cooperstown these ballplayers were home run hitters worthy of remembrance. They and others like them did their damage in the nether regions of baseball: the minor leagues, Negro Leagues, and even the Mexican and Japanese leagues.

Some old-timers claim that **Mule Suttles** was even a better Negro League slugger than the legendary Josh Gibson. At 6′6″, 230 pounds, swinging a bat rumored to weigh as much as 50 ounces, Suttles smashed 20 home runs in 57 recorded games (Negro League statistics are incomplete) during 1930 for the St. Louis Stars and Baltimore Black Sox. Legend has it that one of his shots traveled 600 feet. And in 79 lifetime at-bats against white big-leaguers during exhibition contests, he smashed 11 homers—or one every 7.2 at-bats.

Norman "Turkey" Stearnes was famous for saying that "I never counted my home runs," but historians cite him with 160 round-trippers— the most of any Negro Leaguer. Slight of stature (170 pounds), Stearnes was a league leader in homers on seven occasions and compiled a lifetime slugging percentage of .643.

Chino Smith didn't last as long as Stearnes, but in 1929 he had as great a year as any Negro Leaguer in history with 23 homers, 28 doubles, and a .461 average in just 245 at-bats for the New York Lincoln Giants. His slugging percentage that season was .890, higher than even Babe Ruth's top mark. In 1930, during the first game ever played by black teams at Yankee Stadium, Smith stroked two homers and a triple for six RBI. Chino could have eventually eclipsed all Negro League power records, but after batting .429 that year he died suddenly at age 30.

Hector Espino's career came after Jackie Robinson broke the color line in 1947, so racism may not have been the reason Espino was denied a shot in the majors. Why someone with a minor-league record 484 home runs (481 of which were hit in Mexico) wasn't signed by a big-league club, however, remains a mystery. There is widespread speculation that Hector's own disgust with prejudicial feelings in America kept him from making the jump. During the 25 years he spent playing south of the border, there was no bigger star in the Mexican League.

How players like these would have fared in the major leagues will never be known. Such is not the case for **Bunny Brief, Nick Cullop,** and **Joe Hauser.** These fellows were complete washouts in the majors, although they made their marks as sluggers at other levels. Brief hit just .223 with five homers in the bigs from 1912 to 1917, but in the minors he walloped 40 or more twice and claimed eight home run championships. Cullop hit a mere 11 round-trippers with five major-league clubs from 1926 to 1931, then spent the next 13 summers in the minors —where he crushed 420. Nick also set a minor-league record with 1,857 RBI.

Above: *Japanese slugger Sadaharu Oh, who awaited pitches on one leg, remains the world's home run champion, with 15 long-ball titles in his native country and 868 lifetime homers.* Right: *In 1925 for Salt Lake City, Tony Lazzeri played 200 games and set professional records with 60 homers, 222 RBI, and 202 runs. The runs record has never been broken.*

Hauser was a bit of a different story. His first three years in the majors were actually quite successful. He posted a .304 average from 1922 to 1924 and hit as many as 27 homers in one season. Then a badly broken leg in April 1925 sidelined him for that entire campaign, and in subsequent comebacks he was never able to regain his old touch.

Retreating to the minors in 1930, Hauser wound up compiling some of the most incredible power stats this side of Mark McGwire. He set a professional home run record (for all levels) with 63 during 1930 for Baltimore in the International League. He clubbed 49 for Minneapolis of the American Association in 1932, and in '33 topped his own record with 69 more for Minneapolis. The new mark remained until **Joe Baumann** (a career minor-leaguer) topped it with 72 homers for Roswell of the Longhorn League in 1954. Baumann's homer total and .916 slugging average that year have never been topped at any pro level.

Interestingly, the first man to hit 60 homers in a season was not Babe Ruth. **Tony Lazzeri** clubbed 60 for Salt Lake City of the Pacific Coast League in 1925. Two years later, Lazzeri was Ruth's Yankee teammate when the Bambino slugged 60 round-trippers.

Like the minors, Japan has also proven a haven for failing major-leaguers. **Randy Bass** managed to hit just nine homers during his unmemorable 1977–82 stint in the majors, but they'll never forget the "Great Basu" in Japan. In 1985, suiting up with the Japanese Hanshin Tigers, he hit 54 homers and won the Triple Crown.

Of course, it was a native son who would prove the greatest Japanese slugger of all time—**Sadaharu Oh**. Employing a unique batting stance in which he stood on one leg before the pitch to keep from hitching his swing, Oh was in fact the most prodigious home run hitter ever produced on any continent. Playing from 1959 to 1981, his 15 home run titles and 868 lifetime homers set world records—breaking the legendary marks of Babe Ruth and Hank Aaron in the respective departments.

A nine-time MVP with the Yomiuri Giants, Oh studied martial arts to improve his physical and mental skills as well as to develop patience at the plate. What he apparently didn't learn from his masters was honor. When Bass tied his record of 54 homers in a 130-game season late in 1985, Oh (then Yomiuri's manager) demanded that his pitchers intentionally walk Bass for an entire series rather than let a *gaijin* (foreigner) shoot for a new record.

Joe Hauser enjoyed only fleeting success in the majors, but subsequent years saw him wallop 63 homers in an International League season and 69 during the 1933 American Association campaign.

STRANGEST HOMERS

SOMETIMES IT IS OBVIOUS that a home run has been hit the second the ball leaves the bat. Other times fans anxiously wait to see whether the ball sneaks over the wall or collides with the foul pole before they are able to celebrate a home run. And then there are those times when the ball takes an entirely different route.

One of the oddest homers in history took place at American League Park, which was the home of the Washington Senators from 1904 to 1911. At this particular ballpark there was a doghouse near the outfield flagpole. The grounds crew stored the flag inside the doghouse between games. One afternoon the doghouse door was left open and a member of the Senators hit the ball inside of it. Philadelphia A's center fielder Socks Seybold crawled inside to retrieve the ball and got stuck, allowing the batter to circle the bases for an "inside-the-doghouse" home run.

That wasn't the first time an open door figured into a homer. When the Louisville Colonels visited the Pittsburgh Pirates on May 3, 1899, the Colonels were leading comfortably in the last of the ninth when the Pirates staged a rally. Jack McCarthy had already homered when teammate Tom McCreery drove a ball to the right-field fence. A Pirates employee opened the right-field gate, picked up the ball, and ran off with it. McCreery circled the bases and, despite protests from the Louisville players, the umpire allowed the play to stand. The outcome was a 7–6 Pittsburgh victory. However, later that season at a league meeting, the game was thrown out and did not count in the final National League standings.

In 1911 American League President Ban Johnson attempted to speed up games by eliminating warm-up pitches between innings. On June 27, at the Huntington Avenue Baseball Grounds, the A's Stuffy McInnis capitalized on the rule change when he noticed Boston pitcher Ed Karger tossing warm-ups. McInnis drilled a ball that center fielder Tris Speaker refused to chase because he thought it was hit during warm-ups. McInnis touched them all for a home run. Umpire Ben Egan had no choice but to allow the homer to count because Johnson was sitting in the stands.

In the early 1940s at Ebbets Field, Lonnie Frey of the Cincinnati Reds hit a ball to right field. It bounced off the screen and landed on top of the wall that extended between the scoreboard and foul pole. The ball bounced up and down but never fell back to the field of play, allowing Frey to complete an inside-the-park home run. The same fate would ultimately help the Dodgers in 1950, when Pee Wee Reese duplicated the feat in a game that helped Brooklyn clinch the NL pennant.

Another home run occurred at Ebbets Field that seemed to defy the laws of gravity. George Cutshaw, who played for the Dodgers from 1913 to 1917, hit a line drive to the left-field wall. Apparently the ball had a lot of top-spin on it; when it hit the wall, the ball rolled up and over the fence for a home run.

Above right: During the "pine tar" incident of 1983, a fiery George Brett charged umpire Tim McClelland, who had taken away Brett's home run because there was too much pine tar on his bat. Below: Ebbets Field became the home of at least two odd home runs: Balls hit off the screen and bounced down to the top of the right-field wall—but never returned to the field of play.

Lee MacPhail; the home run counted and the game was replayed.

Sometimes the opposition actually helps the hitter. In May 1993 Cleveland's Carlos Martinez hit a fly ball to right field that bounced off Jose Canseco's head and over the fence for a two-run home run. The gift round-tripper gave the Tribe a 7–6 win over the Rangers.

While that was embarrassing for Canseco, it was at least less frustrating than what happened to Dick Cordell during a minor-league game on August 9, 1952. In the seventh inning of a scoreless game between Denver and Omaha in the Western League, Cordell ran down a long drive off the bat of Denver's Bill Pinckard. Cordell caught the ball before crashing into the left-field wall. The ball was jarred from his glove on impact, ricocheted off the wall, then off his head and over the fence. After a lengthy discussion, the umpire ruled that Pinckard's drive was indeed a homer. It turned out to be the only run of the game.

For Jim Bottomley, one home run wasn't worth all of the grief. Bottomley, who spent 16 seasons in the majors and led the NL with 31 homers in 1928, was once

Above: *Jim Bottomley, once an NL home run king, had to explain one of his homers in a courtroom after it hit a fan in the face. The spectator sued.* Left: *Known more for his power than his defense, Jose Canseco accidentally used his head to turn a fly ball by Carlos Martinez into a memorable home run in May 1993.*

One of the most memorable homers of George Brett's career was disallowed for a brief period of time. Brett's two-out, two-run, ninth-inning homer off Yankees relief ace Goose Gossage was a majestic drive. The game took place on July 24, 1983, at Yankee Stadium, and the blast gave the Royals a 5–4 lead over the Yanks. But after Brett circled the bases, New York manager Billy Martin came out of the dugout and asked the home plate umpire to examine Brett's bat. It was determined that the pine tar on Brett's bat exceeded the legal limit of 18 inches. Brett was called out and the home run was nullified. The umpire was later overruled by American League President

sued after one of his home runs hit a spectator in the face. The suit stated that Bottomley "swung on that ball deliberately and with the intention of creating a situation commonly known as a home run."

During questioning at a deposition, an attorney suggested that a skilled contact hitter could place the ball to whichever part of the field he determined. He then asked Bottomley, "Did you deliberately intend to hit anyone when you batted that ball?"

"No sir," replied Bottomley. "There is no malice in any of my home runs."

INSIDE-THE-PARKERS

THERE WAS A TIME when the inside-the-park home run was the most exciting play in baseball. To successfully negotiate the 360-foot path around the bases required more than just speed. It required nerve.

While today most inside-the-park home runs are a result of a misplayed ball, there was a time when it was an act of defiance against the outfielder. The inside-the-park home run was a dare, a challenge issued by the batter to the opposition. It was baseball's version of the 100-yard dash.

The evolution of stadiums has made the inside-the-park homer less common. The outfield walls are closer to home plate, with no fence deeper than 440 feet, and there are no longer monuments in the field of play at any big-league park. In the past, monuments often aided baserunners vying to win the footrace against the outfield. Casey Stengel, while managing the Yankees, once watched his center fielder try to grab a ball ricocheting between the monuments in Yankee Stadium. Exasperated, Stengel shouted from the dugout, "Ruth, Gehrig, Huggins, someone throw that darned ball in here now!"

One of the biggest obstacles fielders had to face was the scoreboard in center field in Washington Park. The field was home to the National League's Brooklyn Superbas from 1898 to 1912. The scoreboard stood on pillars and, if hit far enough, a ball could roll underneath the scoreboard. Many a center fielder crawled under the scoreboard in a frantic attempt to retrieve the ball before the batter reached home.

The only on-field obstacle today's outfielders contend with is the ivy that adorns the walls of Wrigley Field. On numerous occasions in the park's 84-year history, an outfielder has lost a ball in the ivy, allowing a baserunner to complete an inside-the-park home run. There was even a time when Cubs outfielders would hide a second baseball

Above right: Boston's Mike Greenwell once managed to round the bases without ever hitting the ball into the air. Outfielder Jesse Barfield had crashed trying to field a grounder down the line. Below: Casey Stengel smacked an inside-the-park home run in Game 1 of the 1923 World Series. The ninth-inning dash gave the Giants a 5–4 victory over the Yankees.

in the outfield just in case they couldn't find the one buried in the ivy.

Stengel was the batsman behind one of the most famous inside-the-park home runs in history. He hit two such homers during the 1923 World Series between the New York Giants and New York Yankees, but the first remains legendary. In Game 1 Stengel, a 33-year-old outfielder for the Giants, came to the plate with two outs in the ninth inning and the score tied 4–4. He laced a drive into the left-center gap and circled the bases with the decisive run. It was the first World Series home run hit at Yankee Stadium.

Damon Runyon, the famed New York sportswriter, opened his column the next morning by following Stengel around the bases, thus solidifying the legend of Stengel and his home run. He wrote: "This is the way old Casey Stengel ran running his home run when two were out in the ninth inning and the score was tied, and the ball still bounding inside the Yankee yard. . . . This is the way—His mouth wide open. His warped old legs bending beneath him at every stride. His arms flying back and forth like those of a man swimming with a crawl stroke. His flanks heaving, his breath whistling, his head far back. . . ."

The inside-the-park home run was commonplace in the late 19th century and early 20th century. In fact, when Philadelphia's Ed Delahanty hit four home runs in a game on July 13, 1896, all four (according to some sources) were inside-the-park homers. Several factors contributed to the popularity of the inside-the-parker. Among them were spacious outfields and a ball that didn't travel very far. Hitters also took shorter swings because they used heavier and thicker bats than those used today.

Of the players who notched the most career inside-the-parkers, none played after 1928. The all-time leader is Sam Crawford with 51. Crawford, who played with Cincinnati and

Detroit from 1899 to 1917, had only 97 total home runs for his career. Tommy Leach ranks second with 49 and Ty Cobb is third with 46.

The Mariners' Dan Wilson hit the latest inside-the-park grand slam, in 1998. Hall of Famer Honus Wagner has the most inside-the-park slams with five, while Leach (four) and Joe Jackson (three) rank second and third. In 1990 at Fenway Park, Boston's Mike Greenwell managed a grand slam without lifting the ball in the air. Opposing right fielder Jesse Barfield crashed into the wall trying to field his grounder down the right-field line, allowing Greenwell to circle the bases.

Willie Wilson is clearly the inside-the-park home run king of modern players. Wilson, a switch-hitting center fielder who turned down a football scholarship to play baseball, was a member of the Kansas City Royals from 1979 to 1990. In his rookie season Wilson legged out five inside-the-parkers and fin-

ished with 13 for his career. His teammate, George Brett, a legitimate power hitter with 317 dingers, had seven career homers that failed to leave the yard.

Basestealing demon Lou Brock had nine inside-the-park homers, but other conventional power hitters benefited from the occasional circuit sprint. Babe Ruth had 10 over the course of his career. Mickey Mantle had six, including three in 1958. The only inside-the-park home run of Ted Williams's career clinched the 1946 American League pennant for the Red Sox. Williams, a noted left-handed pull hitter, often faced a shift that saw all but two of the opposing fielders to the right of second base. Williams simply drove the ball to left field and circled the bases.

After the game Williams was asked if that was the easiest home run he had ever hit. "Hell, no," the slugger replied. "It was the hardest. I had to run."

Perhaps the fastest man in baseball in the 1980s, Kansas City's Willie Wilson turned ballgames into track meets with his steals, triples, and 13 career inside-the-parkers.

SLUGGING RECORDS

MOST CAREER HOME RUNS

1	Hank Aaron	755
2	Babe Ruth	714
3	Willie Mays	660
4	Frank Robinson	586
5	Harmon Killebrew	573
6	Reggie Jackson	563
7	Mike Schmidt	548
8	Mickey Mantle	536
9	Jimmie Foxx	534
10	Willie McCovey	521
	Ted Williams	521
12	Ernie Banks	512
	Eddie Mathews	512
14	Mel Ott	511
15	Eddie Murray	504
16	Lou Gehrig	493
17	Stan Musial	475
	Willie Stargell	475
19	Dave Winfield	465
20	Mark McGwire	457
21	Carl Yastrzemski	452
22	Dave Kingman	442
23	Andre Dawson	438
24	Billy Williams	426
25	Darrell Evans	414
26	Barry Bonds	411
27	Duke Snider	407
28	Al Kaline	399
29	Dale Murphy	398
30	Jose Canseco	397
31	Joe Carter	396
32	Graig Nettles	390
33	Johnny Bench	389
34	Dwight Evans	385
35	Cal Ripken	384
36	Frank Howard	382
	Jim Rice	382
38	Orlando Cepeda	379
	Tony Perez	379
40	Norm Cash	377
41	Carlton Fisk	376
42	Rocky Colavito	374
43	Gil Hodges	370
44	Ralph Kiner	369
45	Joe DiMaggio	361
46	Johnny Mize	359
47	Yogi Berra	358
	Fred McGriff	358
49	Lee May	354
50	Dick Allen	351
	Gary Gaetti	351
52	Ken Griffey Jr.	350
53	Harold Baines	348
	George Foster	348
55	Ron Santo	342
56	Jack Clark	340
57	Dave Parker	339
	Boog Powell	339
59	Don Baylor	338
60	Joe Adcock	336
61	Bobby Bonds	332
	Andres Galarraga	332
	Darryl Strawberry	332
64	Chili Davis	331
	Hank Greenberg	331
66	Willie Horton	325
67	Gary Carter	324
	Lance Parrish	324
69	Albert Belle	321
70	Cecil Fielder	319
71	Roy Sievers	318
72	George Brett	317
73	Ron Cey	316
74	Rafael Palmeiro	314
	Reggie Smith	314
76	Greg Luzinski	307
	Al Simmons	307
78	Fred Lynn	306
79	Juan Gonzalez	301
	Rogers Hornsby	301
81	Chuck Klein	300
82	Matt Williams	299
83	Kent Hrbek	293
84	Rusty Staub	292
85	Jimmy Wynn	291
86	Del Ennis	288
	Bob Johnson	288
	Hank Sauer	288
89	Frank Thomas	286
	Frank J. Thomas	286
91	Ken Boyer	282
	Ryne Sandberg	282
93	Ted Kluszewski	279
94	Rudy York	277
95	Brian Downing	275
	Roger Maris	275
97	Bobby Bonilla	273
	Sammy Sosa	273
99	Steve Garvey	272
100	Tom Brunansky	271
	George Scott	271

Ted Williams (left) slugged .634 for his career, better than every player except Babe Ruth (right), who boasted a phenomenal .690 mark.

HIGHEST CAREER HOME RUN PCT.

1	Mark McGwire	8.91
2	Babe Ruth	8.50
3	Ralph Kiner	7.09
4	Juan Gonzalez	7.05
5	Harmon Killebrew	7.03
6	Albert Belle	6.85
7	Ted Williams	6.76
8	Ken Griffey Jr.	6.70
9	Dave Kingman	6.62
10	Mickey Mantle	6.62
11	Jose Canseco	6.57
12	Jimmie Foxx	6.57
13	Mike Schmidt	6.56
14	Frank Thomas	6.49
15	Hank Greenberg	6.37
16	Willie McCovey	6.36
17	Barry Bonds	6.21
18	Cecil Fielder	6.19
19	Darryl Strawberry	6.18
20	Jay Buhner	6.18
21	Lou Gehrig	6.16
22	Hank Aaron	6.11
23	Willie Mays	6.07
24	Mo Vaughn	6.01
25	Hank Sauer	6.01

HIGHEST CAREER SLUGGING AVG.

1	Babe Ruth	.690
2	Ted Williams	.634
3	Lou Gehrig	.632
4	Jimmie Foxx	.609
5	Hank Greenberg	.605
6	Frank Thomas	.584
7	Joe DiMaggio	.579
8	Albert Belle	.577
9	Rogers Hornsby	.577
10	Mark McGwire	.576
11	Ken Griffey Jr.	.568
12	Juan Gonzalez	.568
13	Johnny Mize	.562
14	Stan Musial	.559
15	Willie Mays	.557

Ken Griffey Jr. ranks eighth in career home run percentage, 11th in slugging average, and ninth in homers in a season.

16	Mickey Mantle	.557
17	Barry Bonds	.556
18	Hank Aaron	.555
19	Larry Walker	.552
20	Ralph Kiner	.548
21	Hack Wilson	.545
22	Chuck Klein	.543
23	Mo Vaughn	.542
24	Duke Snider	.540
25	Jeff Bagwell	.538

MOST CAREER RUNS BATTED IN

1	Hank Aaron	2297
2	Babe Ruth	2213
3	Lou Gehrig	1995
4	Stan Musial	1951
5	Ty Cobb	1937
6	Jimmie Foxx	1922
7	Eddie Murray	1917
8	Willie Mays	1903
9	Cap Anson	1879
10	Mel Ott	1860
11	Carl Yastrzemski	1844
12	Ted Williams	1839
13	Dave Winfield	1833
14	Al Simmons	1827
15	Frank Robinson	1812
16	Honus Wagner	1732
17	Reggie Jackson	1702
18	Tony Perez	1652
19	Ernie Banks	1636
20	Goose Goslin	1609
21	Nap Lajoie	1599
22	George Brett	1595
	Mike Schmidt	1595
24	Andre Dawson	1591
25	Rogers Hornsby	1584
	Harmon Killebrew	1584

MOST SINGLE-SEASON HOME RUNS

1	Mark McGwire, 1998	70
2	Sammy Sosa, 1998	66
3	Roger Maris, 1961	61
4	Babe Ruth, 1927	60
5	Babe Ruth, 1921	59
6	Mark McGwire, 1997	58
	Jimmie Foxx, 1932	58
	Hank Greenberg, 1938	58
9	Hack Wilson, 1930	56
	Ken Griffey Jr., 1997	56
	Ken Griffey Jr., 1998	56
12	Babe Ruth, 1920	54
	Babe Ruth, 1928	54
	Ralph Kiner, 1949	54
	Mickey Mantle, 1961	54
16	Mickey Mantle, 1956	52
	Willie Mays, 1965	52
	George Foster, 1977	52
	Mark McGwire, 1996	52
20	Ralph Kiner, 1947	51
	Johnny Mize, 1947	51
	Willie Mays, 1955	51
	Cecil Fielder, 1990	51
24	Jimmie Foxx, 1938	50
	Albert Belle, 1995	50
	Brady Anderson, 1996	50
	Greg Vaughn, 1998	50

No National Leaguer has come within 20 RBI of Hack Wilson's season record of 190.

HIGHEST SINGLE-SEASON HOME RUN PCT.

1	Mark McGwire, 1998	13.75
2	Mark McGwire, 1996	12.29
3	Babe Ruth, 1920	11.79
4	Babe Ruth, 1927	11.11
5	Babe Ruth, 1921	10.93
6	Mark McGwire, 1997	10.74
7	Mickey Mantle, 1961	10.51
8	Hank Greenberg, 1938	10.43
9	Roger Maris, 1961	10.34
10	Sammy Sosa, 1998	10.26
11	Babe Ruth, 1928	10.07
12	Jimmie Foxx, 1932	9.91
13	Ralph Kiner, 1949	9.84
14	Mickey Mantle, 1956	9.76
15	Jeff Bagwell, 1994	9.75
16	Kevin Mitchell, 1994	9.68
17	Matt Williams, 1994	9.66
18	Hack Wilson, 1930	9.57
19	Frank Thomas, 1994	9.52
20	Babe Ruth, 1926	9.49
	Hank Aaron, 1971	9.49
22	Jim Gentile, 1961	9.47
23	Barry Bonds, 1994	9.46
24	Babe Ruth, 1930	9.46
25	Willie Stargell, 1971	9.39

HIGHEST SINGLE-SEASON SLUGGING AVG.

1	Babe Ruth, 1920	.847
2	Babe Ruth, 1921	.846
3	Babe Ruth, 1927	.772
4	Lou Gehrig, 1927	.765
5	Babe Ruth, 1923	.764
6	Rogers Hornsby, 1925	.756
7	Mark McGwire, 1998	.752
8	Jeff Bagwell, 1994	.750
9	Jimmie Foxx, 1932	.749
10	Babe Ruth, 1924	.739
11	Babe Ruth, 1926	.737
12	Ted Williams, 1941	.735
13	Babe Ruth, 1930	.732
14	Ted Williams, 1957	.731
15	Mark McGwire, 1996	.730
16	Frank Thomas, 1994	.729
17	Hack Wilson, 1930	.723
18	Rogers Hornsby, 1922	.722
19	Lou Gehrig, 1930	.721
20	Larry Walker, 1997	.720
21	Albert Belle, 1994	.714
22	Babe Ruth, 1928	.709
23	Al Simmons, 1930	.708
24	Lou Gehrig, 1934	.706
25	Mickey Mantle, 1956	.705

MOST SINGLE-SEASON RUNS BATTED IN

1	Hack Wilson, 1930	190
2	Lou Gehrig, 1931	184
3	Hank Greenberg, 1937	183
4	Lou Gehrig, 1927	175
	Jimmie Foxx, 1938	175
6	Lou Gehrig, 1930	174
7	Babe Ruth, 1921	171
8	Chuck Klein, 1930	170
	Hank Greenberg, 1935	170
10	Jimmie Foxx, 1932	169
11	Joe DiMaggio, 1937	167
12	Sam Thompson, 1887	166
13	Sam Thompson, 1895	165
	Al Simmons, 1930	165
	Lou Gehrig, 1934	165
16	Babe Ruth, 1927	164
17	Babe Ruth, 1931	163
	Jimmie Foxx, 1933	163
19	Hal Trosky, 1936	162
20	Hack Wilson, 1929	159
	Lou Gehrig, 1937	159
	Ted Williams, 1949	159
	Vern Stephens, 1949	159
24	Sammy Sosa, 1998	158
25	Al Simmons, 1929	157
	Juan Gonzalez, 1998	157

MOST WORLD SERIES HOME RUNS

1	Mickey Mantle	18
2	Babe Ruth	15
3	Yogi Berra	12
4	Duke Snider	11
5	Lou Gehrig	10
	Reggie Jackson	10
7	Joe DiMaggio	8
	Frank Robinson	8
	Bill Skowron	8
10	Hank Bauer	7
	Goose Goslin	7
	Gil McDougald	7
13	Lenny Dykstra	6
	Roger Maris	6
	Al Simmons	6
	Reggie Smith	6

FOUR-HOMER GAMES

Bobby Lowe, BOS NL—May 30, 1894
Ed Delahanty, PHI NL—July 13, 1896
Lou Gehrig, NY AL—June 3, 1932
Chuck Klein, PHI NL—July 10, 1936 (10 innings)
Pat Seerey, CHI AL—July 18, 1948 (11 innings)
Gil Hodges, BRO NL—August 31, 1950
Joe Adcock, MIL NL—July 31, 1954
Rocky Colavito, CLE AL—June 10, 1959
Willie Mays, SF NL—April 30, 1961
Mike Schmidt, PHI NL—April 17, 1976 (10 innings)
Bob Horner, ATL—July 6, 1986
Mark Whiten, STL NL—September 7, 1993

Mark McGwire blasted five
home runs on the final weekend
of the 1998 season to finish
with the staggering total of 70.
"I can't believe I did it," he said.
"Can you?"